KOREAN
FOR BEGINNERS

Mastering Conversational Korean

KOREAN
FOR BEGINNERS

Kyubyong Park and Henry J. Amen IV

Illustrations by Aya Padrón

TUTTLE Publishing

Tokyo | Rutland, Vermont | Singapore

Published by Tuttle Publishing, an imprint of Periplus Editions (HK) Ltd.

www.tuttlepublishing.com

Library of Congress Cataloging-in-Publication Data
Amen, Henry J.
 Korean for beginners : mastering conversational Korean / Kyubyong Park & Henry J. Amen IV ; illustrations by Aya Padron.
  159 p. : ill., maps ; 26 cm. + 1 CD-ROM (4 3/4 in.)
  English and Korean.
  ISBN 978-0-8048-4100-9 (pbk.)
1. Korean language--Textbooks for foreign speakers--English.
2. Korean language--Grammar--Problems, exercises, etc. I. Park, Kyubyong. II. Title.
  PL913.A43 2010
  495.7'82421--dc22
                     2009045320

ISBN 978-0-8048-4100-9

First edition
27 26 25 24 23
21 20 19 18 17
2305MP

Printed in Singapore

Cover photo © Christopher Futcher, Dreamstime.com

TUTTLE PUBLISHING® is a registered trademark of Tuttle Publishing, a division of Periplus Editions (HK) Ltd.

"Books to Span the East and West"

Tuttle Publishing was founded in 1832 in the small New England town of Rutland, Vermont [USA]. Our core values remain as strong today as they were then—to publish best-in-class books which bring people together one page at a time. In 1948, we established a publishing outpost in Japan—and Tuttle is now a leader in publishing English-language books about the arts, languages and cultures of Asia. The world has become a much smaller place today and Asia's economic and cultural influence has grown. Yet the need for meaningful dialogue and information about this diverse region has never been greater. Over the past seven decades, Tuttle has published thousands of books on subjects ranging from martial arts and paper crafts to language learning and literature—and our talented authors, illustrators, designers and photographers have won many prestigious awards. We welcome you to explore the wealth of information available on Asia at **www.tuttlepublishing.com**.

Distributed by:

North America, Latin America & Europe
Tuttle Publishing
364 Innovation Drive
North Clarendon, VT 05759-9436 U.S.A
Tel: 1 (802) 773-8930
Fax: 1 (802) 773-6993
info@tuttlepublishing.com
www.tuttlepublishing.com

Japan
Tuttle Publishing
Yaekari Building, 3rd Floor, 5-4-12 Osaki
Shinagawa-ku, Tokyo 141 0032, Japan
Tel: (81) 3 5437-0171
Fax: (81) 3 5437-0755
sales@tuttle.co.jp
www.tuttle.co.jp

Asia-Pacific
Berkeley Books Pte Ltd
3 Kallang Sector #04-01
Singapore 349278
Tel: (65) 6741-2178
Fax: (65) 6741-2179
inquiries@periplus.com.sg
www.tuttlepublishing.com

Acknowledgments

The authors wish to express many thanks to their wives, not just for their support during the process of writing the book, but also for their direct participation: Soyoung Nam assisted in the creation of the audio and video material, and Aya Padrón provided the illustrations that help bring *Korean for Beginners* to life. We would also like to give our heartfelt thanks to our editor, Sandra Korinchak, for her invaluable guidance.

—Kyubyong Park, Seoul, South Korea
—Henry J. Amen IV, Austin, Texas, U.S.A.

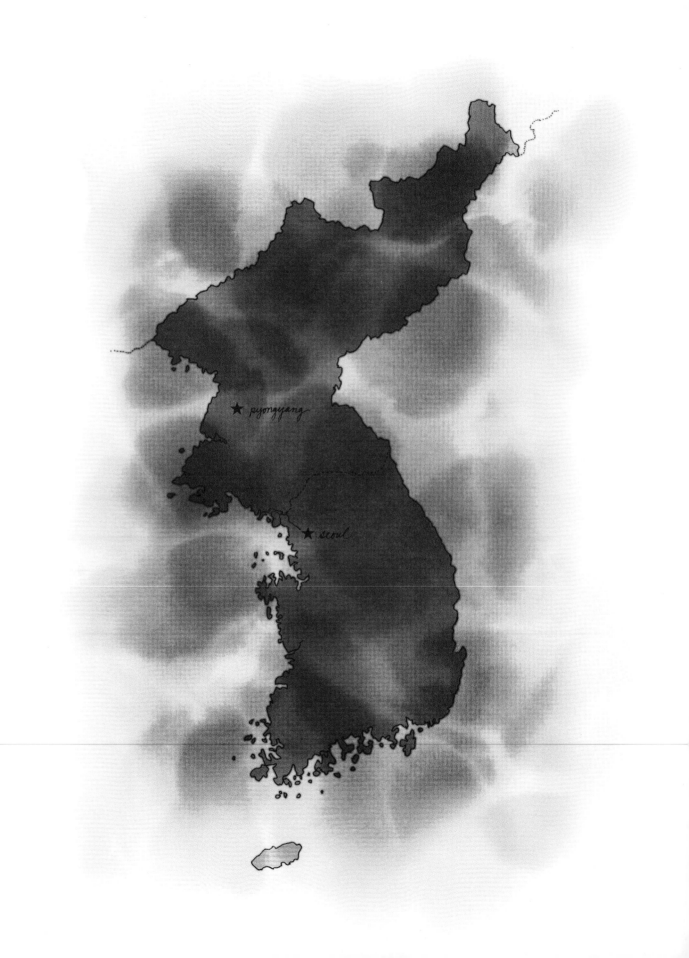

Contents

Acknowledgments v
Preface: Setting the Scene xi

CHAPTER 1: Welcome to Korean! An Introduction to Korean and the Korean Spirit...... **1**
FURTHER VOCABULARY: Korean food 2
KOREAN STYLE: Say what?............................3

CHAPTER 2: Korean Characters
An Introduction to the Korean Characters and Their Pronunciation..................................... **4**
FURTHER VOCABULARY: Taste....................................12
KOREAN STYLE: Korean computer keyboards 13

CHAPTER 3: Reading and Pronouncing Korean Words
Review of the Characters and Some Additional Pronunciation Rules **14**
FURTHER VOCABULARY: Country names 16
KOREAN STYLE: Do you like phlegm?? 17

CHAPTER 4: I You Love
Five Basic Features of Korean: Word Order, Particles, Conjugation, Honorifics, and Omissions and Plurals **18**
FURTHER VOCABULARY: Positive feelings.................21
KOREAN STYLE: You must listen to Korean from the end. 21

CHAPTER 5: My Mother Is Korean, and My Father Is American
All About Particles **22**
FURTHER VOCABULARY: More particles....................27
KOREAN STYLE: Particle play 29

CHAPTER 6: Learn, Learned, Learning
Regular Conjugation Patterns...................... **30**
FURTHER VOCABULARY: Expressions using common endings, part 1 36
KOREAN STYLE: Will you marry *with* me?..............37

CHAPTER 7: Go, Went, Going
Irregular Conjugation Patterns **38**
FURTHER VOCABULARY: Expressions using common endings, part 2 41
KOREAN STYLE: Can I bury something?..................42

CHAPTER 8: My Mother Loves Me
Honorific Endings and Words **43**
FURTHER VOCABULARY: Honorific word forms 47
KOREAN STYLE: Konglish (Korean English) 48

CHAPTER 9: Hello? What to Say in Greeting, in Parting, and in Thanks........................... **49**
FURTHER VOCABULARY: More greetings...................52
KOREAN STYLE: Can Koreans see things over the phone?...52

CHAPTER 10: I, You, We... Do I Know You?
Personal Pronouns and How to Address Strangers.. **53**
FURTHER VOCABULARY: Length, extent, size............56
KOREAN STYLE: Differences between 아저씨 and 오빠, 아줌마 and 아가씨 57

CHAPTER 11: What's This? Demonstrative Pronouns and How to Ask Simple Questions **58**
FURTHER VOCABULARY: Weight, depth, distance......61
KOREAN STYLE: Our wife? 61

CHAPTER 12: To Be, or Not To Be? All About the Verb "To Be"....................................... **62**
FURTHER VOCABULARY: Weather 65
KOREAN STYLE: Yes, I can't?..................................65

CHAPTER 13: My Name Is Hal
Introducing Yourself and Holding Simple Conversations... **66**
FURTHER VOCABULARY: Parts of the body.................68
KOREAN STYLE: Korean family names and given names 69

CHAPTER 14: Father, Mother, Brother, Sister
Korean Nouns and Terms for Family
    Members **70**

FURTHER VOCABULARY: The in-laws 73
KOREAN STYLE: My father enters his bag?? 74

CHAPTER 15: I Don't Want to Eat
Advanced Pronunciation Rules **75**

FURTHER VOCABULARY: Negative feelings 79
KOREAN STYLE: Tongue twisters 80

**CHAPTER 16: Excuse Me, Where's the
Restroom?** Interrogatives: When and
    Where **81**

FURTHER VOCABULARY: Location and direction 85
KOREAN STYLE: Snow water, or eye water? 85

CHAPTER 17: How's Korea? Interrogatives:
How and Why, Reasons and Causes **86**

FURTHER VOCABULARY: Questions? 90
KOREAN STYLE: Korean blind dates 91

CHAPTER 18: I'm from the U.S.
Verb Tenses: Past, Progressive, and Future .. **92**

FURTHER VOCABULARY: Movement 96
KOREAN STYLE: How to multiply your Korean
    vocabulary 97

**CHAPTER 19: Have You Ever Seen a
Korean Movie?** Turning Verbs and
Adjectives into Noun Modifiers **98**

FURTHER VOCABULARY: Dedicated noun
    modifiers 101
KOREAN STYLE: The disaster of misunderstanding
    the word 시원하다 102

CHAPTER 20: I Couldn't Study So Much
Negations **103**

FURTHER VOCABULARY: Health 106
KOREAN STYLE: Word relay 107

CHAPTER 21: I Should Talk to My Wife First
Suggestion, Supposition, Obligation,
    and Prohibition **108**

FURTHER VOCABULARY: Interjections 111
KOREAN STYLE: Korean proverbs 112

**CHAPTER 22: Canada Is Larger than
the U.S.**
Special Adverbs **113**

FURTHER VOCABULARY: More conjunctive
    adverbs 117
KOREAN STYLE: He's an owl. 117

CHAPTER 23: One, Two, Three...
Counting: Numbers and Counting Units **118**

FURTHER VOCABULARY: Counting units 123
KOREAN STYLE: The three-six-nine game 124

CHAPTER 24: How Much Is This? How to
    Shop **125**

FURTHER VOCABULARY: Shopping 128
KOREAN STYLE: Korean euphemisms 128

CHAPTER 25: What Time Is It? Asking
and Telling Time and How Many **130**

FURTHER VOCABULARY: Approximations 133
KOREAN STYLE: A two-year-old newborn!?
    Only in Korea! 134

CHAPTER 26: Today Is August 15
Days, Dates, and Seasons **135**

FURTHER VOCABULARY: Daily words 138
KOREAN STYLE: Which receives deliveries first:
    floor 2 or basement level 2? 139

**CHAPTER 27: I Wish You Would Come
Back to Korea Someday**
Wanting and Wishing **140**

FURTHER VOCABULARY: Korean national holidays ...143
KOREAN STYLE: Crossword puzzle 143

Appendix: Grammar Terms 145
Korean-English Glossary 150
English-Korean Glossary 155

To Download or Stream Bonus Materials:

How to Download the Bonus Material of this Book.
1. You must have an internet connection.
2. Type the URL below into to your web browser.

https://www.tuttlepublishing.com/korean-for-beginners-videos-audio

For support, you can email us at info@tuttlepublishing.com.

PREFACE
Setting the Scene

You're on a sidewalk in the center of Seoul, in the ultra-hip shopping district of Myeongdong. Fresh off the plane, all you can do is stand and stare at the bright neon lights with their funny angular letters. The ample sidewalk is swarming with pedestrians, and the chattering hum of their strange, lilting language is making your head swim.

Just as you're about to pass out from stimulus overload, you get a tap on the shoulder. He has the look of a young professional, maybe late 20s, dressed business casual, smiling widely. "Hello. Can I help you find something?"

Ordinarily, you're wary of friendly strangers you meet in a foreign city, especially when you're there for the first time and don't really know where you're going. But something about this guy tells you he's sincere, that it's okay to trust him. And you're right—because you're in Korea now!

An authentic voice

Congratulations—you just met your **narrator**! You may think you're lucky to have bumped into such a helpful, charming young man. And, well, of course you are! But the truth is many visitors to Korea have this exact experience. As a foreigner, you'll find the Korean people incredibly curious and engaging. They're as excited to learn about you and where you're from as they are to share their own unique culture with you.

This is your narrator in a nutshell, and *Korean for Beginners* is written entirely in his voice. You won't encounter dry grammar lessons or rote vocabulary memorization in these pages. At the same time, you're not going to see things dumbed down or oversimplified. Instead, you'll be learning the basics of the Korean language—and the culture that created it—by way of an **authentic**, one-on-one dynamic. Straight from your narrator's mouth, as it were.

It's this authenticity that makes *Korean for Beginners* the best resource out there for picking up the language as it's being spoken today—short of heading down to Myeongdong and meeting your own guide, that is!

Learning that runs deep

Your authors know the tribulations of language learning—Kyubyong as a Korean studying English and Henry as an American studying Korean. From these struggles and, yes, occasional successes, has come insight, and we're happy to share this insight with you in *Korean for Beginners*.

From how to use **honorifics** to show the proper respect in a conversation, to what exactly a **particle** is. From deciphering **Hangeul**—the Korean writing system—to learning how to say "I can't eat kimchi." These are some of the essentials of Korean language learning, and they'll be illustrated over and over again, along with many others. Heck, by the end we'll have you saying "I CAN eat kimchi!"

Korean for Beginners is divided into 27 chapters, and each includes a core lesson on a fundamental element of the language, with plenty of practical applications thrown in. What's more, each ends in a two-part conclusion. The first is a list of **further vocabulary** related to the subject matter of the chapter, designed to enhance and expand your understanding. And the second offers a relevant **cultural tidbit**, guaranteed to teach you something interesting about the country and its people, be it the layout of a Korean computer keyboard or the rules of a Korean drinking game.

At the back of the book, you'll find a Korean-English/English-Korean glossary with all the terms featured in the chapters. And, perhaps most importantly of all, *Korean for Beginners* comes with a multimedia package that includes **video instruction** on pronouncing the characters and **audio recordings** of the example phrases and sentences in the book.

So crank up the *bulgogi* grill and put a bottle of *soju* on ice—you're about to learn Korean!

Welcome to Korean!

An Introduction to Korean and the Korean Spirit

Welcome! I'm so happy you've decided to learn Korean. Not only will you discover how more than 70 million people on the Korean peninsula communicate with each other, but you'll be learning one of the most systematic languages in the world. Most importantly, though, you're going to be hanging out with me, your faithful guide, as I take you on an in-depth tour of Korean. (This is great for me, too, as it gives me a chance to practice my English with you, something most Koreans are always eager to do!)

But before we start, I have a question for you: What do you know about Korea?

Sports and beef: cultural windows

I'm not sure how closely you follow the news, but you might recall that in 2008, mass demonstrations were held throughout South Korea to protest the purchase of beef from the U.S. But why!? Koreans love beef! Apparently, there were some concerns about the meat not being safe for consumption. What was probably the bigger issue, though, was that Koreans didn't like the idea of their president being "persuaded" by the U.S. to sign onto the deal.

A few years earlier, in 2002, there was another occasion for Koreans to gather by the thousands and show their support for their country. Only this time, the atmosphere was more positive, the intention being to cheer on the national soccer team in the World Cup. Koreans are very enthusiastic and passionate about their country and culture. During the games, all the fans wore red shirts and cheered for victory. Prior to this tournament, the Korean soccer team had never won a single World Cup game. You can imagine the excitement when they made it all the way to the semifinals!

People around the world who've witnessed events like these in the international news must be asking themselves: why are Koreans so passionate?

Korea and Koreans are dynamic

Korea is a small country, similar in size to Great Britain. But there are around 50 million people in South Korea, and 25 million in North Korea. This means the population density on the peninsula is very high. South Korea's capital, Seoul, is one of the largest and most crowded cities in the world. And all of these people are always on the go. The expression 빨리 빨리 [ppalri ppalri] is used by Koreans to sum up the bustling nature of the country and its people. But why are they in such a hurry?

빨리 [ppalri] hurry

Perhaps we can find the answer by looking at the modern history of Korea. You see, after the Korean War of 1950–1953, much of the land and its infrastructure was in ruins. So Koreans became determined and made many sacrifices to rebuild their country as quickly as possible. As a result, in less than 50 years, South Korea was transformed into a developed nation. It joined the Organisation for Economic Co-operation and Development (OECD) in 1996, and in 2008 it was ranked 15th in the world by gross domestic product (GDP).

But even now, Koreans feel they should be doing something more to progress further. This explains why they always seem to be in a hurry and why they're so passionate about their history, their culture, and their homeland.

All systems go...

Just one more thing before we launch ourselves into the world of Korean language. Keep in mind that it's very different from English and other European languages. I'm sure the first thing you'll notice is the **characters**. Korean doesn't use the Roman alphabet, unfortunately, so you're probably worried that it's going to be much more difficult to learn than Spanish, French, German, or other languages you may have studied in school.

But don't worry! Korean characters are formed in a very systematic and straightforward way, so they're easy to pick up. Actually, they're so simple that most Korean children learn them before they even enter school. Sounds good, right? I'll show you what I mean in the next chapter.

Are you ready to begin the adventure? I know I am. Just remember, I'm here to help, and I'll never laugh at you or criticize you along the way (well, maybe a giggle here and there, but hopefully I'll be giggling *with* you). Trust me—I'll take you where you need to go!

Further Vocabulary: Korean food

Another important part of Korean culture is the food! We'd better go over some of the basics.

반찬 side dish

밥 [pap] steamed rice

반찬 [panchan] side dish

김치 [kimchi] kimchi

국 [kuk] soup

김밥 [kimbap] rice rolled in dried laver

　(something like sushi, but much cheaper!)

비빔밥 [pibimbap] a rice bowl with assorted ingredients

볶음밥 [pokkeumbap] fried rice

찌개 [jjigae] stew

갈비탕 [kalbitang] beef-rib soup

삼계탕 [samgyetang] chicken soup with ginseng and

　various ingredients

불고기 [pulgogi] Korean barbecue

떡 [tteok] rice cake

Korean Style: Say what?

Do these "words" look familiar?

lol   btw   omg   imho   cya   ;-)   :P   :(:o

With the spread of modern communication methods, such as texting and online messaging services, languages are constantly being modified for convenience. Tons of creative abbreviations, both for words and emotions, have cropped up in English. Do you know all the ones above? No? Omg, imho you'd better study up! ;-)

Korean is no exception to this phenomenon. If you have a chance to chat with a Korean online or by texting, you're sure to run into a few strange looking words, like this one:

ㄱ ㅅ ㄱ ㅅ

This probably doesn't seem that odd to you, since we haven't even gone over Korean characters yet! But take my word that this is a strange construction indeed. First of all, there aren't any vowels in this "word"! That's because it's an abbreviation, and it stands for 감사감사 [kamsagamsa] ("thank you very much"). Even though this goes against the basic rule of Korean word formation, it's frequently used on the Internet.

There are other types of language peculiarities that have developed as a result of messaging services. Emoticons are one of them. Koreans use emoticons even more frequently than English speakers do, but their emoticons are different. The main thing to notice is that they're made to be viewed vertically, so you don't have to tilt your head to figure them out. Let's take a look.

^;^ -or- ^^ (smile)   : Imagine a smiling face.
ㅠㅠ (crying)   : eyes and tears
-;- (angry)   : Imagine your eyes when you're angry.
ㅋ ㅋ (laughter)   : laughing sound 크크 [keukeu]
ㅎ ㅎ (laughter)   : laughing sound 흐흐 [heuheu]

Many people (mainly the younger generation) enjoy these fun plays on the Korean language. Hey, I have an idea! You want to learn authentic Korean, don't you? Well then keep an eye out, because you might just see some of these emoticons pop up in the chapters ahead. Who knows, seeing them might change your mood from ㅠㅠ to ^;^!

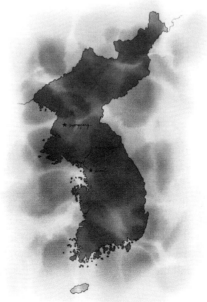

2

Korean Characters

An Introduction to the Korean Characters and Their Pronunciation

The English alphabet is made up of characters—the 26 letters. Likewise, Korean has its own characters, and they're called 한글 [Hangeul]. Due to the strong cultural influence of the Chinese in East Asia, Koreans used to use 한글 in combination with Chinese characters. Nowadays, however, Hangeul is sufficient for almost all communication, and Chinese characters are used much less frequently in Korea.

한글 is probably the easiest East Asian character system to learn. For example, Japanese writing is made up of three different sets of characters: *hiragana*, *katagana*, and Chinese characters (*kanji* in Japanese). And, of course, the Chinese language uses Chinese characters. There are thousands of these, most of them quite complicated, and in order to learn to read and write Chinese, you have to memorize them one by one. Now compare these to the 40 Korean characters, which you'll soon see are formed in a very scientific and commonsense way. No sweat!

한글 is a unique writing system, created in 1444 by King Sejong the Great. His goal was to increase literacy in the country, so obviously he wanted to make 한글 as easy to learn as possible. You only have to look at modern Korea's extremely low illiteracy rate (less than 2%) for proof of the system's success.

Just like the English alphabet, 한글 contains **consonants** and **vowels**. The shape of each one was designed to copy the shape of vocal organs such as the mouth, throat, and tongue when it's spoken, as you'll see in the **videos**. Maybe this clue will help you make sense of the characters.

Something else before we begin. An important key to understanding 한글 is to think in terms of **syllables**. In English, letters are grouped together into syllables. Sometimes just one letter can be a syllable, and there are no rules about the location of vowels and consonants within a syllable. In Korean, on the other hand, syllables are never made up of just one character, and strict formulas govern the creation of syllables. They all contain a combination of <u>C</u>onsonants and <u>V</u>owels, and there are just two patterns for this: C + V and C + V + C.

And finally, keep in mind that the **size** and **location** of the characters can vary depending on which of the above patterns is being used. Sound confusing? Yeah. But it'll make perfect sense once you see the examples below.

Okay, let's check out the consonants first.

Consonants								
Basic	ㄱ g, k	ㄴ n	ㄷ d, t	ㄹ r, l	ㅁ m	ㅂ b, p	ㅅ s, sh	ㅇ Ø/ng	ㅈ j, ch
Double	ㄲ kk		ㄸ tt			ㅃ pp	ㅆ ss		ㅉ jj
Strong	ㅋ k		ㅌ t			ㅍ p		ㅎ h	ㅊ ch

Do you know how many consonants English has? Right, 21. Well, in Korean there are 19 consonants. That's not as many as English, but are you still worried 19 is too many to memorize? There's no need! All you have to do is learn a few simple rules about their shape and pronunciation. We'll start by splitting the 19 consonants into different groups. First, we have the 9 basic consonants.

Basic consonants

The English approximation for each character is shown in [brackets].

An important note! While other books try to teach Korean by spelling out words with English letters, I feel that to truly learn the language, you need to become familiar with the 한글 characters. Each character has a similar sound to a letter or letters in English, but not exactly the same! These are only approximations to help you learn the pronunciation of the characters. So I don't want you to overemphasize the comparisons to English letters. Instead, try to hear and learn each character's sound with fresh ears. Pay close attention to the **videos**.

List of Basic Consonants

ㄱ [g, k] 🎥 2.1

ㄱ is pronounced similarly to [k] at the beginning of a word and at the end of a syllable; in other positions, it's closer to [g].

EX.: 가방 [kabang] bag, 먹다 [meokda] to eat, 미국 [miguk] U.S.A.

ㄴ [n] 🎥 2.2

EX.: 나라 [nara] country/land, 한국 [hanguk] Korea

ㄷ [d, t] 🎥 2.3

ㄷ is pronounced similarly to [t] at the beginning of a word and at the end of a syllable; in other positions, it's closer to [d].

EX.: 다리 [tari] leg/bridge, 믿다 [mitda] to believe, 사다리 [sadari] ladder

ㄹ [r, l] 🎥 2.4

ㄹ is pronounced similarly to [l] at the end of a syllable; in other positions, it's closer to [r]. 🌱

EX.: 별 [pyeol] star, 노래 [norae] song

ㅁ [m] 🎥 2.5 : EX.: 마음 [maeum] heart, mind

ㅂ [b, p] 🎥 2.6

ㅂ is pronounced similarly to [p] at the beginning of a word and at the end of a syllable; in other positions, it's closer to [b].

EX.: 바지 [paji] pants, 잡다 [chapda] to catch, hold, 행복 [haengbok] happiness

ㅅ [s, sh] 🎥 2.7

ㅅ is pronounced similarly to [sh] before the vowels ㅣ, ㅕ, ㅑ, ㅠ, and ㅛ ; in other positions, it's closer to [s].

EX.: 신발 [shinbal] shoes, 사진 [sajin] photo

ㅇ [Ø/ng] 🎥 2.8

ㅇ has no sound when it comes at the beginning of a syllable, 🌱 but is close to [ng] when it's at the end of a syllable.

EX.: 오징어 [ojingeo] squid

ㅈ [j, ch] 🎥 2.9

ㅈ is pronounced similarly to [ch] at the beginning of a word; in other positions, it's closer to [j].

EX.: 조금 [chogeum] a little, 사자 [saja] lion

ㄹ is a tricky one. English speakers will hear it as [r] *or* [l], but Koreans themselves can't hear any difference. This is why Koreans—and other East Asians—find it difficult to differentiate between [l] sounds and [r] sounds when speaking English.

You might wonder why Koreans bother writing ㅇ at the beginning of a syllable if it has no sound. To understand, think about the principal rule I mentioned earlier: Every syllable is composed of at least one consonant and a vowel, remember? Well, what if you want to write a syllable with only a vowel sound? That's when you place ㅇ in the first position. It's a consonant, so it lets you follow the rule of syllable construction, but it has no sound, so it allows the vowel to be pronounced by itself. Understand?

All of these consonants can appear at the beginning of a syllable, at the end of a syllable, or both. Consonants at the end of a syllable (C + V + <u>C</u>) are called **받침** [patchim]. When pronouncing ㄱ, ㄷ, ㅂ, ㅅ, and ㅈ as third-position consonants, you should make them softer than when they're in the first position. It's almost like you're just mouthing the consonant without making any noise. It sounds a bit confusing, I know, but don't worry. I'll explain the concept further in the next chapter.

Double consonants

Next, we have the five double consonants: ㄲ, ㄸ, ㅃ, ㅆ, and ㅉ. Do you recognize the shapes of these? As their name implies, they're doubles of some of the basic consonants. Their pronunciation is harder and thicker than ㄱ, ㄷ, ㅂ, ㅅ, and ㅈ.

Double consonants are perhaps the hardest element of Korean pronunciation for English speakers to hear and mimic, and can lead to some very funny misunderstandings! For example, you might wind up asking a father for his "moon's" hand in marriage instead of his "daughter's" (딸: "daughter," 달: "moon"), and you could then offer to give her a "tail," not a "ring" (꼬리: "tail," 고리: "ring"). Even native Koreans of particular regions sometimes make mistakes in the pronunciation of ㅆ. They sometimes cook "flesh" when what they really wanted was "rice" (살: "flesh," 쌀: "rice").

So don't despair if you can't make out these double consonants at first. They'll take some time. Pay special attention to the **videos**.

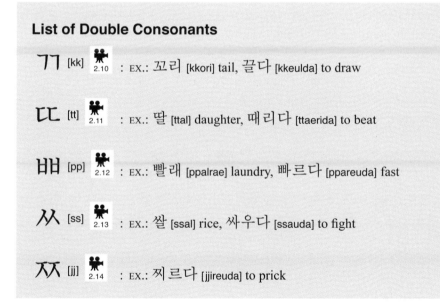

List of Double Consonants

ㄲ [kk] 2.10 : EX.: 꼬리 [kkori] tail, 끌다 [kkeulda] to draw

ㄸ [tt] 2.11 : EX.: 딸 [ttal] daughter, 때리다 [ttaerida] to beat

ㅃ [pp] 2.12 : EX.: 빨래 [ppalrae] laundry, 빠르다 [ppareuda] fast

ㅆ [ss] 2.13 : EX.: 쌀 [ssal] rice, 싸우다 [ssauda] to fight

ㅉ [jj] 2.14 : EX.: 찌르다 [jjireuda] to prick

Strong (aspirated) consonants

The shapes in this final group of five consonants should also look familiar to you now. Each one is formed by adding a line to or slightly modifying one of the basic consonants. For example, ㄱ becomes ㅋ, ㄷ becomes ㅌ, ㅂ becomes ㅍ, ㅇ becomes ㅎ, and ㅈ becomes ㅊ. Pretty simple, right?

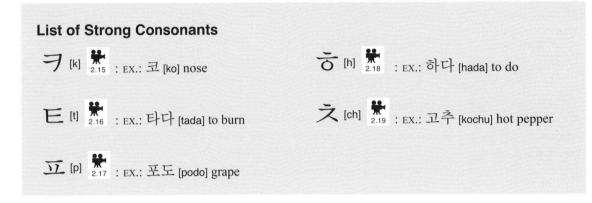

List of Strong Consonants

ㅋ [k] 2.15 : EX.: 코 [ko] nose

ㅌ [t] 2.16 : EX.: 타다 [tada] to burn

ㅍ [p] 2.17 : EX.: 포도 [podo] grape

ㅎ [h] 2.18 : EX.: 하다 [hada] to do

ㅊ [ch] 2.19 : EX.: 고추 [kochu] hot pepper

The consonants in this group are **aspirated**. What does this mean? Well, when you speak them, you should release a puff of air, which gives them a more forceful sound. Does that make sense? Here, try this: put your hand over your mouth. When you pronounce ㄱ [g], ㄷ [d], ㅂ [b], ㅇ [ng], and ㅈ [j], you should only feel a very weak breath of air being expelled from your mouth. Now pronounce the aspirated consonants: ㅋ [k], ㅌ [t], ㅍ [p], ㅎ [h], and ㅊ [ch]. You release a more powerful puff of air for each one, which you should feel on your hand. That's aspiration—got it?

Okay, and just like we talked about with the basic consonants, both double and aspirated consonants can function as 받침, consonants at the **end** of a syllable. Remember to make these softer, like you're just mouthing the consonant without making any noise.

Vowels											
Basic	ㅏ a			ㅓ eo			ㅣ i	ㅗ o	ㅜ u	ㅡ eu
Double	ㅑ ya	ㅐ ae	ㅒ yae	ㅕ yeo	ㅔ e	ㅖ ye		ㅛ yo	ㅠ yu	
	ㅘ wa	ㅙ wae	ㅚ oe	ㅝ weo	ㅞ we	ㅟ wi	ㅢ ui			

In English, there are five vowels: a, e, i, o, and u. But Korean has 21! Oh no! Okay, hold on. You don't have to freak out because, just like the consonants, we can divide up the vowels according to type so they're easier to learn.

Basic vowels

To begin separating the vowels into groups, we have to think back to the two patterns for constructing Korean syllables: C + V and C + V + C. As you can see, no matter which pattern is used, the vowel always goes in the second position.

One defining feature of all vowels is how they are written in relation to the first-position <u>C</u>onsonant. Some are written to the **right** of the <u>C</u>onsonant, while others are placed **below** the <u>C</u>onsonant. So first, let's look at the 3 basic vowels that go to the right of the <u>C</u>onsonant.

And don't forget, the English letters in brackets are just general guides, not exact matches for the Korean sounds. Don't think of the Korean characters as simple substitutions for English letters, but as completely independent and unique sounds. Pay close attention to the **videos**.

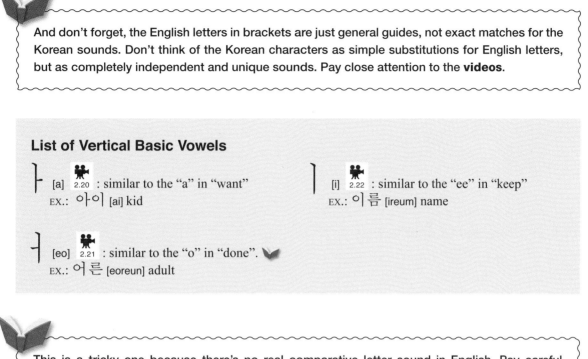

List of Vertical Basic Vowels

ㅏ [a] 2.20 : similar to the "a" in "want"
EX.: 아이 [ai] kid

ㅣ [i] 2.22 : similar to the "ee" in "keep"
EX.: 이름 [ireum] name

ㅓ [eo] 2.21 : similar to the "o" in "done".
EX.: 어른 [eoreun] adult

This is a tricky one because there's no real comparative letter sound in English. Pay careful attention to its pronunciation!

We can refer to these as **vertical** vowels because they look like they're standing up straight. They're placed directly to the **right** of a consonant, as in the word 아버지 [abeoji]. See how the vowels are standing up next to the consonants?

아버지 [abeoji] father, dad

Now for the three basic **horizontal** vowels, which are written like they're lying down.

List of Horizontal Basic Vowels

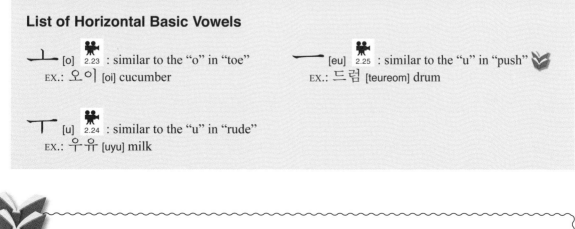

ㅗ [o] 2.23 : similar to the "o" in "toe"
EX.: 오이 [oi] cucumber

ㅡ [eu] 2.25 : similar to the "u" in "push"
EX.: 드럼 [teureom] drum

ㅜ [u] 2.24 : similar to the "u" in "rude"
EX.: 우유 [uyu] milk

This is another tricky vowel, because there's no great English comparison. Watch the **video** a couple extra times for this one.

These vowels are placed directly **below** a consonant, as in the word 스도쿠 [seudoku]. They look like they're lying down, don't they?

> 스도쿠 [seudoku] sudoku (a number puzzle game—do you play it?)

Double vowels (diphthongs)

Have you heard of diphthongs? They're vowels that are a little more complex. They combine two different sounds to create a single new sound. All of the six basic Korean vowels you just learned have diphthongs associated with them.

Let's look first at the diphthongs made from ㅏ, ㅓ, and ㅣ. These are **vertical** vowels, so their diphthongs are also vertical and are written to the right of a consonant.

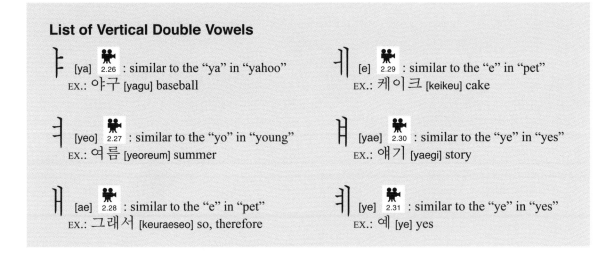

List of Vertical Double Vowels

ㅑ [ya] 2.26 : similar to the "ya" in "yahoo"
EX.: 야구 [yagu] baseball

ㅕ [yeo] 2.27 : similar to the "yo" in "young"
EX.: 여름 [yeoreum] summer

ㅐ [ae] 2.28 : similar to the "e" in "pet"
EX.: 그래서 [keuraeseo] so, therefore

ㅔ [e] 2.29 : similar to the "e" in "pet"
EX.: 케이크 [keikeu] cake

ㅒ [yae] 2.30 : similar to the "ye" in "yes"
EX.: 얘기 [yaegi] story

ㅖ [ye] 2.31 : similar to the "ye" in "yes"
EX.: 예 [ye] yes

Do you remember how we made the aspirated consonants? Right, by adding a line to or slightly modifying one of the basic consonants. Well, the same is true for the formation of these diphthong vowels. Add a line to ㅏ and ㅓ and you get ㅑ and ㅕ. Next, the third and fourth vowels in this list are made by combining two basic vowels. ㅐ is created from ㅏ + ㅣ, and ㅔ comes from ㅓ + ㅣ. Interestingly, though, most Koreans these days can't distinguish between these two vowels because their sounds are so close to each other. The same is true of the final two diphthongs listed here, ㅒ and ㅖ. That means two less sounds for you to learn. Yes!

Okay. Now let's look at two **horizontal** diphthongs that are made from the basic vowels ㅗ and ㅜ. Remember, these are written below the consonant.

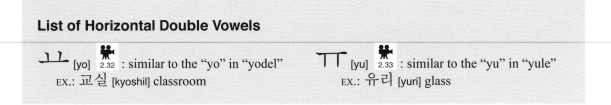

List of Horizontal Double Vowels

ㅛ [yo] 2.32 : similar to the "yo" in "yodel"
EX.: 교실 [kyoshil] classroom

ㅠ [yu] 2.33 : similar to the "yu" in "yule"
EX.: 유리 [yuri] glass

It's easy to see how ㅗ becomes ㅛ, and ㅜ becomes ㅠ.

Great! Just seven more vowels to go! These last diphthongs are a little different, because they're **combinations** of a horizontal vowel and a vertical vowel.

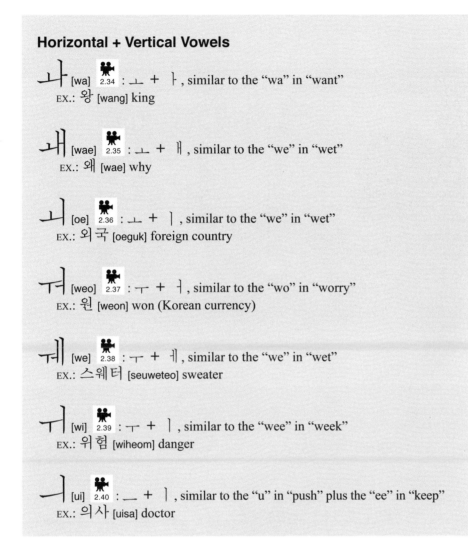

Horizontal + Vertical Vowels

ㅘ [wa] 2.34 : ㅗ + ㅏ, similar to the "wa" in "want"
  EX.: 왕 [wang] king

ㅙ [wae] 2.35 : ㅗ + ㅐ, similar to the "we" in "wet"
  EX.: 왜 [wae] why

ㅚ [oe] 2.36 : ㅗ + ㅣ, similar to the "we" in "wet"
  EX.: 외국 [oeguk] foreign country

ㅝ [weo] 2.37 : ㅜ + ㅓ, similar to the "wo" in "worry"
  EX.: 원 [weon] won (Korean currency)

ㅞ [we] 2.38 : ㅜ + ㅔ, similar to the "we" in "wet"
  EX.: 스웨터 [seuweteo] sweater

ㅟ [wi] 2.39 : ㅜ + ㅣ, similar to the "wee" in "week"
  EX.: 위험 [wiheom] danger

ㅢ [ui] 2.40 : ㅡ + ㅣ, similar to the "u" in "push" plus the "ee" in "keep"
  EX.: 의사 [uisa] doctor

You've made it—nice work! I bet now you might be a little confused about some of the vowels that look similar to each other. But with a little practice and continued exposure, I know you'll find it easy to tell them apart.

And what about their unfamiliar pronunciations? Well, here's a tip for pronouncing those final seven diphthongs. Just think of them as adding together the pronunciations of the two vowels that make up the diphthong, as shown.

Let's practice the most difficult one, ㅢ. Start by loudly making the sound of the first vowel, ㅡ, and then add a quick ㅣ. Do this a couple times, and then say the whole thing faster, and faster, and faster… Soon, you'll be sounding just like a Korean!

Also, you probably noticed that ㅙ, ㅚ, and ㅞ have the same pronunciation. Maybe you're wondering what the point is of having three separate characters for the same sound. Is it just to make it hard on you? Well, yes, but that's not the only reason! Having more characters means the Korean language can contain more words through homophones (words that sound the same but have different spellings and different meanings).

Hmm…are you still thinking, "How am I ever going to be able to remember all these characters and their strange, foreign pronunciations?" Hey, lighten up! You just started, so don't expect to be an expert immediately. No one can do that, not even me. ^^

But if you're still feeling discouraged, let me put things in perspective for you. Picture yourself riding a bus along the hectic, skyscraper-lined streets of Seoul. Outside your window, you're watching all the billboards, street signs, and storefront banners fly by. How cool will it be when you realize you can decipher those alien characters and pronounce all the words you see? It's a gratifying experience, believe me, and one you'll be capable of before you know it.

Further Vocabulary: Taste

I told you food was important. Let's continue our culinary studies by learning how to describe Korean eats.

맛 [mat] taste, flavor

입 맛 [immat] appetite

맛있다 [mashitda] delicious

맛없다 [madeopda] bad

싱겁다 [shinggeopda] bland

짜다 [jjada] salty

달다 [talda] sweet, sugary

맵다 [maepda] spicy

쓰다 [sseuda] bitter

Korean Style: Korean computer keyboards

Have you ever seen a Korean keyboard? If not, have you ever imagined how speakers of other languages use keyboards to write in their language on a computer? Well, studying a Korean keyboard is not only interesting in itself, but it also offers some insight into the relationships between the different Korean characters.

On the English keypad, each letter is assigned a single button. And you make capital letters by holding down the <shift> key. That's only 26 different letter keys, right? Well, as you just learned, in Korean there are 19 consonants and 21 vowels. So how do they fit 40 characters onto those 26 keys? Let's take a look.

Start at the <Q> key in the upper left-hand corner. There are two Korean characters on this button: ㅂ on the bottom and ㅃ above it. Remember that ㅃ is the double consonant of ㅂ? So, while in English you use the <shift> key to make capital letters, in Korean you can type double consonants with <shift>. Does that make sense? Moving to the right in the same row, you can see ㅈ and ㅉ, ㄷ and ㄸ, ㄱ and ㄲ, and ㅅ and ㅆ. All of the consonants that make double consonants are in the upper left section of the keyboard.

Great. And what about aspirated consonants? Well, check out the bottom row of keys. Starting from the left, you have ㅋ, ㅌ, ㅊ, and ㅍ. And the vowels? Most of the basic ones are in the second row to the right, and their diphthongs (double vowels) occupy the keys above them.

But where are ㅘ, ㅙ, ㅚ, ㅝ, ㅞ, ㅟ, and ㅢ? Remember how I told you that each of these seven diphthongs is a combination of two other vowels? With that in mind, can you guess how to type them? Correct! If you want to type ㅘ, you hit ㅗ first, and then ㅏ, which will automatically create the character ㅘ on the screen. ㅙ is ㅗ + ㅐ, ㅚ is ㅗ + ㅣ, and so on.

As you can see, the Korean characters aren't randomly positioned on the keyboard like the English letters are. Because of this, Koreans can type very quickly, and that's one of the many reasons why computers and the Internet are so prevalent in Korean society.

CHAPTER 3

Reading and Pronouncing Korean Words

Review of the Characters and Some Additional Pronunciation Rules

In this chapter, let's practice some of what you've learned so that it'll stick, okay? To do that, we'll take a look at how Korean words are formed and pronounced.

Now, you may remember from when you were young and learning English that there are lots of words that don't fit the typical pronunciation patterns. This probably made it more difficult for you to learn some words (and very difficult for Koreans learning English!). For example, without spending time to think about it, try to pronounce this word: "floccinaucinihilipilification." Can you do it? It's an English word, but I bet many native English speakers would be a little confused as to how it should sound.

Lucky for you, almost all Korean words follow certain fundamental pronunciation rules. Once you learn these rules, you'll be able to pronounce pretty much any Korean word you see. You may not know what it means, but hey, we'll get to that later!

There's even more good news about Korean pronunciation: there are no **accents**. Every syllable of every word is spoken with the same stress. Do you understand what I mean? Think about the word "Canada." In English, we usually accent the first syllable, like this: CA-na-da. Well, in Korean, all syllables receive the same stress, like this: CA-NA-DA.

And finally, the **intonations** in Korean will be similar to those you use in English. There aren't any concrete rules about this, but the main thing to remember is that, just like in English, you let your voice get higher in pitch at the end of a question. Consider how you'd say "Are you having fun?" The intonation of "fun" is higher than that of the rest of the sentence.

Okay. It's time for a pop quiz. How do you pronounce this word:

 음식

Uh-huh, the correct answer is [eumshik]. Let's look at it syllable by syllable. First, we know that ㅇ is silent because it's at the beginning of a syllable, right? Next, do you remember how to pronounce the vowel ㅡ? And then the consonant ㅁ. Look at the shape of ㅁ. It's closed, so your mouth should also be closed. Then, in the second syllable, ㅅ is like [sh], because it's followed by the vowel ㅣ, which makes an [ee] sound. And ㄱ is like [k]. Great!

There's one note of caution with this pronunciation, however. It's actually one of the basic rules I mentioned in the previous chapter. And this rule is about consonants that appear in the third position (C + V + <u>C</u>). Do you remember the name for these consonants? That's right, **받침**! I mentioned a couple times that these have a different pronunciation than consonants in the first position. They're softer, almost like you're simply mouthing the consonant without making any noise.

So in the word 음식, the [k] sound produced by the ㄱ should be **subdued**. Finish the word with your mouth in the correct shape to pronounce this character, but don't actually make the sound. This is very important, because if you make a strong [k] sound, Koreans will hear the word 음시크 instead of 음식. The meaning will be completely different, which is bad, because 음식 is a very essential word. It means "food"!

> 음식 [eumshik] food

Here are a couple more to practice with:

 밥 [pap] steamed rice

 라면 [ramyeon] instant noodles (ramen)

Not too hard, right? Just follow what you learned in chapter 2, and what I just told you about 받침 consonants. 밥 is still the main element in Korean meals, though the younger generation is becoming increasingly fond of Western foods like spaghetti and pizza. And 라면 is the most popular snack in Korea. You've probably seen different versions of it where you live, right? Wow, with all this talk of food, I'm getting pretty hungry! We'd better move on. ^;^

Let's keep looking at those third-position consonants. Here are three very similar one-syllable words:

낫, 낮, 낯

Can you pronounce these? The first two characters are the same in all three, yes? ㄴ is like [n], and ㅏ is the vowel sound [a]. Now, if you add the appropriate 받침 consonants to each one, you get 낫 [nas], 낮 [naj], and 낯 [nach].

But what happens when you apply the pronunciation rule for third-position consonants that I discussed above? Remember, you should shape your mouth as if to pronounce the final consonant but not actually make a sound. How does this affect the pronunciations of these words?

Well, it turns out that the consonants ㅅ, ㅈ, and ㅊ all have the same sound when they're in the third position like this. They all become a soft, non-aspirated [t] sound. Can you hear it? So the pronunciation of each of these words is exactly the same: [nat].

Is this rule confusing? You might think so now, but it's such a common element of Korean that you'll get used to it fast.

So now you've learned some examples of Korean **homophones**—words that sound the same but have different spellings and different meanings. 낫: "sickle," 낮: "day," and 낯: "face."

As you may have noticed, the 받침 pronunciation rule is used when there's no other sound following the third-position consonant. Well, what happens if there is a sound after it? If it's followed by another consonant sound, then the rule still applies. But, if the next sound is a vowel, then something different happens. To demonstrate, let's add the syllable –이 onto the words we just looked at, creating:

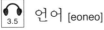 낫이, 낮이, 낯이

What happens now? Well, the third-position consonants revert to their true sound. 낫이 is [nas + i], right? So that's how you pronounce it: [nasi]. Except, in this case, the [s] becomes [sh] according to the pronunciation rules in chapter 2. Likewise, 낮이 is [naji], and 낯이 is [nachi].

Wait a minute! Isn't ㅇ a consonant? You're absolutely right. But remember that at the beginning of a syllable it just acts as a **placeholder**. Because ㅇ has no sound value here, the 받침 consonant jumps over it and connects with the following vowel sound. In other words, the word 낫이 is pronounced the same as the word 나시. Does that make sense? Let's look at two more words where ㅇ is silent:

언어 [eoneo]

한국어 [hangugeo]

언어 is pronounced like 어너, because the [n] sound of ㄴ jumps over the silent ㅇ and connects with the vowel sound of ㅓ. So, [eoneo]. 언어 means "language."

Similarly, 한국어 is pronounced like 한구거. So, [hangugeo]. You know the meaning? No? Hey! What are studying right now? "Korean language," right? Yes, that's 한국어. (한국 means "Korea.")

Both words above share the ending 어. This syllable carries the meaning of "language," although it can't be used independently. Actually, the meaning of 어 originated from a Chinese character. You certainly don't have to learn Chinese characters to learn Korean, but as you study more Korean words, you'll come to know that many of them are based on Chinese characters. In fact, around 70% of Korean vocabulary is related in some fashion to the Chinese language.

Okay, this is a lot to digest, so let's sum up with a short review. When a consonant in the third position is not followed by a vowel, you simply mouth the character without pronouncing it, and this sometimes creates a new sound (like the non-aspirated [t]). If there is a vowel following it, then the consonant retains its true sound, jumping over the ㅇ to join with the vowel sound.

Don't worry! This will be very clear after some more practice. But that will have to wait till the next chapter.

Further Vocabulary: Country names

In Korean, the names of countries sometimes sound a lot different than they do in English. For example, the name for America is 미국, made from two syllables of Chinese origin. 국 means "country" and is used to form the Korean names of many of the world's nations, while 미 means "beautiful." So Koreans refer to the U.S. as "beautiful country"—how sweet!

Likewise, as I mentioned at the end of the chapter, 어 is a Chinese syllable meaning "language," so this is used to name the languages of different peoples.

Nation	Name	Language name
Korea	한국	한국어
China	중국	중국어
U.K.	영국	영어
U.S.	미국	영어
Japan	일본	일본어, 일어
Germany	독일	독일어, 독어
France	프랑스	프랑스어, 불어
Spain	스페인	스페인어
Russia	러시아	러시아어

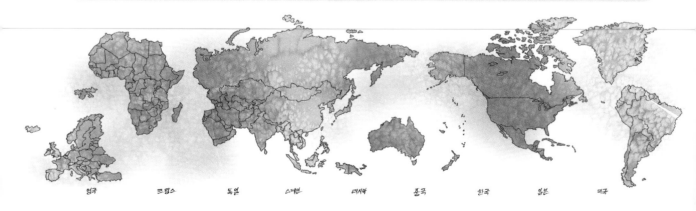

Korean Style: Do you like phlegm??

Some of most difficult pronunciations to differentiate for Westerners learning Korean are ㅋ / ㄲ / ㄱ and ㅌ / ㄸ / ㄷ. I already told you how a simple mistake between basic consonants and their doubles can turn "rice" into "flesh," and a "ring" into a "tail." ㅋ ㅋ But those aren't the only pitfalls to watch out for. Take note:

카레 좋아하세요? [Kare choahaseyo?] Do you like curry?
네? **가래** 좋아하냐고요? [Ne? Karae choahanyagoyo?] What? You want to know if I like phlegm?

우리 **꿀** 먹을까요? [Uri kkul meogeulkkayo?] Why don't we eat some honey?
저는 **굴** 못 먹어요. [Cheoneun kul mot meogeoyo.] Sorry, I can't eat oysters.

이 음식에는 **콩**이 들어갔어요. [I eumshigeneun kongi teureogasseoyo.] This dish has beans in it.
네? 이 음식에 **공**이 들어갔어요? [Ne? I eumshige kongi teureogasseoyo?] What? There's a ball in this food?

이 **달**은 한가해요. [I tareun hangahaeyo.] I'm free this month.
네?? **딸**이 한가하다고요? [Ne? Ttari hangahadagoyo?] What?? Your daughter is free?

카레 [kare] curry
가래 [karae] phlegm
꿀 [kkul] honey
굴 [kul] oyster

콩 [kong] bean
공 [kong] ball
달 [tal] month, moon
딸 [ttal] daughter

I You Love
나는 너를 사랑해. [Naneun neoreul saranghae.]
Five Basic Features of Korean: Word Order, Particles, Conjugation, Honorifics, and Omissions and Plurals

So, we've learned about the Korean characters and how to pronounce them. Technically, you could now read a Korean book out loud and sound pretty good. But would you know what you were reading? No!

Now we must move on to the meaning of the language. And to understand the meaning of any language, you first have to understand its structure, right? So let's go over five important features of the structure of Korean. Just remember, it belongs to an entirely different language family than English, so its structure is going to be very different, too. But maybe this will work to your advantage. You'll be able to learn these rules and features with a fresh mind.

1. Word order
The normal word order in a Korean sentence is: Subject – Object – Verb. So,

🎧 4.1 나는 너를 사랑해. [Naneun neoreul saranghae.] I love you.

> 나 [na] I
> N-는 [neun] topic particle (see chapter 5)
> 너 [neo] you
> N-를 [reul] object particle (see chapter 5)
> 사랑하다 [saranghada] to love
>
> Note: The "N" stands for "noun," as Korean particles attach to nouns. Read on for details.

This sentence is translated into English as "I love you," but if you look at the word order literally, it says "I you love." Strange, isn't it? The verb comes **last**! And it'll always come last. However, the other two elements (the subject and object) can be switched around if you want:

🎧 4.2 너를 나는 사랑해. [Neoreul naneun saranghae.] I love you.

Koreans will understand what you mean by this, even though it'll sound like you're trying to emphasize 너 instead of 나. It would be a little awkward in this case, but the general rule is that the subject can be placed anywhere in the sentence, except at the end.

2. Particles—noun endings

If the word order is so free, how do Koreans know which word is the subject and which is the object? Well, the answer is this: **particles**. These are very important grammatical components of Korean.

Particles are attached to the end of nouns to indicate the function of those nouns, as well as to add meaning to nouns as prepositions do in English. For example, in the sentence we just looked at, 나 means "I," and –는 is a particle letting us know that 나 is the main topic of the sentence. Next, 너 means "you," so can you guess what the particle –를 does? Right! It's the object marker, letting us know that 너 is the object in the sentence.

There are many particles in Korean, and learning them is essential to learning the language. But we don't need to rush it. Let's leave it at this for now, and then in the next chapter we'll discuss these interesting little language elements in greater detail.

3. Conjugation—constant bases vs. variable endings

Korean verbs and adjectives are composed of bases and endings. The bases are constant, while the endings can change. This idea of variable endings attaching to the unchanging bases of verbs and adjectives is called **conjugation**. English verbs conjugate too, but they don't change nearly as much as their Korean counterparts. The purpose of conjugation is to alter the tone of voice, tense, or grammatical function of verbs and adjectives. For example:

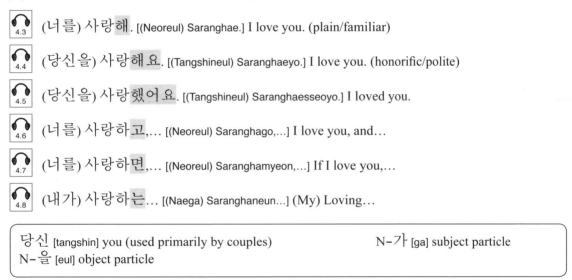

4.3 (너를) 사랑해. [(Neoreul) Saranghae.] I love you. (plain/familiar)

4.4 (당신을) 사랑해요. [(Tangshineul) Saranghaeyo.] I love you. (honorific/polite)

4.5 (당신을) 사랑했어요. [(Tangshineul) Saranghaesseoyo.] I loved you.

4.6 (너를) 사랑하고,... [(Neoreul) Saranghago,...] I love you, and...

4.7 (너를) 사랑하면,... [(Neoreul) Saranghamyeon,...] If I love you,...

4.8 (내가) 사랑하는... [(Naega) Saranghaneun...] (My) Loving...

> 당신 [tangshin] you (used primarily by couples)   N–가 [ga] subject particle
> N–을 [eul] object particle

In all of these sentences and clauses, the verb base (사랑하–) remains constant. (해 and 했 are shortened forms of 하여 and 하였.) Instead, the verb endings decide the precise meaning.

Even though conjugation occurs in English too, I bet reading about it in the context of a foreign language can be pretty overwhelming. But I assure you it'll be crystal clear once you've gotten through chapters 6 and 7. That's where I'll tell you everything you ever wanted to know about conjugation!

4. Honorifics—levels of respect

Korean society is very hierarchical. Everyone has a special place in this hierarchy, which may be higher or lower than the place of someone else, and this cultural trait is reflected in the language. When speaking to someone who is higher up in the hierarchy, you must show the proper respect and politeness through the use of honorifics.

There are two basic levels of respect in Korean: **plain** and **honorific**. Some words have entirely different forms for use in the plain and the honorific, but the difference is most frequently seen in verb and adjective endings. Plain endings are used between friends or when speaking to a child, while honorifics are for those older than you or people you don't know well.

So, in the sentences above, the first and second have the same meaning, but their objects and verb endings are different. 너 is a plain word meaning "you," while 당신  is the honorific form. And 사랑해요 is the honorific form of 사랑해.

> Be careful here, because 당신 is in fact the word usually used between a couple. In general practice, you would use someone's name to show respect rather than either of these versions of "you."

The categories of plain and honorific are further subdivided, with more endings expressing more particular levels of respect for specific situations. But for a beginner, learning the difference between these two basic categories is more than enough! Are you curious about them? Well, don't worry, because before you know it you'll be turning the page to chapter 8, which is all about honorifics.

5. Omissions and plurals

If you've ever studied Spanish, you know it's okay to omit the subject of a sentence in that language. For example, instead of saying "I went to the store," you can just say "Went to the store," and everyone will know what you mean. This is because the conjugation of the verb in the sentence tells who the subject is.

Well, Korean is very similar. Because the verb or adjective ending contains information like tense, tone, and level of respect, specifically identifying the subject of the sentence is sometimes repetitive and unnecessary, as demonstrated in the list of sentences on the previous page. Korean subjects, objects, and their attached particles are often **omitted**.

Omissions can be seen as an easy or difficult language aspect, depending on your point of view, but Korean **plurals** are nothing but simple. In Korean, you don't have to worry about whether nouns are countable or uncountable, or whether you need to add "-s" or "-es" to make a word plural. Most nouns can be used to represent both singular and plural. That's right—you don't have to change them at all! For cases where you really what to emphasize that something is plural, all you need to do is add the suffix –들 onto the end of the word. Not too shabby!

Further Vocabulary: Positive feelings

Aren't you happy that you now know so much about the structure of Korean? Repeat after me:

기분 [kibun] feelings, mood

기쁘다 [kippeuda] glad, happy

즐겁다 [cheulgeopda] pleasant, happy

행복하다 [haengbokada] happy

편하다 [pyeonhada] comfortable

신나다 [shinnada] to be excited

웃다 [utda] to laugh, to smile

재미있다 [chaemiitda] fun, funny

행복해요. I'm happy.

Korean Style: You must listen to Korean from the end.

Of course, it's important to listen to someone carefully when they speak to you. And if you interrupt them, they might get angry. But to Koreans, it's particularly important to listen to the end of a speaker's sentences. There's even a saying about it: "You must listen to Korean from the end." Why is this? Think about what you just learned about the structure of the language. Korean verbs always come at the ends of sentences, and the verbs often contain key information.

Take a look at this example. No, wait…I should say *listen* to what your Korean friend is about to tell you.

나 어제 전지현하고 데이트하는… [Na eoje Cheonchihyunhago teiteuhaneun…] I dated Jihyun Jeon yesterday...

어제 [eoje] yesterday   데이트하다 [teiteuhada] to date
N-하고 [hago] particle meaning "with"

Surprised? You might say "What! You dated Jihyun Jeon? The cute star of the movie *My Sassy Girl*? Unbelievable!" But your friend wasn't finished! The end of his sentence was going to be,

꿈을 꿨어. [kkumeul kkwosseo.] I had a dream.

꿈 [kkum] dream   꾸다 [kkuda] to dream

So all together: 나 어제 전지현하고 데이트하는 꿈을 꿨어. I had a dream I dated Jihyun Jeon yesterday.

Oops! But don't be too disappointed. You can date Jihyun Jeon too, if you want. WHEN PIGS FLY! Haha, I guess you have to listen to English from the end also. ^;^

CHAPTER

5

My Mother Is Korean, and My Father Is American

어머니는 한국 사람이고, 아버지는 미국 사람이에요.

[Eeomeonineun hanguk saramigo, abeojineun miguk saramieyo.]

All About Particles

I gave you a little taste of them in the last chapter, but now it's time to dig into the main course: particles.

Remember, particles are used in Korean to attach to the end of nouns in order to tell listeners what the **functions** of those nouns are, or to act as prepositions and add **meaning** to the nouns. Since this language element is completely foreign to speakers of English, I want to make sure to explain it clearly and with plenty of examples.

In this chapter, we'll go over a handful of particles that you're most likely to come across on a regular basis. Then, once you've mastered the basic concepts, I'll introduce you to other particles throughout the rest of the book. And, just to help you out a little more, I've included a list of all the particles you'll see in this book in the *Further Vocabulary* section at the end of the chapter, which you can refer to anytime. Hey…I aim to please!

Okay, let me describe one more important aspect about particles before we begin. If you've looked ahead at the list already (admit it—I know you have!), you probably noticed that some particles have **two** forms. Why!? Sometimes it seems like Korean just wants to make learning the language as hard as possible, doesn't it?

But actually, there's a very sensible reason for the dual forms. One is attached to nouns that end in a consonant, and the other hooks onto nouns that end with a vowel. This ensures a smoother and easier pronunciation, which is something you can appreciate, right? In fact, you'll see this idea again and again in the next two chapters, which cover conjugation, so it'll pay to get used to it here. I'll use the following abbreviations when explaining:

Nc = noun ending in a consonant
Nv = noun ending in a vowel

Are you ready? Yes, of course you are! Let's start with the most basic particles—those that define the grammatical functions of and relationships between different nouns.

Particles that define grammatical functions and relationships

-이 / -가 [-i/-ga]: Subject particle

Pattern: Nc + 이 / Nv + 가

As you've likely guessed, the job of this particle is to let you know which noun in the sentence is the **subject**. It doesn't get more straightforward than that, does it?

Don't worry about understanding the new vocabulary or grammar points included in this chapter. There will be plenty of time for that later. Right now, just focus on the particles!

5.1 EX. 1: 고향**이** 어디예요? [Kohyangi eodiyeyo?] Where is your hometown?

In this sentence, you can see that the noun 고향, which means "hometown," is the subject of the sentence, and the speaker is asking you where your hometown is located. You're likely to hear this question frequently, as Koreans place a lot of importance on where people are from, both within Korea and abroad.

Also, you'll notice that 고향 ends in a consonant, ㅇ, and that it takes the –이 form of the subject particle. Compare this to the next example:

5.2 EX. 2: 제주도**가** 제 고향이에요. [Chejudoga che kohyangieyo.] Jeju Island is my hometown.

Here, the word 제주도 ends in a vowel, and it takes the particle's –가 form. Do you see the pattern? –이 attaches to nouns ending in a consonant because it starts with a vowel sound. Conversely, –가 latches onto nouns ending in a vowel because it begins with a consonant sound. This is a fundamental and recurring rule in Korean, the pairing of consonants and vowels when adding endings. If you're taking notes, make sure to write that down!

–을 / –를 [-eul/-reul]: Object particle

Pattern: Nc + 을 / Nv + 를

This is another simple particle to grasp. It signifies that a noun is acting as the **object** of the sentence. Take a look:

5.3 EX. 1: 책**을** 읽고 있어요. [Chaegeul ikgo isseoyo.] I'm reading a book.

The word 책, or "book," is the object of the sentence, because the action, "reading," is being done *to* it. Of course, objects can be people too, as in the next example:

5.4 EX. 2: 아내**를** 사랑해요. [Anaereul saranghaeyo.] I love my wife.

Of course I do! And notice the rules governing the use of the two different forms? It's the same as with the subject particle, isn't it? –을 begins with a vowel sound, so it comes after nouns that end in a consonant. And, vice versa, because –를 begins with a consonant, it follows nouns ending in a vowel. Starting to fit together?

–은 / –는 [-eun/-neun]: Topic or contrast particle

Pattern: Nc + 은 / Nv + 는

So far, so good. Now, however, we come to a particle without a direct equivalent meaning in English. Subjects and objects sound pretty familiar, but what's a **topic**? How is that different from a sentence's subject? Rest assured, you're not alone in asking these questions. English speakers have a tough time learning to distinguish between subjects and topics. Basically, you use the topic particle when you want to add particular emphasis to a noun. Let's check it out, shall we?

 EX. 1: 제 이름은 할이에요. [Che ireumeun harieyo.] My name is Hal.

This sentence can be directly translated as "When it comes to my name, it is Hal." Definitely awkward in English, but do you understand the meaning? While 이름, "name," would be considered the subject of this sentence in English, in Korean it occupies the role of the topic because it's being stressed more strongly.

Luckily, the second function of this particle is more intuitive. It can be used to emphasize **contrast** in a sentence where two different nouns are being listed. Check it out:

EX. 2: 어머니는 한국 사람이고, 아버지는 미국 사람이에요. [Eomeonineun hanguk saramigo, abeojineun miguk saramieyo.] My mother is Korean, and my father is American.

Here, the particle attaches to both 어머니, "mother," and 아버지, "father," because these two nouns are being contrasted. One parent is defined as Korean, while the other is American.

어머니는 한국 사람이고, 아버지는 미국 사람이에요.
My mother is Korean, and my father is American.

–도 [-do]: "too," "also," "as well"

Pattern: N + 도

And now we move on to the opposite of contrast, which is **agreement**. It's best to think of this particle as occupying the reverse side of the coin from the particle –은 / –는 in its contrast function, so let's use the same example:

EX.: 어머니도 한국 사람이고, 아버지도… [Eomeonido hanguk saramigo, abeojido…] My mother is Korean, and my father is…

You know what I'm going to say next, don't you? You can guess the last part thanks to the particle –도, which provides us with the hint that the following information is going to match that which came before. So, the final product would be:

어머니도 한국 사람이고, 아버지도 한국 사람이에요. [Eomeonido hanguk saramigo, abeojido hanguk saramieyo.] My mother is Korean, and my father is Korean, too.

Both nouns are being described as the same thing. The –도 particle is used to signify this, and again it's attached to both 어머니 and 아버지. Notice too that there's only one form of this particle. Hurray! So it makes no difference whether the noun ends in a consonant or vowel.

Overall, these particles are pretty handy, aren't they? It's like a little bird is whispering in your ear, telling you the exact grammatical function of each noun. Nice, huh!? They're especially helpful in long, complex sentences where it's essential to understand the relationships between all the different nouns. Take a look at this:

 오늘은 저도 어머니를 도울게요. [Oneureun cheodo eomeonireul toulgeyo.] I *also* will help my mother *today*.

> 오늘 [oneul] today   돕다 [topda] to help

Because of the use of particles, this sentence implies that, on days other than today, someone else helped my mother while I hung around with my friends. Today, though, I suddenly felt very guilty and decided to be a better son, so I'm planning on helping her later. Can you see how this meaning can be understood due to the emphasis placed on the word "today," and the addition of "also"? If you can, then I rate your particle skills as impressive!

Particles comparable to English prepositions

Let's move on. There are many other particles that not only define the grammatical function of nouns but also add meaning to them—much like **prepositions** do in English. In a way, these particles are the Korean version of prepositions, which don't otherwise exist. In fact, in some Korean grammar texts, particles are given the English name "postpositions."

Why "post" instead of "pre"? Any guesses? Well, it's because Korean particles are located **after** their object nouns, whereas English prepositions come **before** them. If you ask me, mastering particles is a whole lot easier than mastering prepositions is for Korean learners of English. So you have a leg up here!

Okay, let's look at three more very common particles.

–에 [-e]: "at," "to," "in" (time, direction, location)

Pattern: N + 에

This versatile little particle can be used to mean any of the three English prepositions listed above. The easiest way to explain this is to show it:

 EX. 1 (time): 보통 몇 시에 일어나세요? [Potong myeot shie ireonaseyo?] *At* what time do you usually wake up?

EX. 2 (direction): 지금 학교에 가고 있어요. [Chigeum hakgyoe kago isseoyo.] I'm going *to* school now.

 EX. 3 (location): 돈이 지갑에 있어요. [Toni chigabe isseoyo.] The money is *in* the purse.

So, with one little particle, we can cover three English words. And, lucky for you, there's only one form, so you don't have to worry about whether the noun ends in a consonant or vowel. Easy!

–에서 [-eseo]: "at," "in," "on" (location), "from" (starting point)

Pattern: N + 에서

The particle –에서 has two basic functions: to describe **location** and to mark the **starting point** of something. Hmm…so are you wondering what the difference is between –에서 and –에 if they can both be used to denote location? Well, unfortunately that's an easy question without an easy answer. The general rule is that, if you have a sentence with a verb that's related to a specific movement or action, –에서 is used more frequently than –에. Yet, there are many exceptions to this principle. So for now, let's just learn –에서 as another way to pinpoint location, sound good? And, of course, to designate a starting point. Have a look:

 EX. 1 (location): 아이가 놀이터**에서** 놀고 있어요. [Aiga noriteoeseo nolgo isseoyo.] A child is playing *on* the playground.

 EX. 2 (starting point): 어디**에서** 왔어요? [Eeodieseo wasseoyo?] Where are you *from*?

–으로 / –로 [-euro/-ro]: "to," "into," "with," "by" (direction, change, means)

Pattern: Nc **+ 으로 / Nv + 로**

> Note: An exception to this is that nouns ending with ㄹ combine with –로, not –으로.

Wow, here's another single particle with all kinds of different possible meanings. And what about "direction, change, means"…do you understand what these mean? No, I don't blame you. We'd better look at some examples, because that's the only way to explain.

EX. 1 (direction): 명동**으로** 가 주세요. [Myeongdongeuro ka chuseyo.] Let's go *to* Myeongdong.

Okay, obviously this is the second particle you've learned that can mean "to." In this sentence, it would be possible to use –에 instead of –으로 / –로. But, just as in the previous explanation, –에 isn't frequently used with action verbs. –으로 / –로 is more natural in this case.

EX. 2 (change): 4호선**으로** 갈아타세요. [Sahoseoneuro karataseyo.] Transfer *to* line 4.

Do you understand the idea of "change" here? You're switching from one thing to another. Of course, it doesn't have to be a subway line that you're changing to. This particle can be used to describe more symbolic changes as well, such as in moods and beliefs.

EX. 3 (means): 저는 자전거**로** 회사에 가요. [Cheoneun chajeongeoro hoesae kayo.] I go to work *by* bicycle.

Hey, cool! I'm jealous that you get to ride your bike to work. Seoul has some nice recreational bicycle paths, but riding in the street from home to the office can be a bit nerve-wracking.

So, how are you feeling about particles now? I know they can seem rather strange to English speakers but, at the same time, they're actually quite easy once you get accustomed to the basic principles of their use.

Of course, I've simplified the explanation just a bit here. For one thing, particles don't only attach to nouns, but also to other particles and adverbs. But if you've made it through this chapter, I'd wager you have just the right amount of particle expertise, and we'll continue to build on it as you learn about other characteristics of this unique language!

Further Vocabulary: More particles

Here it is, just as I promised at the beginning of the chapter: a full list of the Korean particles you'll see in this book!

–의 [-ui]: "of" (possessive)
Pattern: N₁ (modifying noun) + 의 + N₂ (modified noun)
EX.: 이 책의 가격은 아주 비싸요. [I chaegui kagyeogeun aju pissayo.] The price *of* this book is pretty high.

–에게 [-ege]: "to" (preferred in writing)
Pattern: N (person, animal) + 에게
EX.: 누구에게 편지 쓰고 있어요? [Nuguege pyeonji sseugo isseoyo?] *To* whom are you writing a letter?

–한테 [-hante]: "to" (preferred in speech)
Pattern: N (person, animal) + 한테
EX.: 누구한테 편지 쓰고 있어요? [Nuguhante pyeonji sseugo isseoyo?] *To* whom are you writing a letter?

–과 / –와 [-gwa/-wa]: "and," "with" (preferred in writing)
Pattern: Nc + 과 / Nv + 와
EX. 1: 점심으로 김밥과 라면을 먹었어요. [Cheomshimeuro kimbapgwa ramyeoneul meogeosseoyo.] I ate kimbap *and* ramen for lunch.
EX. 2: 어제 친구와 인사동에 갔어요. [Eoje chinguwa insadonge gasseoyo.] Yesterday I went to Insadong *with* my friend.

–하고 [-hago]: "and," "with" (preferred in speech)
Pattern: N + 하고
EX. 1: 점심으로 김밥하고 라면을 먹었어요. [Jeomshimeuro kimbapago ramyeoneul meogeosseoyo.] I ate kimbap *and* ramen for lunch.
EX. 2: 어제 친구하고 인사동에 갔어요. [Eeoje chinguhago insadonge gasseoyo.] Yesterday I went to Insadong *with* my friend.

-만 [-man]: "only," "just"

Pattern: N + 만

EX.: 저는 채식주의자라서 채소**만** 먹어요. [Cheoneun chaeshikjuuijaraseo chaesoman meogeoyo.] I'm a vegetarian, so I eat *only* vegetables.

-부터 [-buteo]: "from"

Pattern: N + 부터

EX.: 오전 9시**부터** 오후 6시까지 일해요. [Ojeon ahopshibuteo ohu yeoseotshikkaji ilhaeyo.] I work *from* 9 a.m. to 6 p.m.

-까지 [-kkaji]: "to," "until," "by"

Pattern: N + 까지

EX.: 오전 9시부터 오후 6시**까지** 일해요. [Ojeon ahopshibuteo ohu yeoseotshikkaji ilhaeyo.] I work from 9 a.m. *to* 6 p.m.

-이나 / -나 [-ina/-na]: "or," "as much/many as"

Pattern: Nc + 이나 / Nv + 나

EX. 1: 아침에는 우유**나** 주스를 마셔요. [Achimeneun uyuna chuseureul mashyeoyo.] I drink milk *or* juice in the morning.

EX. 2: 저는 아침에 우유를 세 잔**이나** 마셔요. [Cheoneun achime uyureul se chanina mashyeoyo.] I drink *as much as* three cups of milk in the morning.

-밖에 [-bakke]: "with the exception of"

Pattern: N + 밖에 + negative expression

EX. 1: 아침에는 우유**밖에** 안 먹어요. [Achimeneun uyubakke an meogeoyo.] I drink *only* milk in the morning.

EX. 2: 지금은 천 원**밖에** 없어요. [Chigeumeun cheon wonbakke eopsseoyo.] I have *only* a thousand won right now.

Literally, 아침에는 우유밖에 안 먹어요 means "I don't drink anything with the exception of milk." You could also say it using the particle -만 (see above): 아침에는 우유**만** 먹어요.

-보다 [-boda]: than

Pattern: N + 보다 + (...더)

EX.: 저는 남편**보다** 키가 더 커요.

[Cheoneun nampyeonboda kiga teo keoyo.]
I'm taller *than* my husband.

저는 남편보다 키가 더 커요. I'm taller than my husband.

-이라고 하다 / -라고 하다 [-irago hada/-rago hada]: indirect quoted speech

Pattern: Nc + 이라고 하다 / Nv + 라고 하다

EX. 1: 저는 할**이라고** 해요. [Cheoneun harirago haeyo.] I'm *called* Hal.

EX. 2: 저는 지우**라고** 해요. [Cheoneun chiurago haeyo.] I'm *called* Jiu.

Korean Style: Particle play

Given the following sentence, which particles would you choose to put in the blanks?

저__ 제 남편__ 사랑합니다.

저 [cheo] I (honorific form of 나)   남편 [nampyeon] husband
제 [che] my (contraction of 저 and the possessive particle –의)

As you just learned, particles are very economical elements of Korean. These tiny little syllables can change the meaning of an entire sentence. Don't believe me? Look at all the possibilities there are for this simple sentence, based only on what you already know:

A. 저**는** 제 남편**을** 사랑해요. [Cheoneun che nampyeoneul saranghaeyo.] I love my husband.

This would be your most basic option. –는 is the particle marking the sentence topic, while –을 signifies the object. So this sentence reads something like, "As far as I'm concerned, ♥ I love my husband."

> Remember how the topic particle adds emphasis to a noun? There's no direct translation for this in English, but "as far as I'm concerned" is a close approximation of the meaning of 저는.

B. 저**는** 제 남편**도** 사랑해요. [Cheoneun che nampyeondo saranghaeyo.] I love my husband, too.

By replacing –을 with –도, we add the meaning of "also" or "too." So you love your husband as well as someone else. Yikes, does your husband know about this!?

C. 저**는** 제 남편**은** 사랑해요. [Cheoneun che nampyeoneun saranghaeyo.] I love my husband and not anyone else.

Ah, that's sweet. The first –는, the one that attaches to 저, or "I," indicates the sentence topic. The second one is used to denote contrast. (Remember, this particle has two functions.) The noun being implicated as the other half of the contrast is not shown, though, so in this case we can infer it means a general "anyone else."

D. 저**를** 제 남편**은** 사랑해요. [Cheoreul che nampyeoneun saranghaeyo.] My husband loves me.

Wow, this is a totally different meaning! You might think this structure isn't possible, but remember what I told you about Korean word order in chapter 4? It's free, because particles let us know which is the subject and which the object. So by simply switching around the particles from example A, we can reverse the meaning of the sentence. Pretty cool, huh!?

Learn, Learned, Learning
배운다, 배웠다, 배우기 [paeunda, paewotda, paeugi]
Regular Conjugation Patterns

Are you ready to **learn** about conjugation? Maybe you **learned** about this concept in school. Well, regardless of what you already know, you're going to be **learning** a lot about Korean conjugation in this chapter.

What can you tell me about the highlighted verbs in the previous sentences? That's right! They're three different forms of the same root verb: "to learn." In both English and Korean, we call this root the **infinitive**. This provides the base stem for all the other different forms of the verb. And that's conjugation—the rules governing the creation of different verb forms.

Now, you were pretty lucky as a kid, because English doesn't have that many conjugation rules to memorize. Take a look:

Present tense	Past tense
I/we **learn**	I/we **learned**
You **learn**	You **learned**
He/she/it **learns**	He/she/it **learned**
They **learn**	They **learned**

See how there's not very much variation at all among the different forms of "to learn"? In many other languages, conjugation is a lot trickier. And—you guessed it—Korean happens to be one of those languages.

For one thing, English verbs conjugate mainly to show differences in **person** (I, you, she, etc.) and **tense** (past, present, etc.). While Korean conjugation does perform these functions, it's also capable of adding dozens upon dozens of different shades of meaning to verbs, as well as different levels of politeness.

Obviously, learning about Korean conjugation is going to be a very important part of your journey, and once you start to get it down, you'll be well on your way to advancing out of the novice stage. But it won't happen all at once. You'll see the information from this chapter again and again throughout the book. After all, practice makes perfect!

Infinitives in Korean

In English, all infinitives have a similar form: they begin with "to." "To go," "to stop," "to eat," "to live." A similar thing happens in Korean, only here the common component comes at the end instead of the beginning. And that common component is -다. Observe:

가다 [kada] to go   먹다 [meokda] to eat
서다 [seoda] to stop   살다 [salda] to live

See how they all end in –다? That's how you can tell they're infinitives.

Great! Now, just as in English the "to" is removed when you want to conjugate the verb, the first step for conjugating a Korean verb is to take off the –다. This gives you the verb **stem**, which never changes no matter what type of conjugation you're doing. Instead, you add different endings onto it. You can think of verb stems as fresh clay in your hands. You can't use them alone, but with a little work you can mold them into whatever meanings you want.

But before we learn how to do that, there's something else you should know…

Adjectives also conjugate in Korean!

Whoa, really?! This is totally different than English, right? I mean, you can't say "it cheaps" or "I distanted," can you? Of course not! But in Korean, this is perfectly acceptable. And what's more, adjectives share the same infinitive and stem characteristics as verbs. Check it out:

싸다 [ssada] cheap   멀다 [meolda] distant
검다 [keomda] black   달다 [talda] sweet

They end in –다, just like verbs! Pretty strange, huh? If it helps, you can think of adjectives as containing the verb "**to be**" within their meaning. For instance, instead of just "cheap," consider 싸다 as translating to "to be cheap." Therefore, the sentence 그것은 싸다 [keugeoseun ssada] doesn't mean "it cheap," but rather "it is cheap." What's more, the same rule applies for removing the –다 when you want to conjugate an adjective, and most of the conjugation patterns for verbs apply to adjectives as well. So it's not really so bad!

Examining stems

Before we talk about the actual conjugation patterns, let's take a look at some important features of verb and adjective stems. In many cases, it's going to be these features that determine the exact pattern of conjugation. Consider these four basic verbs and adjectives: 달리다 [talrida] ("to run"), 먹다 [meokda] ("to eat"), 높다 [nopda] ("high"), and 크다 [keuda] ("big").

1. First, look for whether the stems of these words end in a **consonant** or a **vowel**. Remember, the stems are 달리, 먹, 높, 크. Okay, and they're evenly split, aren't they? 달리 and 크 both end in a vowel, while 먹 and 높 end in a consonant. Just like we learned with particles in the last chapter, consonant vs. vowel endings are going to play a major role in conjugation.

2. Next, regardless of what they end in, pay attention to what the final **vowel sound** is in each stem. Understand? For 달리 it's obviously ㅣ, and for 크 it's ㅡ. But what about the other two? Well, the final vowel sound in 먹 is ㅓ, and for 높 it's ㅗ. Does that make sense?

3. So far, so good. Now for another test. What do these four verbs and adjectives have in common: 살다 [salda] ("to live"), 멀다 [meolda] ("distant"), 달다 [talda] ("sweet"), and 밀다 [milda] ("to push")? Any ideas? Well, as you can see, each of the stems here ends in the character ㄹ.

4. And finally, one more. Tell me if you can spot the similarity between these words: 하다 [hada] ("to do"), 공부하다 [kongbuhada] ("to study"), 생각하다 [saenggakada] ("to think"), 행복하다 [haengbokada] ("happy"). Yes! Each one ends in **하다**!

What's the purpose of all this? Well, these four characteristics—consonant vs. vowel endings, final vowel sounds, verbs/adjectives whose stems end in ㄹ (called ㄹ verbs/adjectives), and verbs/adjectives ending in 하다 (called 하다 verbs/adjectives)—are foundations of some very important rules of Korean conjugation. Don't believe me? Read on and I'll show you!

Conjugation patterns

Finally, we're ready to start conjugating! I bet you're very excited. But remember earlier when I told you Korean conjugation is able to add various shades of meaning to verbs, unlike in English? What did I mean by that? Let's find out.

Let's look at the conjugation ending −자. Let's guess as to its meaning. Let's compare our ideas. And the meaning is…? That's right! It means "let's." When you add −자 to the end of a verb stem, it creates the meaning of "let's do (verb)." So…pop quiz! How would you translate 먹자? If your answer is "let's eat," you're absolutely correct! Now, for bonus points, can you tell me how that verb form was created? It's pretty simple. We start with the infinitive 먹다, drop the ending −다, and in its place add −자.

That, my friend, is Korean conjugation in a nutshell. Of course, it's not always going to be this simple. Conjugation patterns vary depending on what ending you're using, what stem you have, and how their various features relate to each other. Luckily, it's possible to categorize the patterns to make them easier to learn. The following five patterns are used with regular verbs and adjectives. (There are some irregulars, of course, but you don't have to worry about those until the next chapter.)

Okay, 가자—let's go!

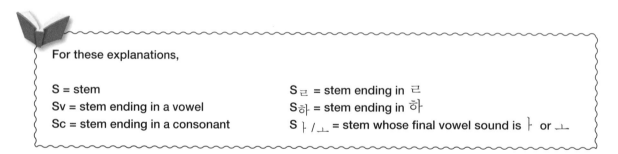

For these explanations,

S = stem
Sv = stem ending in a vowel
Sc = stem ending in a consonant

Sㄹ = stem ending in ㄹ
S하 = stem ending in 하
Sㅏ/ㅗ = stem whose final vowel sound is ㅏ or ㅗ

1. S + ending

This first pattern includes endings that can be stuck directly onto a verb or adjective stem, such as the following:

−고 [-go] (*stem* and)
−거나 [-geona] (*stem* or)
−지만 [-jiman] (*stem* but)
−자 [-ja] (let's *stem*) Note: −자 cannot be used with adjectives.
−기 [-gi] (*stem*-ing)
−지 [-ji] (adverbial form used in negations)

For a better idea of how these endings are used, let's attach them to the verb 가다 ("to go") and the adjective 예쁘다 ("pretty"):

가 + 고   → 가고 (go and)   예쁘 + 고   → 예쁘고 (pretty and)
가 + 거나 → 가거나 (go or)   예쁘 + 거나 → 예쁘거나 (pretty or)
가 + 지만 → 가지만 (go but)   예쁘 + 지만 → 예쁘지만 (pretty but)
가 + 자   → 가자 (let's go)   X
가 + 기   → 가기 (going)   예쁘 + 기   → 예쁘기 (being pretty)
가 + 지   → 가지 (않다) (not go)   예쁘 + 지   → 예쁘지 (않다) (not pretty)

Easy, but also very useful, right? Don't get too cocky, though. After all, this was the first, and simplest, pattern. Let's move on to #2.

2. ① S + ending, ② S̶ㄹ̶ + ㄱㄷ ending

Endings belonging to this second pattern attach directly onto verb and adjective stems, except for stems that end in ㄹ. In this case, the ㄹ is dropped.

The most common ending from this pattern is –는, which turns verbs (and verbs only! –는 doesn't attach to adjective stems) into noun modifiers. When placed next to a noun, a modifier provides an element of description about the noun.

Let's attach the –는 ending to the verb 가다, as we did above, and also to the verb 살다 ("to live"). Pay close attention to what happens to the ㄹ in the stem of 살다—this is what pattern 2 is all about.

① 가 + 는 → 가는 (something that goes)
    EX.: 학교에 **가는** 아이 [hakgyoe kaneun ai] a child who goes to school [6.1]

② 살 + ㄹ̶는 → 사는 (something that lives)
    EX.: 즐겁게 **사는** 사람 [cheulgeopge saneun saram] a person who lives happily [6.2]

학교 [hakgyo] school	즐겁게 [cheulgeopge] happily
아이 [ai] child	사람 [saram] person

Still pretty easy, yeah? Just you wait. They get more complex as we go along.

3. ① Sv + ending, ② S̶ㄹ̶ + ending, ③ Sc + –으– + ending

Pattern 3 endings attach directly onto verbs and adjectives whose stems end in either a vowel or the character ㄹ. Yet, for stems terminating in any other consonant, this pattern calls for the addition of –으– between the stem and the ending. Why? To make the word easier to pronounce, of course!

The conjugative ending –(으)면, lending the meaning of "if" to verbs and adjectives, follows this pattern and is a very handy one to know. To make sure you get a firm grasp of it, we'll attach it to six example words: three verbs and three adjectives.

The first pair should be familiar: the verb 가다 ("to go") and the adjective 예쁘다 ("pretty"). These both have stems that end in a vowel, so you don't need the –으– part of the ending. The same goes for the second pair, 살다 ("to live") and 달다 ("sweet"), because their stems end with ㄹ.

The verb and adjective in the third pair, however, have stems ending in other consonants. So with this pattern 3 ending, you'll have to add –으– for your conjugation of 먹다 ("to eat") and 높다 ("high").

① 가 + 면   → 가면 (if it goes)
　예쁘 + 면 → 예쁘면 (if it's pretty)

② 살 + 면 → 살면 (if it lives)
　달 + 면 → 달면 (if it's sweet)

③ 먹 + 으 + 면 → 먹으면 (if it eats)
　높 + 으 + 면 → 높으면 (if it's high)

4. ① Sv + ending, ② Sㄹ + ≠ ending, ③ Sc + –으–, –느–, –스– + ending

Pattern 4 is somewhat similar to pattern 3. Again, you need to pay attention to whether the final character in the stem is a vowel or a consonant. If the stem of the verb or adjective ends with a vowel, you just stick the ending right onto it. On the other hand, if the stem of the verb or adjective ends with a consonant, you'll add –으–, –느–, or –스– (depending on the ending) between it and the ending. But in this pattern, ㄹ verbs and adjectives lose the final ㄹ of their stems—which is more like pattern 2.

The conjugative ending –ㄴ/–은, which turns verbs and adjectives into past-tense noun modifiers, is one of a few endings we'll be covering in this book that belong to pattern 4. Let's put it to use by attaching it to the same cast of verbs and adjectives we used last time.

Notice how in the first pair the –ㄴ form of the ending is stuck right onto the stem. In the second pair, the final ㄹ of the stem is removed, and then –ㄴ is added. And in the third pair, which features stems ending in other consonants, this ending requires that we add –으– before the –ㄴ.

① 가 + ㄴ → 간 (something that went)
　　EX.: 학교에 **간** 아이 [hakgyoe kan ai] a child who went to school　6.3
　예쁘 + ㄴ → 예쁜 (something that was pretty)
　　EX.: 아주 **예쁜** 여자 [aju yeppeun yeoja] a very pretty woman　6.4

② 살 + ≠ㄴ → 산 (something that lived)
　　EX.: 즐겁게 **산** 사람 [cheulgeopge san saram] a person who lived happily　6.5
　달 + ≠ㄴ → 단 (something that was sweet)
　　EX.: 아주 **단** 과자 [aju tan kwaja] a very sweet cookie　6.6

③ 먹 + 으 + ㄴ → 먹은 (something that ate)
　　EX.: 꿀 **먹은** 벙어리 [kkul meogeun peongeori] a mute who ate honey　6.7
　높 + 으 + ㄴ → 높은 (something that was tall)
　　EX.: 아주 **높은** 건물 [aju nopeun keonmul] a very tall building　6.8

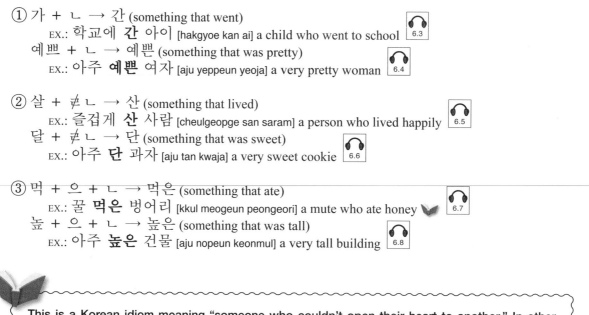

This is a Korean idiom meaning "someone who couldn't open their heart to another." In other words, they couldn't speak because they had a mouth full of honey.

아주 [aju] very, so   꿀 [kkul] honey
여자 [yeoja] woman   벙어리 [peongeori] mute
과자 [kwaja] cookie   건물 [keonmul] building

Very nice! Only one more to go…

5. ① S ㅏ / ㅗ + ending 1 (-아), ② S anything else + ending 2 (-어), ③ S 하 + ending 3 (-여)

Conjugative endings that follow pattern 5 include -아 / -어 / -여, -아요 / -어요 / -여요, -아서 / -어서 / -여서, and -았- / -었- / -였-. Huh? Come again? I can imagine your face right now twisted into a mask of horror. So many confusing, variable endings! But wait. Don't you notice how they all start with -아 / -어 / -여? Just take a second to break them down and they're not so bad, right? I hope…?

Okay, and with these endings, we're going to be concerned with identifying whether or not the final vowel in the stem is ㅏ or ㅗ. Pay no attention to whether the stem ends in a consonant or not; we're just looking at what the last vowel in the stem is. If it's ㅏ or ㅗ, the stem will take the set of endings that start with -아. If it's any other vowel, the -어 endings will be used.

Hey, but what is the -여 group of endings for, then? Well, remember earlier in the chapter (so long ago, I know!), when I told you about 하다 verbs and adjectives? I wasn't just filling your head with useless information! These form their own special group, and in the case of pattern 5 conjugations, they take the -여 endings. Got it?

As for the meaning of these endings, you don't have to worry about them right now. (Phew!) But I'll tell you that the second one, -아요 / -어요 / -여요, is the common honorific conjugative ending you'll see over, and over, and over in this book, especially in chapter 8. Better learn it!

So again, our examples are split into three verb/adjective pairs. As you can see, the first pair includes stems with a final vowel of ㅏ or ㅗ, so they take the ending -아요. In the second pair, the stems of 서다 ("to stop") and 검다 ("black") have a different final vowel. This means the ending -어요 is used. And finally, the third pair contains our 하다 verbs and adjectives, 공부하다 ("to study") and 행복하다 ("happy"). As I said, these take the third ending option, -여요.

① 가 + 아요 → 가요 (it goes)
   높 + 아요 → 높아요 (it is tall)

② 서 + 어요 → 서요 (it stops)
   검 + 어요 → 검어요 (it is black)

③ 공부하 + 여요 → 공부해요 (it studies)
   행복하 + 여요 → 행복해요 (it is happy)

Hmm…wait a minute. Why does 가 + 아요 become 가요 and not 가아요? And, hold on, why is it 서요 instead of 서어요, and 행복해요 instead of 행복하여요? What!? Is Korean just mean and out to get you? No! The answer is simple: **vowel contraction**.

In all conjugation patterns, when you have a vowel that connects directly to another vowel, they usually contract into something new. Why? Yes, for ease of pronunciation! The same holds true for English contractions; think about how much easier it is to say "I'm" than "I am."

You certainly don't need to memorize these now. Just skim the list below quickly to familiarize yourself with the idea of vowel contraction. Then, when you meet them one by one later on in the book, you won't be taken by surprise.

Rule of Vowel Contraction	Example
ㅏ + ㅏ → ㅏ	가다 (to go): 가 + 아 → 가
ㅓ + ㅓ → ㅓ	서다 (to stop): 서 + 어 → 서
ㅗ + ㅏ → ㅘ	오다 (to come): 오 + 아 → 와
ㅜ + ㅓ → ㅝ	주다 (to give): 주 + 어 → 줘
ㅡ + ㅓ → ㅓ	쓰다 (to write): 쓰 + 어 → 써
ㅣ + ㅓ → ㅕ	가지다 (to have): 가지 + 어 → 가져
ㅐ + ㅓ → ㅐ	꺼내다 (to take out): 꺼내 + 어 → 꺼내
ㅔ + ㅓ → ㅔ	세다 (to count): 세 + 어 → 세
ㅚ + ㅓ → ㅙ	되다 (to become): 되 + 어 → 돼
하 + ㅕ → 해	하다 (to do): 하 + 여 → 해

That's it! You've learned the five patterns! I don't want to get all emotional here, but I'm really, really proud of you for sticking with it through this chapter. Conjugation's not easy...I know! But armed with this knowledge, you're nearly ready to step up to a new level of Korean apprenticeship and start making some real headway with the language.

Yet, my grasshopper, one or two challenges still block your path. And, don't look now, but one of them is waiting for you in the next chapter: irregular conjugations. Ahhh! Don't fear, though, because compared to what you just went through, this should be a breeze.

Further Vocabulary: Expressions using common endings, part 1

The following are common expressions you'll see later in this book that utilize endings you just learned.

-고 (Pattern 1)

V-고 있다 / 계시다   to be V-ing (progressive tense, chapter 18)
V-고 싶다   want to V (chapter 27)

-기 (Pattern 1)

A/V-기 때문에   because ... A/V (chapter 17)
V-기 싫다   hate V-ing (chapter 27)

-지 (Pattern 1)

A/V-지 않다   not A/V (chapter 20)
V-지 못하다   not be able to V (chapter 20)
V-지 말다   Don't V (chapter 21)

-(으)면 (Pattern 3)

V-(으)면 안 되다   shouldn't V (chapter 21)

Korean Style: Will you marry *with* me?

In English, there are two main types of verbs: transitive and intransitive. Transitive verbs act on objects (nouns), while intransitive verbs do not (see the examples and explanations below). Korean also has both transitive and intransitive verbs. "So what?" you may be asking. Well, when we're talking about objects, we're also talking about object *particles*. So, in other words, a sentence with a transitive verb is going to feature an object particle, whereas a sentence with an intransitive verb won't. Is your head spinning yet? Don't worry, here's what I'm talking about:

저는 빵을 좋아해요. [Cheoneun ppangeul choahaeyo.] I like bread.
그 사람은 갑자기 사라졌어요. [Keu sarameun kapjagi sarajyeosseoyo.] He suddenly disappeared.

As you see above, in the first sentence 좋아하다 ("to like") is a transitive verb, and its object is 빵 ("bread"). So 빵 has the object particle attached to it. Conversely, the verb 사라지다 ("to disappear") doesn't take an object because it's intransitive—hence, no object particle in the sentence.

Apparently, verbs that are transitive in English are transitive in Korean, and intransitives are the same too, right? No, wait! Sometimes you'll run across a verb that's one type in English and the other in Korean. Look:

Will you marry me?

In English, "to marry" is a transitive verb, right? In this sentence, it takes the object "me." But in Korean, the verb 결혼하다 is actually intransitive! And instead of the object particle, the noun in the sentence is going to have the particle –과 / –와 ("with") attached to it. Because when you marry, you're taking an action "with" someone else. Get it? So,

~~나를 결혼할래요?~~
나와 결혼할래요? [Nawa kyeolhonhalraeyo?] Will you marry me?

If you want to propose in Korean, please remember this. Generally, if you were to make a mistake between the particles –을 / –를 (object) and –과 / –와 ("with"), it would be overlooked. But in this case, you really want the person you're proposing to to understand you, right!?

나를 결혼할래요?
Will you marry me?
(With incorrect particle)

Go, Went, Going

가다, 갔다, 가기 [kada, katda, kagi]

Irregular Conjugation Patterns

In the previous chapter, we goed over the basics of Korean conjugation. I telled you about five patterns for use with regular verbs and adjectives. It ised a bit confusing, but I gived you assurance that you would pick it up in time.

Hmm…has your friend and faithful guide through the world of Korean finally lost his mind? Well, that's always a possibility, but in this case I'm just trying to show you that there are no rules without exception.

I'm sure you can pick out the mistakes in the sentences above: goed → went, telled → told, ised → was, gived → gave. But why? I mean, why don't verbs like "to go," "to tell," "to be," and "to give" follow regular conjugation patterns? Believe me, as someone who's studied English for years, I've asked this question many times. But I haven't found anyone yet who can give a definitive answer. That's just the way those verbs work, right? All I know is this: verbs that conjugate irregularly tend to be those used very frequently, and you just have to memorize their irregular conjugations one by one.

Like English, Korean contains plenty of verbs and adjectives that break the rules we learned in the last chapter. Let me tell you, I'd rather not have to burden you with explanations of these unruly words. In fact, it even makes me, a native speaker, dizzy! But I have a duty to instruct you in the ways of Korean; and, just like in English, the exceptions happen to be very common words that you'll hear and use most every day.

Hey, but like we've done before, we can divide these verbs and adjectives into groups to make them easier to learn. You see, there happen to be five main types of irregular conjugators. We're not going to learn any new endings here; I'll explain the five types using conjugative endings you already know, and then give you a couple examples of verbs and adjectives that are included in each type. Ready?

1. ㅅ irregular verbs / adjectives

These are verbs and adjectives whose stems end with ㅅ. What's irregular about them? Well, if you're attaching an ending that begins with a vowel, these stems will lose that final ㅅ.

Let's look at the example of 붓다 ("to pour"). Remember the ending -(으)면, from conjugation pattern 3? Since the stem 붓 ends with a consonant, we're going to choose the -으면 form of that ending. Ordinarily, this would give us 붓으면, right? But it's an ㅅ irregular verb, so we need to drop the ㅅ. The final product? 부으면.

Verb / Adjective	Ending	Example
붓다 ("to pour")	–(으)면 (pattern 3)	붓 + ㅅ 으면 → 부으면
	–ㄴ / –은 (pattern 4)	붓 + ㅅ 은 → 부은
	–아요 / –어요 / –여요 (pattern 5)	붓 + ㅅ 어요 → 부어요
낫다 ("better")	–(으)면	낫 + ㅅ 으면 → 나으면
	–ㄴ / –은	낫 + ㅅ 은 → 나은
	–아요 / –어요 / –여요	낫 + ㅅ 아요 → 나아요

The following words look like ㅅ irregular verbs/adjectives, but they're not. They follow regular conjugation rules:

벗다 ("to take off"), 웃다 ("to laugh"), 씻다 ("to wash")

2. ㅂ irregular verbs / adjectives

Next, we have ㅂ irregular verbs/adjectives, whose stems end with ㅂ. Similar to what happened in the last group, they lose their final ㅂ when attached to endings beginning with a vowel. Yet, something else happens with these irregulars. They're going to grow either an 오 or 우 to replace that ㅂ.

For an example, we'll look at the verb 돕다 ("to help"). Using that same ending, –(으)면, we need the –으면 form because the stem 돕 ends in a consonant. Under the normal rule, this would result in 돕으면, but not here! The ㅂ in 돕 is dropped, and the 으 from the ending turns into 우. 도우면 is the correct outcome.

Verb / Adjective	Ending	Example
돕다 ("to help")	–(으)면 (pattern 3)	돕 + ㅂ 우 + 으면 → 도우면
	–ㄴ / –은 (pattern 4)	돕 + ㅂ 우 + 은 → 도운
	–아요 / –어요 / –여요 (pattern 5)	돕 + ㅂ 오 + 아요 → 도와요
곱다 ("beautiful")	–(으)면	곱 + ㅂ 우 + 으면 → 고우면
	–ㄴ / –은	곱 + ㅂ 우 + 은 → 고운
	–아요 / –어요 / –여요	곱 + ㅂ 오 + 아요 → 고와요

The following words look like ㅂ irregular verbs/adjectives, but they're not. They follow regular conjugation rules:

잡다 ("to take"), 뽑다 ("to pull out"), 입다 ("to wear"), 넓다 ("large"), 좁다 ("narrow")

3. ㄷ irregular verbs

ㄷ irregular verbs have stems that end in…you guessed it—ㄷ. But I bet you can't guess what happens to the ㄷ when you combine the stem with an ending beginning with a vowel? Do you drop it? Nope, it becomes ㄹ! Pretty strange, I know.

What shall we use for an example this time…how about 걷다 ("to walk")? As I'm sure you know, if this were not an irregular verb, it would combine with the ending -(으)면 to create 걷으면. But, no. The ㄷ at the end of the stem becomes ㄹ in this case, so what you get is 걸으면. Take note: there are no ㄷ irregular adjectives.

Verb	Ending	Example
걷다 ("to walk")	-(으)면 (pattern 3)	걷 + ㄷ̸ ㄹ + 으면 → 걸으면
	-ㄴ / -은 (pattern 4)	걷 + ㄷ̸ ㄹ + 은 → 걸은
	-아요 / -어요 / -여요 (pattern 5)	걷 + ㄷ̸ ㄹ + 어요 → 걸어요
묻다 ("to ask")	-(으)면	묻 + ㄷ̸ ㄹ + 으면 → 물으면
	-ㄴ / -은	묻 + ㄷ̸ ㄹ + 은 → 물은
	-아요 / -어요 / -여요	묻 + ㄷ̸ ㄹ + 어요 → 물어요
듣다 ("to hear")	-(으)면	듣 + ㄷ̸ ㄹ + 으면 → 들으면
	-ㄴ / -은	듣 + ㄷ̸ ㄹ + 은 → 들은
	-아요 / -어요 / -여요	듣 + ㄷ̸ ㄹ + 어요 → 들어요

The following verbs look like ㄷ irregular verbs, but don't be fooled! They follow regular conjugation rules:

받다 ("to take"), 닫다 ("to close"), 얻다 ("to get"), 믿다 ("to believe")

4. 르 irregular verbs / adjectives

This category covers verbs/adjectives whose stems end with 르, which makes them different than the other three types we've looked at. Why? Because their stems end with a vowel, which means they'll be taking conjugative endings that start with a consonant. Okay, so what's irregular about these guys? Well, the ㅡ in the 르 has to be cut when an ending beginning with a vowel is attached. Not only that, but you then have to add another ㄹ before the ending!

Since there aren't too many instances where vowel-ending stems take vowel-beginning endings, our table is going to look a little different. Check it out:

Verb / Adjective	Ending	Example
자르다 ("to cut")	-아요 / -어요 / -여요 (pattern 5)	자르 + ㅡ̸ ㄹ + 아요 → 잘라요
다르다 ("different")	-아요 / -어요 / -여요	다르 + ㅡ̸ ㄹ + 아요 → 달라요

5. ㅎ irregular adjectives

Okay, you're doing great! Our last group makes up the ㅎ irregular adjectives, adjectives whose stems end with ㅎ. That's right, there aren't any ㅎ irregular verbs!

For these, the ㅎ is dropped from the stem when adding endings beginning with a vowel. But that's not all. If the ending begins with the vowel ㅏ or ㅓ, this character will change to 애. The table will explain all...

Adjective	Ending	Example
까맣다 ("black")	–(으)면 (pattern 3)	까맣 + ㅎ + 으면 → 까마면
	–ㄴ / –은 (pattern 4)	까맣 + ㅎ + 은 → 까만
	–아요 / –어요 / –여요 (pattern 5)	까맣 + ㅎ + 아요 → 까매요
이렇다 ("like this")	–(으)면	이렇 + ㅎ + 으면 → 이러면
	–ㄴ / –은	이렇 + ㅎ + 은 → 이런
	–아요 / –어요 / –여요	이렇 + ㅎ + 어요 → 이래요

> The following adjectives look like ㅎ irregular adjectives, but they're not. They follow regular conjugation rules:
> 좋다 ("good"), 싫다 ("hateful"), 많다 ("many"), 괜찮다 ("fine")

Don't you feel a little weird after studying all these *irregulars* for so long? Hey, let's not give them a hard time. After all, they can't help being what they are, and the fact is that they're all very useful words! But I promise we'll go over something more *normal* in the next chapter. ^;^

And besides, you can now breathe a sigh of relief. Your conjugation studies are over! (For now...)

Further Vocabulary: Expressions using common endings, part 2

More expressions! These are some handy ones...

–아 / –어 / –여 (Pattern 5)

V–아 / –어 / –여 주다 / 드리다 to do V-ing for someone (chapter 24)
V–아 / –어 / –여 보다 to try V-ing (chapter 24)
V–아도 / –어도 / –여도 되다 to be allowed to V (chapter 24)

–ㄴ / –은 (Pattern 4)

V–ㄴ / –은 적이 있다 / 없다 to have ever/never done V-ing (chapter 19)

–ㄹ / –을 (Pattern 4)

V–ㄹ / –을 수 있다 / 없다 to/not to be able to V (chapter 19)
V–ㄹ / –을 거다 to be going to V (chapter 18)
V–ㄹ / –을 거 같다 I guess it is going to V (chapter 18)
V–ㄹ / –을 줄 알다 / 모르다 to know/not to know how to V (chapter 19)

Korean Style: Can I bury something?

Hey, are you wondering what would happen if you didn't follow the irregular conjugation rules I told you about in this chapter? I bet it could lead to some funny misunderstandings, right? Let's see.

뭐 좀 **물어** 봐도 돼요? means "Can I ask something?" in Korean. Because 묻다 ("to ask") belongs to the category of ㄷ irregular verbs, what happens when it takes the ending –아 / –어 / –여? That's right, it becomes 물어, not 묻어. Yet, what would I be talking about if I made a mistake and actually said 뭐 좀 **묻어** 봐도 돼요?

Grammatically, there's nothing wrong with this sentence, because there in fact exists a verb 묻다 that follows regular conjugation rules. So, with the ending –아 / –어 / –여, it would conjugate to 묻어. But it means something completely different than "to ask." Yup, it's "to bury"! So you're asking your friend, "Can I bury something?" I bet his face turns pretty white when he hears that one!

As we learned, 닫다 ("to close"), 얻다 ("to get"), and 믿다 ("to believe") are regular verbs, despite the fact that their stems end with ㄷ. But what happens if you treat them as irregulars?

창문 좀 **닫**아 주세요. [Changmun chom tada chuseyo.] Close the window.
창문 좀 **달**아 주세요. [Changmun chom tara chuseyo.] Hang the window. (Huh?)

며느리 **얻**었다면서요? [Myeoneuri eodeotdamyeonseoyo?] I heard you got a daughter-in-law.
며느리 **얼**었다면서요? [Myeoneuri eoreotdamyeonseoyo?] I heard your daughter-in-law got frozen.
  (What happened? She didn't pay her heating bill?)

저를 제발 **믿**어 주세요. [Cheoreul chebal mideo chuseyo.] Please trust me.
저를 제발 **밀**어 주세요. [Cheoreul chebal mireo chuseyo.] Please push me. (Off a cliff, maybe?)

창문 [changmun] window
좀 [chom] please
달다 [talda] to hang, hoist
며느리 [myeoneuri] daughter-in-law

얼다 [eolda] to be frozen
제발 [chebal] please
믿다 [mitda] to trust, believe
밀다 [milda] to push

뭐 좀 묻어 봐도 돼요?
Can I bury something?

CHAPTER
8

My Mother Loves Me
어머니는 저를 사랑하세요. [Eomeonineun cheoreul saranghaseyo.]
Honorific Endings and Words

If you know any Koreans, you probably also know that they study English with a passion. Pretty much every Korean has a dream to speak English fluently. Yet, despite all their hard work, most of them feel very embarrassed at their English ability and are terrified of making mistakes when they speak. They're always second guessing themselves: "Oh no, did I say that correctly?"

But hey, it's only natural to make mistakes when you're learning something as complex as a new language system. And this goes for you as well as for all those Koreans. Even though your knowledge of Korean is quite incomplete, don't be afraid to use it. No one's going to laugh at you. Well, maybe sometimes. But it won't be out of malice, but rather compassion and pride that you've decided to learn their language. They'll feel closer to you because of your adorable Korean and be more willing to offer a helping hand.

When I'm talking to my Korean friends in English, one peculiarity I notice is that they use the word "please" too often. Or they'll insert the words "Could you…?" in front of a sentence that doesn't need them. Why is this? Well, it comes from a habit of politeness they've inherited from their native tongue. Being polite and showing respect is very important to Koreans, remember?

Now, I want you to think back to chapter 4. Flip the pages if you have to…whatever it takes to recall what I told you about honorifics. Ah, yes! Korean society is hierarchical, right? And how you speak to people depends on your relative positions within the hierarchy. When talking to someone above you, you use the **honorific** form; for someone lower, the **plain** form is okay.

Like I said, there are more levels of respect than just these two—Korean has four in total, actually. Does that sound scary? Believe me, for little children learning proper speech etiquette it can be, but not for you! I'm going to briefly introduce you to the four levels here, but for the rest of the book we'll mainly focus on just one, semi-universal form—not too polite, but not too rude either.

Why just one? Hey, you don't have to draw your sword just to swat a mosquito, do you? ㅋㅋ That's a traditional Korean expression meaning, basically, don't overdo it if you don't have to. Our goal is to jumpstart your basic Korean, not train you as a linguistic scholar!

For examples of the four levels of respect, we'll use a verb you should recognize by now: 사랑하다. Koreans LOVE this word, so you should too!

Plain form 1

 사랑해. [Saranghae.] I love you.

For use in: conversation among friends, or when speaking to children

Say this when you kiss your daughter goodnight before putting her to bed. Or, when you've had one too many with your buddy and need to slap him/her on the back and confess, "I love you, man!"

Plain form 2

 사랑한다. [Saranghanda.] I love you.

For use in: books, newspapers, websites, and other written media

In Korea, books talk to you in this plain form because they think they're better than you. Not this book, though!

Honorific form 1

🎧 사랑해요. [Saranghaeyo.] I love you.

For use in: regular conversation

Say this to that special someone you met three nights ago in a bar but can't quite remember his or her name.

Honorific form 2

🎧 사랑합니다. [Saranghamnida.] I love you.

For use in: formal situations like job interviews, conference presentations, speeches from the president, or on the news

Shout this one through your tears as you profess your undying love to someone who's way out of your league. Or during a job interview to butter up your boss so you can then slack off for the next year.

As you can see, the plain forms are used between close friends or are directed to children, while honorifics need to be pulled out for your elders, superiors, or people you don't know that well.

But now that I've shown you the four levels, I'm happy to report that, as a beginner, you really only need to learn one: Honorific form 1. As I said, this form is like Goldilocks' porridge—not too rude, not too polite, but juuuuust right.

Think about it: many circumstances in day-to-day life call for this form. Whether it's asking someone the time on the street, saying hello to your coworkers as you sit down to your desk, or chatting with the taxi driver on the way home, this mildly honorific form carries a friendly politeness without sounding too stuffy. Plus, as a foreigner, you won't be expected to know the other forms anyway. So learn this one, and (for the most part) that's that!

Great, you say, but how do I employ this honorific form? Well, see how the four different forms above rely on different endings added to the same verb stem? You guessed it—it's more **conjugation**! You should be a pro at this by now, right? The ending for this particular form is -아요 / -어요 / -여요. It belongs to pattern 5, if you'll remember. So if the final vowel in the verb or adjective stem is either ㅏ or ㅗ, -아요, will be used. Stems with other final vowels take -어요. And, of course, 하다 verbs and adjectives require -여요.

So we have: 살다 → 살아요, 죽다 → 죽어요, 하다 → 해요. It's all coming back, right?

-(으)시: Honorific suffix

You must be feeling pretty good at only having to remember one honorific form, huh? Well, I hate to throw a monkey wrench into the plans, but…

…there's another honorific element that's very frequently used by Koreans, and it's the honorific suffix -(으)시. Most other books on Korean don't address this important little guy. Instead, they'll teach you expressions that every Korean knows require -(으)시, but leave it out. That's not helpful! So I'm going to explain it to you right here, right now. Hey, what are friends for?

So, why do Koreans frequently use -(으)시? It's because it's a relatively simple way to show a little **extra respect** to someone. By adding -(으)시 between the stem and conjugative ending of a verb or adjective, you're conferring respect on whoever the subject of your sentence is. Let me show you.

Using our favorite Korean verb again, 사랑하다, let's talk about how much our mothers love us. Because if we're going to show respect to anyone, it should be our mothers, right!? So in this case, you'd better add the -(으)시 suffix to the original verb. The stem, 사랑하, ends in a vowel, so we're only going to take the 시 part of the suffix, creating the infinitive 사랑하시다. And the sentence would go like this:

🎧 8.5 어머니는 나를 사랑하세요. [Eomeonineun nareul saranghaseyo.] My mother loves me.

어머니 [eomeoni] mother

Since "mother" is the subject of the sentence, she's the recipient of your sincere respect. But wait a minute!? What happened to the verb 사랑하시다? We had to conjugate it, of course, so it changed a little bit. Shall we analyze?

To the honorific infinitive 사랑하시다 we added the ending we just learned about above, -아요 / -어요 / -여요. This gives us 사랑하시어요 (we use the second ending option, -어요, because the stem ends in the vowel ㅣ). But what happens in this case? That's right, 시어 is contracted to 세. So we wind up with 사랑하세요.

Get it? If you do, then you now understand why I spent so much time explaining conjugation rules in the previous chapters. If not…well, don't worry, it takes some time to pick these rules up. Feel free to go back and have another look at those chapters, especially chapter 6, but also know that we'll be reinforcing your knowledge of Korean conjugation throughout the rest of the book. Don't fret, I'm here to help!

Anyway, if you were to say 어머니는 나를 사랑해요, foregoing the honorific suffix, it would certainly make sense and you'd be understood. But using -(으)시 properly will really impress people, because as I've told you again and again, showing respect is very important in this language! If you want to learn authentic Korean, don't overlook this aspect.

By the way, aren't you sick of using the verb 사랑하다? Me too. Let's create another example with the honorific suffix, only this time we'll use the adjective 예쁘다, which means "beautiful" or "cute." All you guys out there, you can use this sentence when you meet a pretty girl for the first time:

🎧 **8.6** 참 예쁘세요. [Cham yeppeuseyo.] You're so beautiful.

> 참 [cham] very, so

You're paying her a double compliment, right? First by talking up her looks and second by showing her respect with the honorific suffix!

Sorry, ladies, but Korean men won't respond so positively to that one. They'll take it as a critique of their manliness! Instead, you can say:

🎧 **8.7** 참 멋지세요. [Cham meotjiseyo.] You're so handsome.

> 멋지다 [meotjida] handsome

But actually, don't say this, or you'll turn him into a spoiled prince. ^^

Honorific words

Oops, I almost forgot! I can't give you the full 100 points for composing the sentence 어머니는 나를 사랑하세요. Hey! Why not? Well, the problem here has to do with 나. You see, there's yet another way that Koreans show respect, and that's by using entirely different **word forms**. This happens with pronouns a lot: there's one version for plain use and a totally different one for situations where honorifics are required. For the word "me," 나 is the plain form, so in our sentence you'd be better off using 저, the honorific  one. This gives you a final product of:

🎧 **8.8** 어머니는 **저**를 사랑하세요.

I know this is intimidating. Two different words for the same thing!? But there really aren't that many for you to learn. I'll show you a few of the most important ones in the *Further Vocabulary* section coming up next, and then we won't worry too much more about them.

> Keep in mind that you're not honoring yourself here by using the honorific form of "me." With honorifics, the respect is always being paid to the person you're talking to or about, not you!

Further Vocabulary: Honorific word forms

When you want to show respect for someone (either talking to them directly or talking about them with someone else), you need to use the honorific forms of words. Compare the plain and honorific forms of some common terms below.

	When you... (plain)	When your mother... (honorific)
eat(s)	먹다 [meokda]	드시다 [teushida]
exist(s)	있다 [itda]	계시다 [kyeshida]
sleep(s)	자다 [chada]	주무시다 [chumushida]
talk(s)	말하다 [malhada]	말씀하시다 [malsseumhashida]

	For your... (plain)	For your mother's... (honorific)
age	나이 [nai]	연세 [yeonse]
house, home	집 [chip]	댁 [taek]
name	이름 [ireum]	성함 [seongham]
speech	말 [mal]	말씀 [malsseum]

	When you talk to a child about yourself... (plain)	When you talk to your mother about yourself... (honorific)
I	나 [na]	저 [cheo]
we	우리 [uri]	저희 [cheohui]
to ask	묻다 [mutda]	여쭈다 [yeojjuda]
to meet, to see	보다 [poda]	뵙다 [poepda]
to give	주다 [chuda]	드리다 [teurida]
to talk	말하다 [malhada]	말씀드리다 [malsseumdeurida]

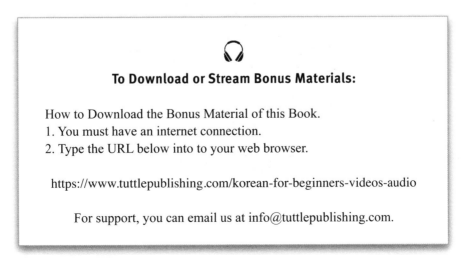

🎧
To Download or Stream Bonus Materials:

How to Download the Bonus Material of this Book.
1. You must have an internet connection.
2. Type the URL below into to your web browser.

https://www.tuttlepublishing.com/korean-for-beginners-videos-audio

For support, you can email us at info@tuttlepublishing.com.

Korean Style: Konglish (Korean English)

English is the most influential language in the world. It started in Europe but has spread around the globe, and it's still going! Each country it's entered has taken bits and pieces and adapted it to its own local language. This is true of Korean, which contains many newly introduced words you might recognize…or will you? Koreans call this Konglish, which means KOrean eNGLISH. Here are some examples:

- Koreans live in APARTs. (아파트 [apateu], which means "apartment")
- Koreans enjoy doing HEALTH in a gym. (헬스 [helseu], which means "fitness")
- Koreans cheer on someone by shouting, "FIGHTING!" (파이팅 [paiting], which means "Go!")
- Koreans wear Y-SHIRTS under their business suits. (와이셔츠 [waisyeocheu], which means "dress shirts")
- Korean drivers look into the BACK MIRROR when they put their car in reverse. (백미러 [paengmireo], which means "rearview mirror")
- Koreans turn the HANDLE when they drive. (핸들 [haendeul], which means "steering wheel")
- In Korean universities, CUNNING is a very serious offense. (컨닝 [keonning], which means "cheating")
- Koreans usually write with a BALL PEN. (볼펜 [polpen], which means "ballpoint pen")
- Koreans jot notes in a NOTE. (노트 [noteu], which means "notebook")
- In Korea, NOTEBOOKs are usually more expensive than desktops. (노트북 [noteubuk], which means "laptop")
- In Korea, you can find a DRIVER at the hardware store. (드라이버 [teuraibeo], which means "screwdriver")
- In Korea, you insert an electrical plug into the CONSENT. (콘센트 [konsenteu], which means "outlet," or "socket")
- In Korea, SUPERs are everywhere. (슈퍼 [shyupeo], which means "supermarket")

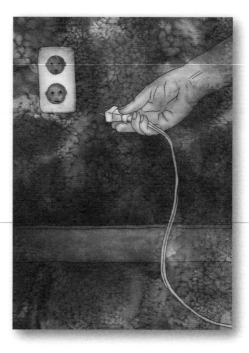

CHAPTER
9

Hello?

안녕하세요? [Annyeonghaseyo?]
What to Say in Greeting, in Parting, and in Thanks

Hello? Are you still there?

Wow. I realize you've been studying some heavy, heavy stuff in the last few chapters. Why have I been torturing you with all these difficult concepts like particles, conjugation patterns, and honorifics? It's simple, really. These are the **building blocks** of the Korean language. While it would've been fun to teach you little Korean niceties back in chapter 4, it would've been like cheating, right? Because you wouldn't have understood how the words and sentences were formed or where they fit into the grand scheme of the language. This isn't just a phrasebook, after all. My goal is to take your hand and lead you through the jungle of Korean…deep into the heart of it!

And guess what. Now you're there. You've arrived! Your comprehension of the structure of the language is at a point where you can start learning more practical things. Yes! So let's take a nice, long break from the heavy stuff and get into something far less complex. How does that sound? Yeah, I thought you'd like that. ^^

So…no matter where you are or who you're talking to, you have to start off the same way, right? With a **greeting**! English has lots of greetings, doesn't it? "Hi," "Hello," "Hey," "What's up"…and it even varies according to the time of day. "Good morning," "Good afternoon," etc.

Well, consider yourself lucky, because Korean has only one greeting, which can be used anytime, anywhere:

🎧 9.1 안녕하세요? [Annyeonghaseyo?] Hello. / How are you?

The Korean 안녕하세요 is truly a universal greeting. When talking to close friends or children, it's okay to simply say 안녕 (a plain form). For people you don't know well, however, the polite thing to use is the full 안녕하세요, which you'll probably notice includes the **honorific suffix** we discussed last chapter. And there's one more element to this greeting: the bow. Koreans usually greet each other with a deep bow while saying 안녕하세요.

Okay, and another important expression to learn in any language is "**thank you**." For Korean people, saying "thank you" frequently in casual conversation facilitates the building of relationships. So pay attention to this one! (Or should I say two…?)

🎧 9.2 감사합니다. [Kamsahamnida.] 🕊 Thank you.

🎧 9.3 고맙습니다. [Komapseumnida.] 🕊 Thank you.

> **Pay attention to the pronunciation of these. It's 합니다 [hamnida] and 습니다 [seumnida], not [hapnida] and [seupnida]. Why? Sorry, but you'll have to wait till chapter 15 to find out!**

As you can see, there are actually two ways to say "thank you." Which one you use is up to you. Now, English speakers like to add "very much" or "really" when they say "thank you." You can do this in Korean by putting the word 정말 [cheongmal] before 감사합니다 or 고맙습니다. But be careful! This isn't a traditional Korean speech pattern, so it'll make your Korean sound less authentic. Just saying 감사합니다 or 고맙습니다 with a smile is enough for Koreans.

And now, what do you think would naturally follow "thank you"? Yes! In English, the proper response when someone thanks you is to say "you're welcome," right? Well, it's possible to say this in Korean as well:

 천만에요. [Cheonmaneyo.] You're welcome.

But again, Koreans don't typically use this phrase. Instead, they just smile or say this shyly:

 뭘요. [Mweoryo.] You're welcome. (*Lit.* "It's nothing.")

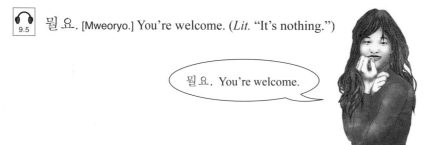

So far, so good: one main greeting, two simple ways to express thanks, and no real need to say "you're welcome." What are we missing…? Ah! How about an **apology**? This could come in pretty handy, I think, because you might be nervous when you first arrive in Korea and feel the need to apologize a lot. Well, we're only human, after all, and we all make mistakes. So even if you don't suffer from an excess of nerves, it's important to know how to apologize.

Just as there are two ways to express thanks, Koreans have two options for saying they're sorry:

 죄송합니다. [Choesonghamnida.] I'm sorry.

 미안합니다. [Mianhamnida.] I'm sorry.

Either is fine, but 죄송합니다 is more polite. So when talking to parents, teachers, or other elders, it's better to use 죄송합니다.

And what do you do when someone apologizes to you? You can't just stand there with a blank look on your face! If you say nothing, the person who apologized will feel even worse, thinking you're angry with them. So you'd better learn this one:

 괜찮아요. [Kwaenchanayo.] It's okay.

 (If this pronunciation guide looks like nonsense to you, don't worry. It'll all be explained in chapter 15!)

Ah, it's great to see that everything's fine between you two again. Now we can move on to the last salutation of today's journey.

When you part company with someone, you have to say **goodbye**. This is where Korean is more complex than English, but not by much. There are two ways to say goodbye, and which one you use depends on whether you're the one staying or the one going. And, just like with "hello," both of these contain the honorific suffix. I told you it was important to learn!

When you're staying and someone else is going, you say:

 안녕히 가세요. [Annyeonghi kaseyo.] Goodbye.

Conversely, when you're the one going and the person you're speaking to is staying, the correct phrase is:

안녕히 계세요. [Annyeonghi kyeseyo.] Goodbye.

Two ways of saying goodbye?! Do you think that's confusing? Well, if you look closely, there's only one syllable that's different between the two phrases: 가 and 계. The direct translation of 안녕히 **가**세요 is "go peacefully," and 안녕히 **계**세요 translates to "stay peacefully." As you can see, the word 안녕 is very often used in Korean salutations.

안녕히 [annyeonghi] peacefully   계시다 [kyeshida] to be, to stay (honorific form of 있다 [itda])

Actually, one funny thing that some English speakers encounter when they first visit Korea is that it can be hard to distinguish between "hello" and the two "goodbyes." All three are pretty similar, right? It can be particularly difficult when the Korean speaker is someone in the service industry who utters these words to customers all day long and has gotten used to saying them very fast.

You might be headed for the door after buying some dried squid in a convenience store, only to hear what you think is 안녕하세요 from the clerk. "What? Hello? But I'm leaving!" Well, it's okay to be confused, but rest assured that the clerk actually just gave you a super quick 안녕히 가세요.

So now that you know the secrets of Korean greetings and niceties, it's time for a short review as we say goodbye. See you in the next chapter!

안녕히 가세요. 안녕히 계세요.

Further Vocabulary: More greetings

"Hello" by itself can get a little bland, don't you think? Here are some alternatives for the phrases we learned in this chapter.

어서 오세요! [Eoseo oseyo!] Welcome! (This is often used when shopkeepers greet their customers.)

오랜만이에요. [Oraenmanieyo.] Long time no see.

축하해요. [Chukahaeyo.] Congratulations! (For anyone who has something to celebrate!)

Korean Style: Can Koreans see things over the phone?

What's the first thing you say in English when you pick up the phone? I'm guessing it's probably "Hello?" Well, in this chapter we learned how to say "hello" in Korean, so can you guess what Koreans say on answering the phone? 안녕하세요?

Um…no, unfortunately. If you say 안녕하세요, the caller will think you're being way too friendly, and he or she will get all sheepish and embarrassed. Instead, there's a particular word of greeting that's used over the phone: 여보세요 [yeoboseyo].

And what does that mean? Good question! Most Koreans will be reluctant to give you an answer, because actually it means nothing. Well, there is an explanation, but it's a strange one. 여보세요 originally came from 여기를 보세요 ("Look at this"). In modern times, though, it's almost never used except as a phone greeting. And over the phone, there's no way for you to see what the other person would be pointing out, right? So really, this is just an idiom.

여기를 보세요.
Look at this.

As long as we're on the subject of phone etiquette, there's one other thing that might trip you up when you talk on the phone with a Korean. Unlike in English-speaking cultures, Koreans often hang up without saying goodbye! But why!? Well, it doesn't make any sense to say 안녕히 가세요, because as you know this means "Go peacefully." What? Go where? Likewise, 안녕히 계세요 wouldn't work.

However, while there's no official way to say goodbye over the phone in Korean, people have made up their own methods for doing this. For example, some will give you the long "yes": 네~~~. Others might say 끊을게요 [kkeuneulgeyo] (I'll hang up).

But in my experience, the strangest telephone goodbye would have to be 들어가세요 [teureogaseyo], which means "enter." Huh? What do you want me to enter? The phone? I've asked a lot of people what they think this means, but no one can give me a straight answer, even though it's pretty commonly used. Just another crazy idiom, I suppose!

CHAPTER

10

I, You, We... Do I Know You?
나, 너, 우리 [na, neo, uri]
Personal Pronouns and How to Address Strangers

Do you remember the first word you ever learned? Maybe it was "mama" or "dada"? Of course, it's different for everybody, but one thing we all have to learn early on is how to refer to the people around us.

With this in mind, it's time to take a look at **personal pronouns** in Korean. You've already been exposed to a few of them through the various example sentences I provided in previous chapters. After all, it's hard to say much without personal pronouns! These simple little words allow us to reference people without directly stating their name, profession, or other descriptive features—very handy. Personal pronouns are divided by person (1st, 2nd, and 3rd) and by number (singular and plural).

Singular Personal Pronouns		
	Plain	**Honorific**
1st person	나 ("I") 🎧 10.1	저 ("I") 🎧 10.4
2nd person	너 ("you") 🎧 10.2	~씨 ("Mr." or "Mrs.") 🎧 10.5
3rd person	그 사람 ("he" or "she") 🎧 10.3	그 분 ("he" or "she") 🎧 10.6

In English, the first-person singular pronoun is "I." Well, in Korean there are two words that can be used for this pronoun. Can you guess why? Thinking back to chapter 8, you know that some Korean words vary depending on who you're talking to and how much respect you're supposed to show that person. There's **plain** and **honorific**, remember? And your use of pronouns definitely needs to reflect this.

When you want to say "I," 나 [na] is plain, and 저 [cheo] is honorific (used when you need to show respect to the person you're talking *to* or *about*). So, if you're speaking to a child or your friend, you can say 나. With your seniors, you'd do better to use 저.

Next, we'll move on to the second-person singular pronoun: "you." Oh, wait, wait... We're forgetting something, aren't we? There's another form related to the first-person pronoun: "me." This is used when the pronoun is the **object** of the sentence. So can you guess how it's created? That's right, with a particle! Since "me" is a sentence object, you simply add the object particle, -을 / -를, to 나 or 저. This gives you 나를 [nareul] and 저를 [cheoreul]. Remember this trick, because you can use it to create objects with all the other pronouns I'm going to show you, too.

Okay, where were we? Oh, right! The second-person pronoun, "you." In Korean, it's 너 [neo]. Well, actually 너 is the counterpart of 나; they're both in the plain form. So what's the counterpart of 저, the "you" used to show respect? As it turns out, there's no single honorific form of "you." It's best just to say the person's name and add 씨 [ssi] after it. For example, when talking to 규병, you can address him as 규병 씨 [Kyubyong ssi]. This is roughly equivalent to saying "Mr. Kyubyong."

Okay, and there's one point we need to note before moving on. When 나, 저, and 너 are combined with the subject particle –가, they're going to transform to 내, 제, and 네, respectively. (Interestingly, these are the exact same forms as the possessive pronouns we'll look at on the next page!) So that would make 내가, 제가, and 네가—got it?

Wow, we're just rolling along! We've already come to the third-person singular pronouns. In English, these are "he" and "she." For Korean, 그 [keu] means "he," and 그녀 [keunyeo] is "she." There's a similarity to English here, isn't there? You make the word "she" by adding "s" to "he," and in Korean, you get 그녀 by adding 녀 to 그. What a coincidence!

But here's the thing. Neither of these third-person pronouns is used much in Korean conversation. They're mainly for written language. Instead, Koreans typically say 그 사람 [keu saram] or 그 분 [keu bun]. 그 in this case means "that" or "the," and 사람 means "person." What's 분? You guessed it: the honorific form of 사람. You can use these regardless of the gender of the person you're talking about.

We're halfway done! Actually, more than halfway, because plural personal pronouns are even simpler. Shall we take a look?

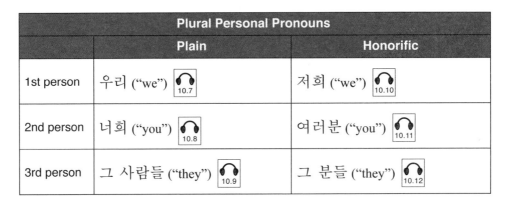

Plural Personal Pronouns		
	Plain	**Honorific**
1st person	우리 ("we") 🎧 10.7	저희 ("we") 🎧 10.10
2nd person	너희 ("you") 🎧 10.8	여러분 ("you") 🎧 10.11
3rd person	그 사람들 ("they") 🎧 10.9	그 분들 ("they") 🎧 10.12

Remember what I said back in chapter 4? Compared to English, Korean doesn't place as much emphasis on the difference between singular and plural. With many nouns, it's very simple to make a singular into a **plural**: just add –들 [deul] to the end.

Does this hold true with pronouns? Well, what is "we" in Korean? 나들? Good guess…but in this case, no. We need a new word for the first-person plural pronoun, "we", and it's 우리 [uri]. Again, this is the plain form. To be respectful, you'd use 저희 [cheohui]. I'm sure you can see the similarity between 저, the honorific first-person singular pronoun, and 저희.

Moving on to the second person, what's the plural of "you"? Well, the plain form is 너희 [neohui], and then you have the honorific 여러분 [yeoreobun]. If you take apart this honorific pronoun, 여러 means "several," and 분 is, as you know, the honorific form of the word "person." Put these together and 여러분 is one honorific word meaning "you all." Got it?

And at last, we come to the third-person plural pronouns, which correspond to the word "they" in English. Thankfully, these are pretty simple. Just add –들 to 그 사람 or 그 분, making: 그 사람들 [keu saramdeul] and 그 분들 [keu pundeul]. Remember, the first one is plain, the second honorific. Easy!

Possessive Personal Pronouns		
	Plain	**Honorific**
1st person (singular)	나 + 의 → 나의, 내 ("my") 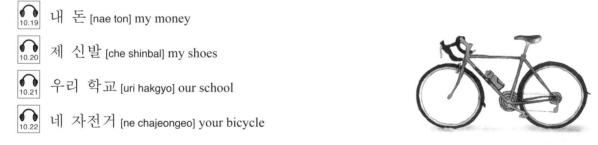10.13	저 + 의 → 저의, 제 ("my") 10.16
1st person (plural)	우리 + 의 → 우리 (의) ("our") 10.14	저희 + 의 → 저희 (의) ("our") 10.17
2nd person (singular)	너 + 의 → 너의, 네 ("your") 10.15	~씨 + 의 → ~씨 (의) ("your") 10.18

We've covered the basic pronouns, and I also told you how to make them into the object of a sentence (remember, just use –을 / –를, the object particle!). But there's one more form these pronouns can take, and that's the **possessive**. You know what possessives are in English, right? The _____ *of* somebody, or somebody's _____. In Korean, the particle –의 attaches to the end of the noun that's exercising the possession. As I've said, we'll slowly but surely be learning all about particles and their applications. How exciting!

So how does this relate to personal pronouns? Well, the first-person singular possessive pronoun (how's that for a name? ^^) is "my" in English. How would you form this in Korean? Could it be as simple as adding the possessive particle to 나 and 저? Yes! How easy! So this creates 나의 [naui] and 저의 [cheoui]. Only, here we run into cases of **vowel contraction**. This is because, when the character 의 is used as a particle, its pronunciation is allowed to be [e] instead of [ui]. Most people follow this alternate pronunciation. Then, the pronouns contract even further: 나의 becomes 내 [nae] and 저의 becomes 제 [che]. It's all about making things easier to say—can't argue with that!

Following this, I bet you can guess how to create a possessive out of the second-person pronoun 너. Yep, just tack on the possessive particle –의 to create 너의, which contracts to 네 [ne].

For all the other pronouns we learned, the possessive particle attaches without any vowel contractions taking place. For example, 우리 ("we") becomes 우리의 ("our"), and 너희 ("you," plural) becomes 너희의 ("your," plural). But in most cases, the possessive particle just disappears, leaving 우리 ("our"), and 너희 ("your," plural). Remember, as I warned you in chapter 4, Koreans like to omit things!

For practice, here are some examples of phrases using possessive pronouns. Are you getting accustomed to the different contractions yet?

10.19 내 돈 [nae ton] my money

10.20 제 신발 [che shinbal] my shoes

10.21 우리 학교 [uri hakgyo] our school

10.22 네 자전거 [ne chajeongeo] your bicycle

Since it's difficult to tell the difference between the pronunciations of 네 [ne] ("your") and 내 [nae] ("my"), most people pronounce 네 as 니 [ni].

돈 [ton] money
신발 [shinbal] shoes
학교 [hakgyo] school
자전거 [chajeongeo] bicycle

Addressing strangers

Okay, very good. We've gone over personal pronouns. Now, how would you address someone you happened to bump into on the street? This is a bit complicated to figure out in Korean. Why? Think back to the hierarchy. You can't be sure what level of respect you're supposed to show a stranger without first learning more about him or her (i.e., their position in the hierarchy relative to yours). Actually, due to this problem, Koreans simply tend not to address someone directly in such a situation. Instead, they use other expressions to attract the person's attention. It's not really too different from English. When you address a stranger on the street, what do you say?

🎧 **10.23** 실례합니다. [Shilryehamnida.] Excuse me.

This allows you to speak to someone without making a presumption about their status relative to yours. But, because it's still important to be polite, it's customary to use honorific form 2 in this expression. Recognize the ending? After saying 실례합니다, you can just continue with whatever comment or question you wanted to put to that person.

So, this is good for situations where you want to avoid using a title to address a stranger, but there are many other instances where it's okay to do so. Generally, you can call men you don't know 아저씨 🎧 **10.24**, and women 아줌마 🎧 **10.25**, 아주머니 🎧 **10.26**, or 아가씨 🎧 **10.27**.

Originally, 아저씨 meant "uncle" and 아주머니 meant "aunt." But nowadays, these words are used most often to address strangers, clerks, waiters and waitresses, taxi drivers, etc. That is, people you don't know and with whom you aren't establishing a personal relationship.

아저씨 [ajeossi] Sir	아줌마 [ajumma], 아주머니 [ajumeoni] Madam
아가씨 [agassi] Miss	

But be careful. Don't use 아저씨 or 아주머니 for people who aren't married. Of course, there's no way of telling this about a stranger, so typically if you think he or she is fairly young, it's best to avoid these terms. For example, if you call a teenage girl 아줌마, she'll probably get angry and shout this:

🎧 **10.28** 저는 아줌마가 아니에요! [Cheoneun ajummaga anieyo!] I'm not a married woman!

Yikes! Looks like you've ruined your chances of friendship with this 아가씨!

Further Vocabulary: Length, extent, size

Let's continue building your Korean vocabulary with these terms for describing how big or small something is.

길이 [kiri] length	좁다 [chopda] narrow, small
길다 [kilda] long, lengthy	크기 [keugi] size, bulk
짧다 [jjalda] short	크다 [keuda] big, large
넓이 [neolbi] area, extent	작다 [chakda] small, little
넓다 [neolda] large, extensive	

Korean Style: Differences between 아저씨 and 오빠, 아줌마 and 아가씨

Want to know a famous cultural joke in Korea? Allow me to explain. As I told you in this chapter, 아저씨 literally refers to a man that is married. But by extension, it can be used humorously to mean a man who looks old for his age. So if a teenage girl addresses a guy in his mid-20s as 아저씨, she's letting him know that she thinks he looks old, that there seems to be a generation gap between him and her. Otherwise, she'd call him 오빠 (which means "elder brother"). Here are some sure-fire ways to tell an 아저씨 from an 오빠:

- If you clip your cell phone to your belt, you're an 아저씨.
  If you keep your cell phone in your pocket, you're an 오빠.
- If you go to a barbershop, you're an 아저씨.
  If you go to a stylist, you're an 오빠.
- If you get happy when someone calls you 오빠, you're an 아저씨.
  If you don't think anything of someone calling you 오빠, you're an 오빠.

But wait, because this applies to women as well. Like we learned, married women are called 아줌마, while young women should be addressed as 아가씨. Here's how you can tell them apart:

- If you tell your beautician to give you a long-lasting perm, you're an 아줌마.
  If you ask for a good-looking perm, you're an 아가씨.
- If you look around *after* taking a vacant seat on the subway, you're an 아줌마.
  If you look around *before* taking a vacant seat on the subway, you're an 아가씨.
- If you wear white gloves while driving, you're an 아줌마.
  If you wear sunglasses while driving, you're an 아가씨.

So...which are you?

11

What's This?

이게 뭐예요? [Ige mweoyeyo?]
Demonstrative Pronouns and How to Ask Simple Questions

When you go to a foreign country for the first time, you're almost like a baby, aren't you? You don't know the culture, the history, and, most importantly, the language! But don't worry—in Korea, babies are always welcome!

When you pose questions to Korean people with your limited Korean, they'll be very pleased and answer you with a smile. And just like a curious infant, you'll probably want to ask many questions. But how do you do this in Korean? Well, after I'm done with you in this chapter, you'll know exactly what to say.

Asking questions with demonstrative pronouns

Let's begin with the most basic questions:

🎧 11.1 이게 뭐예요? [Ige mweoyeyo?] What's this?

🎧 11.2 그게 뭐예요? [Keuge mweoyeyo?] What's that (nearby)?

🎧 11.3 저게 뭐예요? [Cheoge mweoyeyo?] What's that (far away)?

First, notice that to make a question sentence in Korean, all you have to do is change the ending of the verb or adjective and stick a question mark after it. Unlike in English, there's no fumbling with extra words like "do" or "does" or switching up the word order. How simple!

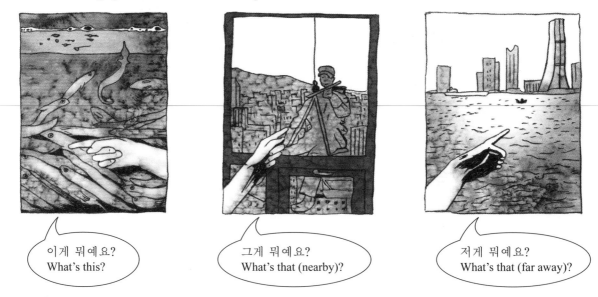

이게 뭐예요?
What's this?

그게 뭐예요?
What's that (nearby)?

저게 뭐예요?
What's that (far away)?

Next, pay close attention to the translations above. You're not saying "what is" but "what's." That's a **contraction**, right? As we've seen, Korean frequently allows for the use of contractions. But what's actually being contracted here?

Well, the **demonstrative pronouns** ("this" and "that") are, for one thing. In their unabbreviated forms, "this" is 이것 [igeot], "that" (nearby) is 그것 [keugeot], and "that" (far away) is 저것 [cheogeot]. The contractions occur when the subject particle –이 is added onto each of these demonstrative pronouns. So, for "this," instead of saying 이것이, Koreans shorten it to 이게. Likewise, 그것 + 이 = 그게, and 저것 + 이 = 저게. Understand?

And what about the rest of the sentence, the 뭐예요? Remember, the verb comes at the end of the sentence in Korean, so this is literally the "what's" in the English translation. And it's a contraction as well. The full form of the word "what" is 무엇 [mueot]. –예요 [yeyo] is an alternate form of the verb ending –이에요 [ieyo], which means "to be." 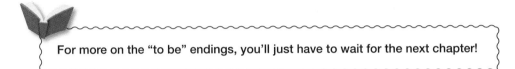 When you put the two full forms together to create 무엇이에요, they contract into 뭐예요. See? And there you have a very complex explanation of three very simple question sentences. Great!

> For more on the "to be" endings, you'll just have to wait for the next chapter!

Okay, you may have noticed that we differentiated between two forms of the English word "that"—one that signifies something nearby, and the other something farther away. This is because in Korean, as in many other languages, demonstrative pronouns vary depending on the object's distance from the speaker and listener.

As you learned with the above questions, there are three categories: 이 (close to the speaker / "this" in English), 그 (closer to the listener, or relating to something from earlier in the conversation / "that" in English), and 저 (distant from both speaker and listener / "that" in English).

For example, consider a situation where you're talking to a salesperson in a clothing store. You point out a pair of jeans that's next to you and ask,

🎧 11.4   이게 뭐예요? [Ige mweoyeyo?] What's this?

The salesperson answers,

🎧 11.5   그건 ✌ 청바지예요. [Keugeon cheongbajiyeyo.] That's a pair of jeans.

> The contraction 그건 in this sentence results from 그것 + 은, where –은 is the topic particle.

청바지 [cheongbaji] jeans

Is that clear? Right. Let's continue this enlightening conversation:

🎧 11.6   그게 뭐예요? [Keuge mweoyeyo?] What's that? (pointing out an item close to the salesperson)

🎧 11.7   이건 ✌ 핸드폰이에요. [Igeon haendeuponieyo.] This is a cell phone.

🎧 11.8   저게 뭐예요? [Cheoge mweoyeyo?] What's that? (pointing out an item distant from both of you)

🎧 11.9   저건 ♥ 휴지통이에요. [Cheogeon hyujitongieyo.] That's a wastebasket.

핸드폰 [haendeupon] cell phone   휴지통 [hyujitong] wastebasket

Needless to say, 이건 = 이것 + 은, **and** 저건 = 저것 + 은.

Okay. So we've learned how to ask about objects using the word "**what**." Let's move on to asking questions about people, shall we? After all, you don't want to refer to a person as "what"! And which demonstrative pronoun do we use in this situation? That's right: "**who**." Look at the example below.

🎧 11.10   저 분은 누구예요? [Cheo puneun nuguyeyo?] Who's that?

I bet you can figure out this sentence's structure using things you've already learned. Want to try? Let's go.

First, what does 저 mean? It should be fresh in your mind, because we just went over it. It's the demonstrative meaning "that" (far away). Okay, for the next word, you may have to think back to the previous chapter. Any guesses about the meaning of 분? Excellent! It's the honorific form of the word "person." And now what's the function of –은? Come on, I know you can do it. Right! It's the topic particle, signifying that the word "person" is the main topic of this sentence.

Okay, so far so good. Now for the part you haven't learned yet. Even though you don't know it, you can probably guess that 누구 [nugu] is the Korean word for "who," right? But unlike 무엇 ("what"), 누구 doesn't contract when you add the –예요 ending to it. It simply becomes 누구예요. Got it?

So, how to answer 저 분은 누구예요? Let's say the person in question is your teacher. You'd respond:

🎧 11.11   (저 분은) 우리 선생님이에요. [(Cheo puneun) Uri seonsaengnimieyo.] That is my teacher.

선생 [seonsaeng] teacher   –님 [-nim] sir, dear (showing politeness or respect)

The 저 분은 is in parentheses here because you don't have to repeat it. It'll be understood because it was in the question. And of course you can see that 선생 is the word for "teacher," but you should always attach –님 after 선생, because teachers are highly respected in Korea. Me, on the other hand, I'm just your friend. So don't worry about it!

And finally, do you recognize the word 우리? We're getting back into the personal pronouns with this one, right? As you learned in the last chapter, 우리 means both "we" and "our." But wait—why is it used here, where the English translation says "my," not "our"? What's going on?

Well, we've uncovered another interesting feature of Korean. Koreans sometimes use "our" instead of "my." In the above sentence, the teacher being pointed out is not the teacher of both the speaker and listener, but only of the speaker. And yet, the speaker says 우리, not 제.

But, but why? Sorry, this is one of those times when you just have to take the language as it comes. And remembering this feature can be pretty important, as you'll see very shortly…

Further Vocabulary: Weight, depth, distance

More handy description words!

무게 [muge] weight

무겁다 [mugeopda] heavy

가볍다 [kabyeopda] light

깊이 [kipi] depth

깊다 [kipda] deep

얕다 [yatda] shallow

거리 [keori] distance

멀다 [meolda] far, distant

가깝다 [kakkapda] close, near

Korean Style: Our wife?

It definitely doesn't make sense in English to say "our home" or "our school" to someone that doesn't have the same home or school as you. So you probably find it strange that Koreans routinely say 우리 집 and 우리 학교 to mean "my home" and "my school." Some scholars believe this linguistic characteristic is a result of Korean culture's emphasis on the whole rather than the individual. There's no real way to confirm this theory, so all that matters to you is that you remember this interesting custom of the Korean language.

There are many more examples in addition to the ones mentioned above. Perhaps the most famous (or infamous) are 우리 아내 ("my wife") and 우리 남편 ("my husband"). If you translate these literally, you get "our wife" and "our husband." But hey! Korea is a monogamous society, so don't get the idea that Koreans share wives and husbands! That would certainly be frowned upon!

집 [chip] house, home   아내 [anae] wife   남편 [nampyeon] husband

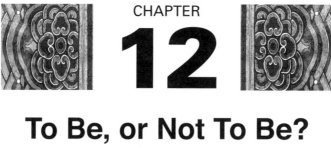

To Be, or Not To Be?
이다, 아니다? [ida, anida?]
All About the Verb "To Be"

It's time to learn one of the most essential verb and adjective endings in Korean: –이다 [-ida]. This carries the meaning of "to be." Have you ever thought about the verb "to be"? No? Not even a little? Of course, it's one of the most basic constructions in any language. But many times it's the simplest parts of a language that are the most important. So we'll have to look at this ending very closely.

To be

In English, the verb "to be" has two main functions. The first is to express that something **exists**, as in the sentence "There are two books." The word "are" is a conjugation of the verb "to be," and it's telling us that two books exist. The second function is to turn nouns or adjectives into **predicates** so they describe something, as in the sentence "I am an author." In this sentence, the noun "author" is acting as a predicate and is linked to the word "I" by the verb "to be." This second example is comparable to the function of –이다 in Korean, with one important difference: –이다 is only attached to nouns or noun phrases—not adjectives—to make a predicate.

So, what can you tell me about the format of –이다? Notice what it ends with: –다. Looks familiar, yeah? Is it coming back to you? Right! We learned in chapter 6 that –다 signifies an infinitive. And in this case, even though –이다 isn't an independent verb in its own right, that's still what it's telling us.

So to use this construction in a sentence, we're going to need to take off the –다 and conjugate the stem. Its everyday, polite form winds up being –이에요 / –예요 [-ieyo/-yeyo]. 🦋 Which of these two options you use depends on…anybody?…right—whether the noun you're attaching it to ends with a consonant or a vowel.

> **Contrary to what it looks like, this ending isn't formed by added the honorific form 1 ending, –아요 / –어요 / –여요, to the stem. It's simply a unique ending belonging to –이다.**

Remember in the previous chapter when we discussed how 무엇이에요 becomes 뭐예요? This is a perfect example of the fact that nouns ending with a consonant take –이에요, while vowel-ending nouns get –예요.

For example, the word 겨울 ends with what? Yes, ㄹ, a consonant. So:

🎧 지금은 겨울**이에요**. [Chigeumeun kyeourieyo.] It's winter.

And what about a word like 간호사, which means "nurse"? It ends with ㅏ, a vowel, so you would say:

 이 분은 간호사**예요**. [I puneun kanhosayeyo.] This person is a nurse.

지금 [chigeum] now	겨울 [kyeoul] winter	간호사 [kanhosa] nurse

Didn't I tell you that consonant vs. vowel ending rule would come in handy? It's all over the place!

Not to be

Okay. We've learned how to say what something **is**. What about what something **isn't**? Well, the negative form of the –이다 ending is the adjective 아니다 [anida]. It isn't an ending, but rather a separate, stand-alone adjective, and its polite conjugation is 아니에요 [anieyo].

Like we saw above, this conjugation isn't the result of adding the honorific form 1 ending. It's just a unique ending belonging to 아니다.

Now, when you use this verb to say what something isn't, you also have to add the subject particle to the end of the noun you're talking about. So:

 지금은 겨울**이** 아니에요. 봄이에요. [Chigeumeun kyeouri anieyo. Pomieyo.] It's not winter. It's spring.

 이 분은 간호사**가** 아니에요. 선생님이에요. [I puneun kanhosaga anieyo. Seonsaengnimieyo.] This person is not a nurse. This person is a teacher.

봄 [pom] spring

Got it? Remember that in Korean, words can be **omitted** if the meaning is clear without them. In both pairs of sentences above, words have been left out of the second sentence. 지금은 and 이 분은 are omitted because the listener already knows what's being referred to.

지금은 겨울이 아니에요.
봄이에요.
It's not winter. It's spring.

This cruel *existence*

Now you've learned one function of "to be" in Korean. You use –이다 and 아니다 to say what something is or is not in order to describe it. But what about the other function of "to be" I told you about at the beginning of the chapter? In English, we also use "to be" to express that something exists. Well, you can do this in Korean as well, but you have to use a different adjective: 있다 [itda]. This is another one you're going to see over, and over, and over again.

Imagine this scenario: At a library, you ask, "Where are the Korean books?" The librarian replies,

🎧 12.5 한국어 책은 저기에 있어요. [Hangugeo chaegeun cheogie isseoyo.] The Korean books are over there.

> 책 [chaek] book   –에 [-e] location particle—remember?
> 저기 [cheogi] over there (distant from both speaker and listener)

The adjective 있어요 in this sentence is the honorific form 1 (–아요 / –어요 / –여요) conjugation of 있다. The last vowel in the stem is ㅣ, so it gets the –어요 ending. Make sense?

Actually, 있다 has two meanings in Korean: "to be" (**exist**), and "to have" (**possess**). So, an immigration official at the airport might say this to you:

🎧 12.6 여권이 있으세요? [Yeogweoni isseuseyo?] Do you have your passport?

> 여권 [yeogweon] passport

Be careful! It doesn't mean "Does your passport exist?" It means "Do you have your passport?" with the implied meaning of "Please show me your passport." Notice how the honorific suffix –(으)시– is added to the adjective to create 있으세요. So if the meaning were "Does your passport exist?" the official would be expressing respect to your passport. That's nonsense! On the other hand, with the meaning of "Do you have your passport?" the respect is being shown to you, the listener, not the passport.

Um, you'd better answer the question. This guy's getting impatient! I expect you have your passport, right? So,

🎧 12.7 네, 있어요. [Ne, isseoyo.] Yes, I have it.

🎧 12.8 예, 있어요. [Ye, isseoyo.] Yes, I have it.

> 네 [ne] yes   예 [ye] yes

And what about the opposite of 있다, an adjective meaning "**to not be**" and "**to not have**"? Well, this is 없다 [eopda], and its usage is exactly the same as that of 있다. So if you need to say you don't have your passport, you'd say:

🎧 12.9 아니요, 없어요. [Aniyo, eopsseoyo.] No, I don't have it.

> 아니요 [aniyo] no

Whoops! Where's your passport? I hope you can find it, because if not, you'll have to turn around and go home!

Further Vocabulary: Weather

If you want to master the art of chitchat, you have to know how to talk about the weather!

날씨 [nalssi] weather

따뜻하다 [ttatteutada] warm

덥다 [teopda] hot

더위 [teowi] (the) heat

춥다 [chupda] cold

추위 [chuwi] (the) cold

맑다 [makda] clear, sunny

흐리다 [heurida] cloudy

Korean Style: Yes, I can't?

Did you know that in some countries, nodding your head means "no" and shaking your head means "yes"? Fortunately, you don't have to worry about this confusion in Korea. Nodding is "yes" and shaking your head means "no," which is probably what you're used to. However, there's another area where English and Korean differ in the use of "yes" and "no."

Suppose you go to a Korean restaurant with your Korean friend. Kimchi, the most popular side dish in Korea, is served with your meal. Your friend asks you, 김치 먹을 수 있어요? ("Can you eat kimchi?") You don't want to eat kimchi because it's too spicy, so you answer, 아니요. 못 먹어요. ("No, I can't eat it.") Your friend is surprised because she thought you could. So she asks again, 정말요? 김치를 못 먹어요? ("Really? Can't you eat kimchi?") You want to say, "No, I can't. It's too spicy." But when you say this in Korean, you must use 예 ("yes") instead of 아니요 ("no").

In English, you can answer the questions, "Can you eat kimchi?" and "Can't you eat kimchi?" in the same way. You can just say "No." But in Korean, you have to pay attention to whether the question is worded in the positive or negative. If it's negative, your answer will be the opposite of what you're used to. Because the Korean words 예 / 아니요 contain the meaning "what you said is correct/incorrect." So, 예, 못 먹어요 really means "It's true that I can't eat kimchi." Mixing up the "yes" and "no" when answering a negative question is one of the most frequent mistakes when Koreans learn English, and vice versa.

recipe for: 김치   from the kitchen of: 송현주

ingredients:

cabbages

green onions

sea salt

lots of red pepper flakes!

fresh minced garlic

chopped fresh ginger

anchovy

preparation:

1. wash the cabbage leaves and then chop them up into long pieces.

2. salt the cabbage leaves well and allow to marinate for about 5 hours.

3. season the cabbage leaves with the green onions, garlic, red pepper flakes, ginger and anchovy. (you might want to wear gloves to prevent the red pepper flakes from burning your hands!)

4. put the seasoned cabbage leaves in a container aside for several days.

5. store the final product in the refrigerator. enjoy!

13

My Name Is Hal

저는 할이라고 합니다. [Cheoneun harirago hamnida.]

Introducing Yourself and Holding Simple Conversations

In chapter 9, we studied greetings in Korean. Do you remember? Please repeat after me,

🎧 13.1 안녕하세요? [Annyeonghaseyo?] Hello.

But what comes next? You can't just say "hello" and expect that to be the extent of your conversation, right? Maybe you'd like to say "Nice to meet you" and introduce yourself. There are two common ways to do this in Korean:

🎧 13.2 처음 뵙겠습니다. [Cheoeum poepgetseumnida.] *Lit.* This is the first time I've met/seen you.

🎧 13.3 (만나서) 반갑습니다. [(Mannaseo) Pangapseumnida.] Nice (to meet you).

처음 [cheoeum] first (time)	만나다 [mannada] to meet
뵙다 [poepda] to see, to meet (honorific form of 보다 [poda])	반갑다 [pangapta] glad

The first expression may sound a bit odd in English, but the important part is the verb 뵙다, conjugated here according to honorific form 2. It's the respectful form of 보다. Therefore, you're implying that it's a double honor to see, or meet, the listener for the first time, as you're using both the honorific verb form and the most honorific ending. How nice of you!

As for the second expression, 반갑습니다 also utilizes honorific form 2 and means "I'm glad." 만나서 translates to "meeting you" or "to meet you," so you're actually saying "I'm glad that I've met you." But this expression has become so common that it's entirely okay to omit 만나서.

Great! What's the next step? Well, you might want to tell the person your name with one of these expressions:

🎧 13.4 제 이름은 할입니다. [Che ireumeun harimnida.] My name is Hal.

🎧 13.5 저는 할입니다. [Cheoneun harimnida.] I am Hal.

🎧 13.6 저는 할이라고 합니다. [Cheoneun harirago hamnida.] I am called Hal.

이름 [ireum] name	N-(이)라고 하다 [N-(i)rago hada] to be called N (particle expression)

In English, you'd probably choose one of the first two rather than the third one. But in Korean, it's the opposite. Koreans usually use the last one. That said, whichever expression you use, it's okay!

What wouldn't be okay is if you were to use 내 or 나는 instead of 제 or 저는 in this situation. Remember, 나 is the plain form for "I," whereas 저 is the honorific. Because you want to make a good impression on this person you're meeting for the first time, you should be polite and use the honorific form. That's also why each of these expressions includes the most honorific conjugation form.

So, now the listener has met you and knows your name. How do you ask for his or her name? If you can do this well, the listener will think your Korean is quite sophisticated. In English you'd say, "What's your name?" This can be translated to 이름이 뭐예요? [Ireumi mwoyeyo?] But in Korean this is rude, because 이름 is a plain word. Again, you must be mindful of the difference between **plain** and **honorific** words.

Of course, because you're a foreigner, your mistakes will be forgiven. But why not use the proper words when greeting someone and make a great impression? It's the only first impression you'll ever make, after all, and it'll determine how that person sees you. So, instead of 이름이 뭐예요?, say:

🎧 13.7 성함이 어떻게 되세요? [Seonghami eotteoke toeseyo?] What's your name?

> 성함 [seongham] name (honorific form of 이름)   어떻게 [eotteoke] how, like what
> 되다 [toeda] to become

어떻게 means "how," and 되세요 is the honorific conjugation of a verb translating to "to become." When you put these English translations together, the words don't make sense, do they? It's just an **idiom**, or expression, you should learn as a whole: N-이 / 가 어떻게 되세요? It's used to politely inquire about something. Here are some more examples using this idiom:

🎧 13.8 직업이 어떻게 되세요? [Chigeobi eotteoke toeseyo?] What do you do? (What's your occupation?)

🎧 13.9 연세가 어떻게 되세요? [Yeonsega eotteoke toeseyo?] How old are you?

🎧 13.10 가족이 어떻게 되세요? [Kajogi eotteoke toeseyo?] What is your family like?

> 직업 [chigeop] job, occupation   가족 [kajok] family
> 연세 [yeonse] age (honorific form of 나이)

Now we're really getting into some good conversation, aren't we? Let's look at some possible examples of how to answer the first question above.

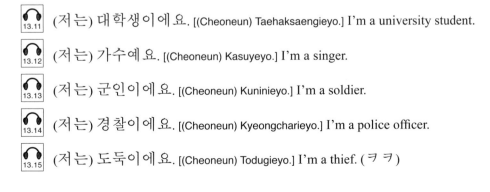

🎧 13.11 (저는) 대학생이에요. [(Cheoneun) Taehaksaengieyo.] I'm a university student.

🎧 13.12 (저는) 가수예요. [(Cheoneun) Kasuyeyo.] I'm a singer.

🎧 13.13 (저는) 군인이에요. [(Cheoneun) Kuninieyo.] I'm a soldier.

🎧 13.14 (저는) 경찰이에요. [(Cheoneun) Kyeongcharieyo.] I'm a police officer.

🎧 13.15 (저는) 도둑이에요. [(Cheoneun) Todugieyo.] I'm a thief. (ㅋㅋ)

대학생 [taehaksaeng] university student
가수 [kasu] professional singer
군인 [kunin] soldier

경찰 [kyeongchal] police
도둑 [toduk] thief

What? Excuse me?

Have you ever pretended to understand what someone said even though you didn't really? If you don't know how to say "What? What did you say? Excuse me?" in Korean, you may have to pretend a lot, right? Well, there's good news! It's very simple to ask someone to repeat themselves in Korean. Just say,

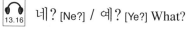 네? [Ne?] / 예? [Ye?] What?

As you know, 네 and 예 mean "yes." But if you pronounce either of them with a rising intonation, it means "Can you say that again?"

Are you ready to move on to the next chapter and work hard to learn about Korean nouns? 네? 예? Hey, that's not going to work—I know you heard me!

Further Vocabulary: Parts of the body

Just in case you want to describe your body to someone…easy, tiger!

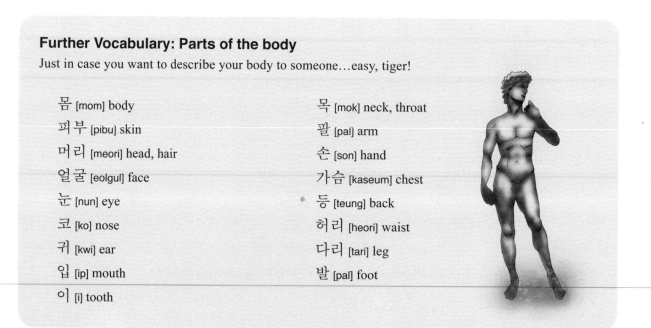

몸 [mom] body
피부 [pibu] skin
머리 [meori] head, hair
얼굴 [eolgul] face
눈 [nun] eye
코 [ko] nose
귀 [kwi] ear
입 [ip] mouth
이 [i] tooth

목 [mok] neck, throat
팔 [pal] arm
손 [son] hand
가슴 [kaseum] chest
등 [teung] back
허리 [heori] waist
다리 [tari] leg
발 [pal] foot

Korean Style: Korean family names and given names

A full Korean name consists of both a family name and a given name. Family names are usually one syllable, given names two. (Rarely, though occasionally, the family name could be two syllables and the given name one or three syllables.) In English, the given name precedes the family name, but in Korean, the order is the opposite. This probably has something to do with traditional Korean culture, which emphasizes family and society over the individual.

Originally, a Korean's family name represented a close tie to a specific group, so if a Korean met somebody with the same family name, he or she would feel very close to that person. These days, this aspect of Korean culture is disappearing, mostly because you'll meet people with the same family name all the time. There are millions of Koreans, but not even 300 family names!

Among the already short list of names, just a handful account for a considerable percentage. The most frequent is 김 [Kim], around one in five! Do you know who won the Nobel Peace Prize in 2000? It was Korea's former president 김대중 [Kim Daejung]. He's one of many with the family name of 김. The second most frequent is 이 [I] (often romanized as "Lee" or "Yi"), and after that it's 박 [Pak] (often romanized as "Park").

> Koreans usually don't put a space between their surnames and given names.

Let me tell you about a strange coincidence related to the surname 박. It seems many Korean sports stars have that family name. There's the Korean former MLB pitcher 박찬호 [Park Chanho], woman golfer 박세리 [Park Seri], Manchester United soccer player 박지성 [Park Jisung], and famous swimmer 박태환 [Park Taehwan]. Is there a 박 conspiracy going on here?! Probably not, but with the small number of family names in Korea, it's easy to see patterns like this.

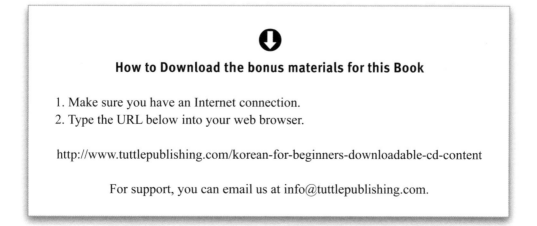

How to Download the bonus materials for this Book

1. Make sure you have an Internet connection.
2. Type the URL below into your web browser.

http://www.tuttlepublishing.com/korean-for-beginners-downloadable-cd-content

For support, you can email us at info@tuttlepublishing.com.

CHAPTER 14

Father, Mother, Brother, Sister...
아버지, 어머니, 형제, 자매...
[abeoji, eomeoni, hyeongje, chamae...]
Korean Nouns and Terms for Family Members

"Person," "language," "school," "notebook," "idea," "excellence"...what are these? **Nouns**, of course! In many languages, nouns are perhaps the most fundamental components. In the Korean language, nouns differ from those in English in two key areas.

1. Any **modifiers** of a noun (e.g., adjectives) must come **before** the noun.
2. Nouns don't have **articles** ("a," "an," "the").

In English, noun modifiers sometimes are placed before the noun and sometimes after it. But in Korean, they can only come before! (Rest assured, we'll study noun modifiers in greater detail later, in chapter 19.) And you've probably already noticed that there aren't any words for "a" or "the" in Korean. These are the two main rules you need to know about Korean nouns. They're pretty easy in comparison to other languages...no changes according to case, gender, etc.

Let's take a look at some basic Korean nouns, shall we? How about "man" and "woman"? These would be 남자 and 여자, respectively. But sometimes these words alone sound a little impolite when referring to somebody. So 남자분 🎧 14.1, and 여자분 🎧 14.2, are better to use in those instances.

남자(분) [namja(bun)] man   여자(분) [yeoja(bun)] woman

Those are two pretty fundamental nouns, right? Let's move on to some others: terms for **family members**. What do you call your father? Father? Dad? Daddy? Papa? There are several ways to refer to a father in English. But in Korean, there are just two:

🎧 14.3   아빠 [appa] dad

🎧 14.4   아버지 [abeoji] father

Okay, let's keep going!

🎧 14.5 엄마 [eomma] mom

🎧 14.6 어머니 [eomeoni] mother

🎧 14.7 할아버지 [harabeoji] grandfather

🎧 14.8 할머니 [halmeoni] grandmother

🎧 14.9 아들 [adeul] son

🎧 14.10 딸 [ttal] daughter

🎧 14.11 부모님 [pumonim] parents

Do you see how 할– is added to 아버지 to mean "grand-"? But be careful. There's no 할어머니. The shorter 할머니 is the correct term for "grandmother." And in the word for "parents," 부모님, 부 signifies *father* and 모 is *mother* (these come from Chinese characters), with the respectful ending –님 that we learned about in chapter 11.

Moving on. What about your **siblings**? Well, I hate to say it, but in Korean this topic is kind of confusing. In English, there are just two words, "brother" and "sister," right? But Koreans use different terms depending on the relationship between the speaker and his or her sibling. If an older sibling is the speaker, he or she will simply call the sibling by name. However, for a younger sibling, this isn't looked highly upon. Instead, younger siblings use these terms:

If you are the...	call your elder sister	call your elder brother
younger brother	누나 [nuna] 🎧 14.12	형 [hyeong] 🎧 14.14
younger sister	언니 [eonni] 🎧 14.13	오빠 [oppa] 🎧 14.15

Phew! Maybe at first you'll think this is too complicated and wonder why it's even necessary to follow these rules. But it's a perfect example of the cultural characteristics of Korea. I don't have to explain again that Koreans feel showing the proper respect for someone is very important, and they believe such respect begins with what you call that person. Using the words above to address your elder siblings indicates your respect for them and the value you place on your relationship with them. And it's rules like these that facilitate smooth and comfortable social relationships among Koreans.

Okay, like I said above, if you're the elder sibling, you can just call your younger brother or sister by name. But if you want to refer to them when talking to someone else, you use these terms:

🎧 14.16 남동생 [namdongsaeng] younger brother

🎧 14.17 여동생 [yeodongsaeng] younger sister

Recognize 남 and 여? These syllables appear in the words for "man" and "woman" too. Obviously, they're closely related to **gender**. Yet, you don't have to specify the gender of your younger sibling if you don't want to. Instead, just say:

 동생 [tongsaeng] younger sibling

And here's how to do it if you want to refer to a sibling without specifying an age relationship:

 형제 [hyeongje] brother/sibling (no gender)

자매 [chamae] sister

All right! That's a lot of new vocabulary to take in, so let's practice using it in a conversational context, which will help it stick in your brain. Ready?

가족이 어떻게 되세요? [Kajogi eotteoke toeseyo?] What is your family like?

할아버지, 할머니하고 부모님, 누나, 제가 있어요. [Harabeoji, halmeonihago pumonim, nuna, chega isseoyo.] There's my grandfather and grandmother, my parents, my elder sister, and I.

형제가 어떻게 되세요? [Hyeongjega eotteoke toeseyo?] Do you have any siblings?

언니랑 남동생이 있어요. [Eonnirang namdongsaengi isseoyo.] I have an elder sister and a younger brother.

| N-하고 [-hago] and (particle) | N-(이)랑 [-(i)rang] and (particle) |

Very nice! What a lot of simple but useful words and expressions you've learned over the last few chapters, don't you think? If you ask me, you're no longer a Korean novice! I think you're ready for something more, and I have faith that you can conquer it. So, for the second half of this book, I'm going to lead you to the uppermost extent of the beginner category. Sound good?

First, though, we need to go back and cover something I oversimplified in the early chapters. What is it? Well, you'll just have to wait and see…

Further Vocabulary: The in-laws

Oops! We can't forget these folks! Your mother-in-law would be so mad…

여보 [yeobo] your wife

장인어른 [changineoreun] or 아버님 [abeonim] your wife's father

장모님 [changmonim] or 어머님 [eomeonim] your wife's mother

처형 [cheohyeong] your wife's older sister

처제 [cheoje] your wife's younger sister

처남 [cheonam] your wife's brother

여보 [yeobo] your husband

아버님 [abeonim] your husband's father

어머님 [eomeonim] your husband's mother

아주버님 [ajubeonim] your husband's older brother

도련님 [toryeonnim] or 서방님 [seobangnim] your husband's younger brother

형님 [hyeongnim] your husband's older sister

아가씨 [agassi] your husband's younger sister

Korean Style: My father enters his bag??

In Korean text, the spacing of words is a little tricky. Even Koreans are confused by it sometimes. If you're not careful and make mistakes with your word spacing, you can wind up writing something very different than what you intended.

The rule is that each word should stand alone, but that particles should be attached to whatever words they're related to. Remember what I've told you about particles? Because word order in Korean is somewhat free, particles tell us whether a noun is the subject, object, etc. of a sentence. And a particle should always hook onto the end of its noun.

So what happens if you make a mistake in the spacing of a particle? Let's find out:

아버지가 방에 들어가신다. [Abeojiga pange teureogashinda.] My father enters the room.

> 방 [pang] room　　　　　　　　들어가다 [teureogada] to enter

You can identify the particles in this sentence, right? –가 denotes the subject, and –에 in this case means "to" or "into." So the sentence translates to "My father enters the room."

But look what happens if you attach –가 to the beginning of the second word instead of the end of the first, like this:

아버지 가방에 들어가신다. [Abeoji kabange teureogashinda.] My father enters his bag.

가방 means "bag." So the sentence now says "My father enters his bag." Funny? Okay. How about this one?

아버지가 죽을 드신다. [Abeojiga chugeul teushinda] My father eats soup.

> 죽 [chuk] soup　　　　　　　　드시다 [teushida] to eat (honorific form of 먹다)

What are the particles here? Yes, we have the subject particle just like last time, and then there's the object particle, –을. So our sentence says "My father eats soup." But transfer the subject particle again and you get this:

아버지 가죽을 드신다. [Abeoji kajugeul teushinda.] My father eats leather.

가죽 means "leather." Your father eats leather? How odd!

CHAPTER
15

I Don't Want to Eat
밥 먹기 싫어요. [Pap meokgi shireoyo.]
Advanced Pronunciation Rules

I know what you're thinking—we already learned pronunciation rules! Don't worry, I remember, even though it was ages ago in chapters 2 and 3. And, rest assured, with what I taught you back then, you can probably pronounce about 80% of Korean words correctly. Why 80% instead of 100? Well, the thing is, I didn't want to burden you by getting into the exceptions to those rules. As we've seen so often throughout this book, every rule has its exception, right? But now, you've come so far and done so well that I feel you're ready to take on these pesky exceptions.

It just so happens that each of the special rules we're going to look at deals with a sound change caused by 받침 consonants. You remember what 받침 are, don't you? Yes, of course, they're consonants that appear in the third position in a syllable. So let's see what happens to 받침 consonants ㅌ, ㄱ, ㄴ, and ㅎ in certain situations.

받침 ㅌ + 이 → [치 (chi)]

Remember what happens to a 받침 consonant that's followed by a syllable beginning with a vowel? Right, the sound of the 받침 jumps to the next syllable and connects with that vowel sound. The 받침 ㅌ does this as any other 받침 would, but something special happens when the vowel starting the next syllable is 이. The ㅌ changes its pronunciation to ㅊ [ch], giving us 치 [chi] instead of 티 [ti]. For example,

🎧 15.1 우리 같이[가치] 공부해요. [Uri **kachi** kongbuhaeyo.] Let's study together.

> 같이 [kachi] together

What's the reason for this sound change? Well, as usual, it makes for smoother pronunciation during fast speech. Let's look at another example:

🎧 15.2 끝이에요[끄치에요]? [**Kkeuchieyo**?] Are we finished?

> 끝 [kkeut] end

No, we're not finished. We just started! So let's keep going.

받침 ㄱ before ㄴ or ㅁ → [ㅇ (ng)]

Behold, the syllable following a 받침 consonant doesn't have to start with a vowel to bring about a change in pronunciation. Take the case of the 받침 ㄱ: when it comes before a syllable beginning with ㄴ, ㄹ, or ㅁ, it's pronounced as ㅇ [ng], not ㄱ [k]:

🎧 15.3   먹이를 먹는[멍는] 고양이 [meogireul **meongneun** koyangi] a cat eating food

🎧 15.4   한국말[한궁말] 잘하시네요. [**Hangungmal** chalhashineyo.] You speak Korean well.

> 먹이 [meogi] (an animal's) food   고양이 [koyangi] cat   잘하다 [chalhada] to do well

Does this seem like a strange, arbitrary pronunciation rule? If so, spend some time thinking about it, because it provides one of the clearest examples of why these kinds of changes take place. Try saying 먹는 three times fast, keeping the true pronunciation of ㄱ [k]. See how your mouth just wants to turn it into ㅇ [ng]? I think that's pretty neat.

받침 ㄴ before ㄹ → [ㄹ (l)]

So far, so good. Let's move on to the 받침 ㄴ. When this 받침 is followed by the consonant ㄹ, it creates a pronunciation that is very hard for Koreans. So, for example, if your name is Henry and you want to write it in Hangeul as 헨리, get ready to have a lot of people calling you "Halley." That's because Koreans change the sound of ㄴ [n] into ㄹ [l] in this case.

Even if you're not named Henry, you'll run into this rule when you take the green line of the Seoul subway. There's a stop you're likely to pass: 선릉[설릉] [Seolreung]. Take my advice—if you're lost and are looking for this station, don't ask for "Seonreung." All you'll get is a blank stare!

받침 ㅎ + ㄱ, ㄷ, ㅈ → [ㅋ (k), ㅌ (t), ㅊ (ch)]
받침 ㅎ before ㅇ → [Ø (silent)]

The last 받침 consonant that's worth mentioning is ㅎ. In fact, this is the only aspirated consonant (pop quiz—what are the other four??) that frequently appears as 받침. Hmm…it must be pretty lonely then, don't you think? Maybe that explains the effect it has on consonants that follow it. You see, when a 받침 ㅎ comes right before the consonants ㄱ, ㄷ, or ㅈ, they become aspirated from the influence of the ㅎ, changing to [ㅋ, ㅌ, and ㅊ]. See how the ㅎ makes itself some new aspirated friends?

🎧 15.5   이름이 어떻게[어떠케] 되세요? [Ireumi **eotteoke** toeseyo?] What are you called?

🎧 15.6   할머니는 머리가 하얗다[하야타]. [Halmeonineun meoriga **hayata**.] My grandmother's hair is white.

🎧 15.7   몸이 좋지[조치] 않아요. [Momi **chochi** anayo.] I don't feel good.

머리 [meori] hair, head, brain
하얗다 [hayata] white
몸 [mom] body

좋다 [chota] good
않다 [anta] not (negation)

There's one more thing to remember about the 받침 ㅎ, but it's easy…almost common sense, in fact. When it's followed by the character ㅇ, it becomes silent. Watch:

🎧 15.8   저는 이 책을 좋아해요[조아해요]. [Cheoneun i chaegeul **choahaeyo**.] I like this book.

좋아하다 [choahada] to like

Oh, do you really like the book? I'm flattered! You've given me new motivation to teach to the best of my ability. Let's learn more rules!

Double 받침

Okay, are you ready for another exception to a basic rule? Remember how I told you that Korean syllables are built according to one of two patterns: C + V or C + V + C? Well, it just so happens that occasionally that second pattern will actually have **two** consonants at the end instead of just one. We call these double 받침, since they function together as a pair as the syllable's 받침 consonant.

Now, before you start crying and yelling about how I misinformed you, let you down, etc., there's one thing to keep in mind: double 받침 are pretty rare. In fact, even native Korean speakers feel a little awkward when they have to use them! Because of this, I'm not going to cover all of them in this book. Instead, let's take a look at some of the basic features of double 받침—kind of like a double 받침 FAQ—and then we'll go over a couple of the least rare of the rare. Is that okay? Have I redeemed myself? I hope so. ^^

1. Double 받침? What's the need!?

Good question! Lucky for you, the answer is quite straightforward. Simply put, employing double 받침 allows the Korean language to contain more words. Think about it: You have a limited number of character combinations available to use in the syllable pattern C + V + C. However, by increasing the number of third-position consonant possibilities, the amount of potential syllables increases as well, as does the number of possible words. The more words, the greater the expressive potential of the language. Got it?

2. How many double 받침 are there? Can any consonant combine with any other to form a double 받침?

No. There are only 13 of these in total. And we already know two of them. That's because two of the five double consonants we learned—ㄲ and ㅆ—can be used as double 받침. (Pop quiz—what are the other three double consonants??) So that leaves 11 more: ㄳ, ㄵ, ㄺ, ㄽ, ㄾ, ㅄ, ㄻ, ㄼ, ㄿ, ㄶ, and ㅀ.

3. How do I write double 받침?

As you can see in the list above, you have to write both consonants directly beside each other and **half** the size of a regular consonant.

4. Okay, so how do I pronounce double 받침, wise guy? Does each one have its own new, unique pronunciation?

Guess what…no! You don't have to learn any new pronunciations for double 받침. Remember the basic pronunciation rule for 받침 consonants, that when they encounter a syllable starting with a vowel, they hop over the ㅇ and join with the vowel sound? This rule still holds true with double 받침, but it's only the second consonant in the pair that jumps to the next syllable; the first one remains where it is. Observe:

🎧 15.9 이 책 읽어[일거] 주세요. [I chaek **ilgeo** chuseyo.] Read this book for me.

🎧 15.10 우리 집은 마당이 넓어요[널버요]. [Uri chibeun madangi **neolbeoyo**.] My house has a wide yard.

🎧 15.11 아무 문제 없어요[업써요]. 🌱 [Amu munje **eopsseoyo**.] No problem.

🎧 15.12 공부를 조금밖에[바께] 못 했어요[해써요]. 🌱 [Kongbureul **chogeumbakke** mot **haesseoyo**.]
I couldn't study so much.

> 읽다 [ikda] to read
> V-아 / 어 / 여 주다 [-a/eo/yeo chuda] to do something for someone
> 마당 [madang] yard, garden
> 넓다 [neolda] large, big
> 아무 [amu] no (with negative expression)
> 문제 [munje] problem
> 공부 [kongbu] studying (noun)
> 조금 [chogeum] a little (bit)
> N-밖에 [bakke] with the exception of (particle)
> 못 [mot] (can)not

> 📖 When ㅅ is the second consonant in a double 받침, it takes on an [ㅆ] sound after it jumps to the next syllable.

> 📖 ㄲ and ㅆ are exceptions to the rule. They do not separate, but rather are both transferred to the following syllable.

Great—not so tough, is it? But what happens when the following syllable begins with a consonant? Or, better yet, when there is no following syllable? These are certainly valid questions. The answer is that one of the consonants in the double 받침 will be voiced and the other will be silent. Unfortunately, there's no simple rule to tell you which will happen to which 100% of the time. But don't worry. As I told you, these are rare elements of the language and are confusing even for Koreans. My advice: don't sweat it. Instead, just learn the pronunciations of some of the more common double 받침 words, case by case. Like these:

🎧 15.13 여덟[여덜] [yeodeol] eight

🎧 15.14 값[갑] [kap] price

🎧 15.15 삶[삼] [sam] life

받침 ㄶ / ㅀ

Let's close out this discussion with a look at two somewhat common double 받침. We've already gone over the 받침 ㅎ and how it turns consonants into aspirated friends, and both of these pairs have ㅎ as their second consonant: ㄶ and ㅀ. The good news here is that the pronunciation of these two double 받침 is relatively simple, because it's based on what you already know about the 받침 ㅎ.

받침 ㄶ / ㅀ + ㄱ, ㄷ, ㅈ → [ㄴ / ㄹ (n / l)] + [ㅋ (k), ㅌ (t), ㅊ (ch)]
받침 ㄶ / ㅀ before ㅇ → [ㄴ / ㄹ (n / l)]

So, when you have a 받침 ㄶ or ㅀ that's followed by a syllable beginning with ㄱ, ㄷ, or ㅈ, the ㅎ is going to convince the ㄱ, ㄷ, or ㅈ to go aspirated: ㅋ, ㅌ, or ㅊ. Remember, ㅎ is lonely! Okay, but then what happens to the ㄴ / ㄹ part of the pair? Well, it just stays put at the end of the first syllable.

For examples of this rule, let's take the words 많다 ("plenty") and 싫다 ("hateful") and see what occurs when we add the endings –고, –다, and –지만 onto their stems:

많고[만코] [manko]   싫고[실코] [shilko]
많다[만타] [manta]   싫다[실타] [shilta]
많지만[만치만] [manchiman]   싫지만[실치만] [shilchiman]

Great! And now, what about when these two double 받침 encounter a syllable starting with a vowel? According to the rules we've learned, the second consonant in the pair jumps into the second syllable, while the first consonant stays put. And that's what happens here. But, as we learned before, the consonant ㅎ goes silent when it hits ㅇ. So actually, these two characters cancel each other out into silence, leaving room for the remaining ㄴ or ㄹ to hop over to the second syllable. Sounds complicated, but let's simplify with some examples:

🎧 15.16 괜찮아요[괜차나요]. [Kwaenchanayo.] It's okay.

🎧 15.17 밥 먹기 싫어요[시러요]. [Pap meokgi shireoyo.] I don't want to eat.

Congratulations! You now know how to pronounce 100% of Korean words! Oh, you don't believe me? Okay, okay…I guess it's more like 98%. But come on, that's incredible!

Further Vocabulary: Negative feelings

Ahh…don't feel so down. The confusing pronunciation lesson is over!

슬프다 [seulpeuda] sad

괴롭다 [koeropda] pained, distressed

우울하다 [uulhada] gloomy, depressed

화나다 [hwanada] to get angry

짜증스럽다 [jjajeungseureopda] irritated

귀찮다 [kwichanta] troublesome, tiresome

울다 [ulda] to cry, to weep

재미없다 [chaemieopda] boring, dull

Korean Style: Tongue twisters

I'm sure you know some tongue twisters in English, right? For example, "Shall she sell seashells by the seashore?" And, "Peter Piper picked a peck of pickled peppers." We all learn these when we're kids, don't you remember? I don't know why exactly…maybe just because they're fun to say. And maybe because it's nice to remind ourselves that, even though we may speak a language fluently, it can still trip us up sometimes.

Korean also has many well-known tongue twisters, and they're really funny. Sometimes, Koreans compete to see who can pronounce the sentences quickest and most accurately. Also, professional announcers practice these sentences to warm up their mouths before an event.

Here's one famous Korean tongue twister: "간장 공장 공장장은 강 공장장이고, 된장 공장 공장장은 공 공장장이다" [Kanjang kongjang kongjangjangeun kang kongjangjangigo, toenjang kongjang kongjangjangeun kong kongjangjangida] ("The chief of the soy sauce factory is Mr. Kang and the chief of the soybean paste factory is Mr. Kong"). The meaning is nonsensical, of course, which adds to the humor. Can you say it?

How about this one: "내가 그린 기린 그림은 긴 기린 그림이고 네가 그린 기린 그림은 안 긴 기린 그림이다" [Naega keurin kirin keurimeun kin kirin keurimigo nega keurin kirin keurimeun an kin kirin keurimida] ("The picture that I painted is of a long giraffe and the picture that you painted is of a not-long giraffe.") Funny but difficult, aren't they?

Like I said, tongue twisters show us that even native speakers have trouble speaking their mother tongues. Keep that in mind as you continue learning Korean, and remember that even if you're talking to native Korean speakers, they won't laugh at your mistakes. In fact, Koreans are always eager to instruct learners in the pronunciation of Korean.

Excuse Me, Where's the Restroom?

저기요, 화장실이 어디예요? [Cheogiyo, hwajangshiri eodiyeyo?]
Interrogatives: When and Where

Are you ready to continue a discussion we had back in chapter 11? You remember, don't you? We talked a bit about interrogatives, focusing on two main question words: 무엇 ("what"), and 누구 ("who"). Now I'm going to introduce you to two more: "when" and "where."

When?

When you travel abroad, one of the things you want to make sure to do is investigate the country's medical system. Nothing can spoil a trip like getting sick in an unfamiliar place and realizing you can't make a doctor's appointment because you don't speak the language!

Lucky for you, Korea has an excellent healthcare system. There are clinics everywhere, and they're consistently staffed with helpful, friendly personnel. You can even find facilities where they speak English! But hey, you don't need that, do you? With what I'm going to teach you right now, you'll be able to do it like a real Korean.

So, what's the first thing you'll need to do? Make an appointment to see the doctor, of course. When you call, they'll probably ask you:

🎧 16.1 언제가 편하세요? [Eeonjega pyeonhaseyo?] When is good for you?

> 언제 [eonje] when   편하다 [pyeonhada] good, comfortable

Maybe you're hoping to get in tomorrow, so let's tell them that.

🎧 16.2 저는 내일이 괜찮아요. [Cheoneun naeiri kwaenchanayo.] Tomorrow will be good for me.

> 내일 [naeil] tomorrow

And just like that, you've got yourself a doctor's appointment! You'll be able to kick that cold in no time.

Okay, let's practice some more with the interrogative 언제. Say you've made a new Korean friend, and you're curious about when her birthday is. Birthdays are always a good topic of conversation, aren't they? In this case, you'd say:

🎧 16.3 생일이 언제예요? [Saengiri eonjeyeyo?] When is your birthday?

생일 [saengil] birthday

Or maybe you want to ask your friend about the weather in Korea, another nice conversational tool. You could say something like this:

🎧 16.4   한국은 언제 비가 많이 와요? [Hangugeun eonje piga mani wayo?] When is the rainy season in Korea?

비 [pi] rain   오다 [oda] to come   많이 [mani] much

Actually, Korea typically has a short but intense rainy season that's called 장마 [changma] and occurs throughout the month of July. It rains almost every day. Ask your new friend about it—I'm sure she'll be more than happy to have someone to complain to about 장마.

Where?

From **time**, let's move on to a **space**-oriented interrogative. Consider this: you've just arrived at Incheon International Airport, Korea's main hub and one that's frequently been rated as a top world airport. It's not actually in Seoul, but rather about an hour west on the coast. Seoul is a crowded city, remember? We can't have big planes flying this way and that all day as 10+ million people go about their business. That would be distracting. So the main airport is in Incheon.

Anyway, you've arrived at the airport, and now what do you do? Is a friend meeting you there to help guide you? Of course, I wish I could be there to meet you, but I've been so busy working on this book. ^^ So perhaps you're all alone in a big airport in a strange new country. Don't worry. Korea's transportation system is well organized, and you have many options for getting to Seoul, or wherever you want to go.

But before you can arrange where to go, you have to know where you are, right? Well, do you? If not, don't hesitate to ask:

🎧 16.5   여기가 어디예요? [Yeogiga eodiyeyo?] Where is this?

여기 [yeogi] here, this place   어디 [eodi] where

Of course, a person might think you're a bit odd for asking such a question at the airport. Didn't the flight attendants tell you where you were landing!? But remember, Koreans are very helpful, so I bet you'll get a straight answer.

Now that you know where you are, it's time to arrange transport to where you want to be. Many people catch a taxi from the airport. It's a little pricier, but the convenience and comfort can't be beat. After you've thrown your bags in the trunk and hopped into the back seat, the driver will ask you:

🎧 16.6   어디 가세요? [Eodi kaseyo?] Where are you going?

어디 가세요?
Where are you going?

What do you think is missing in this sentence? Anything? If you were constructing this question, wouldn't you put a particle (such as –에, or –(으)로, or –까지) on the end of 어디? Well, you wouldn't be wrong to do so. Your cabbie is simply **omitting** it because, in this situation, the meaning of 어디 is understood without it.

> N–에 [-e] to, at (particle)   N–까지 [-kkaji] to, by, until (particle)
> N–(으)로 [-(eu)ro] to (particle)

Congratulations! You've successfully taken a taxi and arrived at your destination. Don't you feel great that you've accomplished this all in a foreign language? Well, you should.

Uh-oh, wait a minute. It was a long ride from the airport to downtown Seoul, and you didn't use the restroom before you left. Now you've really got to go! What do you do!? First of all, relax. You're in a land of nice restrooms, and unlike in many countries of the world, you don't have to pay to use them! So all you have to do is pop into a café and ask:

🎧 16.7 (실례지만) 화장실이 어디예요? [(Shilryejiman) Hwajangshiri eodiyeyo?] (Excuse me,) Where's the restroom?

> 화장실 [hwajangshil] restroom

It's okay to just say 화장실이 어디예요? But in order to draw the employee's attention, you'll want to begin your question with 실례지만, which is another way to say "excuse me." Surprised and pleased by your fluent Korean, the barista will no doubt inform you of the location of the restroom with a smile.

To understand his response, however, you're going to need to think back again to chapter 11 and the demonstrative pronouns "this" and "that." Hmm…I can tell by the look on your face you'd appreciate a review. Shall we?

Remember that in English these are only two words, but in Korean we have three. The demonstrative 이 translates as "this," referring to something close to the speaker. The other two both signify the English "that," but differ depending on the specific location of what exactly it is you're talking about. 그 is used for something close to the listener, while 저 is for an object distant from both speaker and listener.

It's all coming back to you now, right? Well, the barista's directions will probably include one or more of these pronouns, but there will be another element as well: 쪽 [jjok]. 쪽 actually has a number of different uses, but when you add it to the end of demonstrative pronouns, it creates the meaning of "this/that direction." I bet you can figure out these translations:

🎧 16.8 이 쪽 [i jjok] this way

🎧 16.9 그 쪽 [keu jjok] that way (closer)

🎧 16.10 저 쪽 [cheo jjok] that way (more distant)

And lastly, we'll need a particle…but which one? Of course, the particle indicating "in the direction of" is called for, which is –(으)로. So finally we have the barista's answer:

🎧 16.11 이 쪽으로 가세요. [I jjogeuro kaseyo.] Go this way.

🎧 16.12 그 쪽으로 가세요. [Keu jjogeuro kaseyo.] Go that way. (closer by)

저 쪽으로 가세요. [Cheo jjogeuro kaseyo.] Go that way. (more distant)

But wait, what if the restroom is on a totally different floor? Oh no! Oftentimes in Korea's multi-story buildings, the restrooms for multiple businesses will be located on a separate floor, or the men's and women's will be in different places. So your barista may need to direct you to an upper or lower floor, like this:

 남자 화장실은 위 층에 있어요. [Namja hwajangshireun wi cheunge isseoyo.] The men's room is on the next floor up.

여자 화장실은 아래 층에 있어요. [Yeoja hwajangshireun arae cheunge isseoyo.] The women's room is on the next floor down.

위 [wi] upper   아래 [arae] lower   층 [cheung] floor, story

Notice these sentences are a little different than the three listed above. Here, the barista isn't telling you to go a certain way, but rather is relating *where* the restrooms *are*. So, in place of the **directional** particle –(으)로, you need the particle of **location**, –에. Make sense?

I bet you really have to go to the restroom now, don't you!? But there's still one more way the barista could respond to your question, and we should cover all the bases, right? Any ideas what else he might say? Well, he could tell you to go straight or to turn left or right:

이 쪽으로 죽 가서 왼쪽으로 도세요. [I jjogeuro chuk kaseo oenjjogeuro toseyo.] Go straight this way and then turn left.

죽 [chuk] straight
V–아서 / 어서 / 여서 [-aseo/eoseo/yeoseo] and then (conjugative ending, pattern 5)
왼 쪽 [oenjjok] left (direction)
돌다 [tolda] to turn

Ahhhhhh…you found the restroom! Well, I won't keep you, then, but I just want to mention something about 왼 and its opposite, 오른. These are related to "left" and "right," respectively, but you can't use them alone. They always have to be paired with a second word to create meaning. This could be 쪽 ("way"), which you've already learned, or perhaps 손 [son] ("hand"), or 발 [pal] ("foot"), which would give you the following: 왼쪽 ("left"), 오른쪽 ("right"), 왼손 ("left hand"), 오른손 ("right hand"), 왼발 ("left foot"), 오른발 ("right foot").

Okay, you must be bursting now, so I'll leave you to it!

Further Vocabulary: Location and direction

More words to help you figure out where you're going in life.

앞 [ap] (the) front
앞쪽 [apjjok] front (direction)
뒤 [twi] (the) back, (the) rear
뒤쪽 [twijjok] back, rear (direction)
옆 [yeop] (the) side
옆쪽 [yeopjjok] side (direction)
안 [an] (the) inside
안쪽 [anjjok] inside (direction)
바깥 [pakkat] (the) outside
바깥쪽 [pakkatjjok] outside (direction)
동쪽 [tongjjok] east
서쪽 [seojjok] west
남쪽 [namjjok] south
북쪽 [pukjjok] north

(In Korean, you always list the cardinal directions in the order east, west, south, north.)

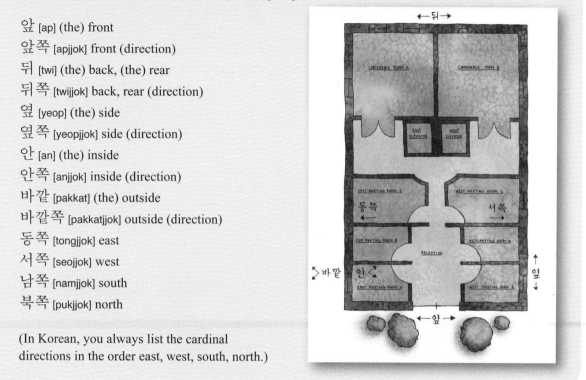

Korean Style: Snow water, or eye water?

Oops! You forgot to check the weather forecast this morning. Don't worry, just ask your Korean friend, 오늘 비 와요? ("Will it rain today?"). But don't be confused if your friend puts on a mischievous grin and replies, 아니요, 비는 지금 미국에 있어요. ("No, Rain is in the U.S. right now."). This is a common joke in Korean, playing on the double meaning of 비 to mean both the precipitation rain and the Korean singer Rain.

Words like this are called homonyms—they sound the same and are spelled the same but have different meanings. English has them too, of course, lots of them. Consider the words "fly," "matter," and "bear," for starters. In Korean, homonyms are used to make some great puns, like this one:

눈에 눈이 들어가니 눈물일까, 눈물일까?

The word 눈 has two meanings. The first is "snow," and the other is "eye." So can you guess what the sentence above means? It says, "When snow gets in your eye and melts, is the water eye water or snow water?"

Here are some more good ones:

다리가 너무 아파서 다리에서 쉬었어요. [Tariga neomu apaseo tarieseo shieosseoyo.]
머리를 다쳐서 머리가 빠져요. [Meorireul tachyeoseo meoriga ppajyeoyo.]
배에서 배를 먹었더니 배가 아파요. [Paeeseo paereul meogeotdeoni paega apayo.]

Answers?　　I rested on a **bridge**, for my **legs** hurt.
My **hair** has been falling out since I hurt my **head**.
I developed a **stomach**ache after I ate a **pear** on the **ship**.

17

How's Korea?
한국 어때요? [Hanguk eottaeyo?]
Interrogatives: How and Why, Reasons and Causes

Now that you're back from the restroom, are you ready to learn how to ask more questions? Asking questions is good, right? As the saying goes, you'll never know if you don't ask. Well, I want you to know! So I'm going to show you how to ask questions using two more useful question words: "how" and "why."

How?

Do you have any foreign friends? If so, I bet you've asked them what they think of your country. You'll run into the same thing when you come to Korea and talk to your new Korean friends. They'll always want to know:

🎧 17.1 한국 어때요? [Hanguk eottaeyo?] How's Korea?

> 어떻다 [eotteota] how

Here, the word 어떻다 is an adjective, so when you're curious about someone's feelings or opinion on a subject, you can say N-이 / 가 어때요? Remember, 어떻다 is a ㅎ irregular adjective, so when you conjugate it with the pattern 5 ending –아요 / –어요 / –여요, you drop the final ㅎ. That's how you get 어때요, right? Great. Let's practice.

🎧 17.2 이 음식점 분위기가 어때요? [I eumshikjeom punwigiga eottaeyo?] How's the restaurant's atmosphere?

🎧 17.3 오늘 기분이 어때요? [Oneul kibuni eottaeyo?] How're you feeling today?

> 음식점 [eumshikjeom] restaurant   분위기 [punwigi] air, atmosphere, ambience, mood
> 기분 [kibun] feeling, mood

Pretty easy, right? But wait, because there's more we can do with the adjective 어떻다. For example, we can make an **adverb** out of it: 어떻게. As I'm sure you know, adverbs modify verbs or adjectives, so using this adverb, we can come up with a different way to say 한국 어때요? Check it out:

🎧 17.4 한국(을) 어떻게 생각하세요? [Hanguk(eul) eotteoke saenggakaseyo?] What do you think of Korea?

> 생각하다 [sanggakada] to think

Notice that the literal translation is "How do you think…," but of course in English we would say "what" instead. Anyway, the adverb 어떻게 is modifying the verb "think" in this sentence, isn't it? This just gives us a somewhat more long-winded way of saying "How's Korea?"

The 어떻게 adverb can be really useful in other circumstances—especially if it's your first time in Korea, because you're likely to get lost a few times. Don't lose your cool! Just remember 어떻게, and you can find help.

Say you're trying to find your way to Insadong, Seoul's famous traditional district that's full of atmospheric teashops and handicraft stores. Oh no, you forgot your map at home! What do you do? Well, just flag down a friendly pedestrian and ask:

🎧 17.5 인사동(까지) 어떻게 가요? [Insadong(kkaji) eotteoke kayo?] How can I get to Insadong?

The passerby will kindly inform you that you can get there on the subway:

🎧 17.6 지하철을 타세요. [Chihacheoreul taseyo.] Take the subway.

| 지하철 [chihacheol] subway | 타다 [tada] to ride, to take |

So make sure to take note of the handy 어떻게 adverb. It just might save your day!

But we're still not done exploring the usefulness of the adjective 어떻다, because there's yet another form: 어떤 [eotteon]. 어떤 is a noun modifier—it modifies whatever noun is written directly after it. Now, its meaning is a little different from that of 어떻다 and 어떻게, but we're going to learn it anyway because it's a great word to know. Instead of "how," 어떤 translates into "what (kind of)," or "which."

Need some context? I think so. Let's say you're on a blind date in Korea, and your date wants to know your preferences for dinner. He might ask you:

🎧 17.7 어떤 음식을 좋아하세요? [Eotteon eumshigeul choahaseyo?] What kind of food do you like?

By the way, do you know much about Korean food? I'm sure you've heard of kimchi, at least from me, but you can't use this as an answer to the question. Kimchi is a side dish, not a main dish. So what else? Do you know bulgogi? It's Korean barbeque—sliced meat marinated in a special mixture of sauces and spices and grilled over charcoal. It's terrific; I bet you'll love it! So why don't you tell your date this:

🎧 17.8 저는 불고기를 사랑해요. [Cheoneun pulgogireul saranghaeyo.] I love bulgogi.

Oops! He's starting to laugh at you! Why? Well, I admit, I played a little trick on you. The Korean verb for "to love" is definitely 사랑하다, but typically it's only used to talk about people you love, not food or other inanimate objects. In these cases, use 좋아하다 instead. So let's revise your statement:

🎧 **17.9** 저는 불고기를 좋아해요. [Cheoneun pulgogireul choahaeyo.] I like bulgogi.

Hey, this is pretty good. You've made your date laugh, the tension has been eased, and everything's looking up. So, come on, keep the mood going. Make some conversation. Um…how about the weather? The weather? Are you sure? Well, here goes:

🎧 **17.10** 오늘 날씨 어때요? [Oneul nalssi eottaeyo?] How's the weather today?

> 날씨 [nalssi] weather

Oh boy! What does he look like, the weatherman? I don't know if any date has ever been successful following a conversation about the weather. Good luck!

Why?

Why? Why did you act so foolishly last night? Hey, I'm just kidding, I'm sure your date understood that your conversational skills were simply a result of your beginner Korean, not your personality. Is there anything they said that you didn't understand? Maybe they asked you why you came to Korea. Or, better yet, they probably asked why you're learning Korean.

In Korea, learning English is taken very seriously and viewed as a necessary, yet incredibly difficult, task. Koreans look at native English speakers like you and think you're very lucky to have learned the language as a child. On the other hand, since Korean is not a major international language like English, they wonder why English speakers would choose to study it. So they might ask you:

🎧 **17.11** 한국어를 왜 배우세요? [Hangugeoreul wae paeuseyo?] Why do you learn Korean?

> 왜 [wae] why   배우다 [paeuda] to learn

As you can see, the Korean word for "why" is 왜. Of course, in English "why" always appears at the beginning of the sentence, but in Korean 왜 should be placed in front of the sentence's verb. Why? Because it's an **adverb** in Korean, so it technically modifies the verb. However, if you really want to put 왜 at the beginning of the sentence (e.g., 왜 한국어를 배우세요?), it doesn't matter. Remember? In Korean, the word order is relatively free.

By the way, why *are* you learning Korean? For some people, they study the language for romantic reasons. So they might answer:

🎧 **17.12** 여자 친구가 한국 사람이어서 한국말을 배워요. [Yeoja chinguga hanguk saramieoseo hangungmareul paeweoyo.] I'm learning Korean because my girlfriend is Korean.

> 친구 [chingu] friend

Ah, the power of love! It's as great a reason as any for learning a second language, don't you think!

Reasons and causes

What about the conjugative ending –아서 / –어서 / –여서 in the sentence above? If you recall, in the last chapter we used it to mean "and then," but here, it's signifying the **reason** for a certain action. Both meanings are possible with this ending. (You'll have to wait till chapter 22 for a more thorough explanation.)

Another way to say this sentence would be:

 여자 친구 때문에 한국말을 배워요. [Yeoja chingu ttaemune hangungmareul paeweoyo.]
I'm learning Korean because of my girlfriend.

> 때문 [ttaemun] because of (reason for an action or state of being)

Similar to the ending –아서 / –어서 / –여서, the word 때문 is used to express the reason or cause for an action or state of being. It's placed after the noun that's being identified as the reason. See how that works?

Great! And do you want to learn one more way to say this? If so, then it's time to introduce you to the wonderful trick for transforming verbs and adjectives into **nouns**. Koreans do this all the time. In English it's like adding "-ing" onto a verb (e.g., changing "to learn" into "learning," for use in the sentence "Learning is fun.").

It's simple. All you have to do as add the ending –기 onto the verb or adjective stem. I introduced this briefly back in chapter 6, do you remember? It's a pattern 1 ending…the easiest!

So, for the special verb ending –이다, which means "to be," what's the noun form? Yes, 이기! We can then say:

 여자 친구가 한국 사람이기 때문에 한국말을 배워요. [Yeoja chinguga hanguk saramigi ttaemune hangungmareul paeweoyo.] I'm learning Korean because of my girlfriend *being* Korean.

It's rather clunky in English, I know, but in Korean it's perfectly natural! So there you have three different ways of explaining the reason for something.

And now, what about you? What's your reason for learning Korean?

Further Vocabulary: Questions?

Ask away!

Questions using 어때요

당신 생각은 어때요? [Tangshin saenggageun eottaeyo?] What do you think?

제 머리 모양 어때요? [Che meori moyang eottaeyo?] How do you like my hairdo?

커피 대신 차를 마시는 게 어때요? [Keopi taeshin chareul mashineun ke eottaeyo?] Why don't you have tea instead of coffee?

생각 [saenggak] thought   대신 [taeshin] instead
모양 [moyang] shape   차 [cha] tea
커피 [keopi] coffee   마시다 [mashida] to drink
게 [ke] thing (shortened form of 것 ["thing"] + subject particle –이)

Questions using 어떻게

요즘 어떻게 지내세요? [Yojeum eotteoke chinaeseyo?] How are you doing these days?

불고기는 어떻게 먹어요? [Pulgogineun eotteoke meogeoyo?] How do you eat bulgogi?

요즘 [yojeum] these days, nowadays
지내다 [chinaeda] to live

Questions using 어떤

그 사람은 어떤 사람이에요? [Keu sarameun eotteon saramieyo?] What is he like?

어떤 일을 하세요? [Eotteon ireul haseyo?] What's your job?

일 [il] work, job

Questions using 왜

왜 우세요? [Wae useyo?] Why are you crying?

왜 그렇게 생각해요? [Wae keureoke saenggakaeyo?] Why do you think so?

울다 [ulda] to cry
그렇게 [keureoke] so, in this/that way

불고기는 어떻게 먹어요?
How do you eat bulgogi?

Korean Style: Korean blind dates

Traditionally, marriages were arranged in Korea. Parents would set up a meeting for a son or daughter who'd reached a certain age, and if both agreed to it, they'd get married. (Sometimes they married even though they didn't want to, of course, because they were raised to obey their parents.) Nowadays, parents can't force their children to marry, but these kinds of meetings still take place.

What about more casual meetups? There are two types of these: 미팅 and 소개팅. 미팅 is a direct adoption of the English word "meeting," but it has a more specific meaning. It refers to meetings between young men and women who are searching for a partner, and they occur especially in college.

And then there's the 소개팅. This is close to the concept of a blind date in the West. The word is related to 미팅, as 소개 means "introduction," and 팅 is taken straight from 미팅. So obviously, it means meeting someone through a third party's introduction.

Will you have a chance to go on a 소개팅 or 미팅 in Korea? Who can say? It's highly possible, if that's what you're looking for. But if you're a guy, you have to remember two things. First, you need to pay. And second, you have to drop her off at her home (or at least offer to). Otherwise, don't expect a second date!

🎧

To Download or Stream Bonus Materials:

How to Download the Bonus Material of this Book.
1. You must have an internet connection.
2. Type the URL below into to your web browser.

https://www.tuttlepublishing.com/korean-for-beginners-videos-audio

For support, you can email us at info@tuttlepublishing.com.

CHAPTER

18

I'm from the U.S.

미국에서 왔어요. [Migugeseo wasseoyo.]
Verb Tenses: Past, Progressive, and Future

If you had to guess, how many foreigners would you say are living in South Korea right now? Actually, the best anyone can do is guess, because the number isn't known exactly, but estimates suggest that as much as 2% of the population is made up of non-nationals. That's a pretty big number in a country of 50 million.

But still, Koreans will see you, a person from a faraway land who's studying hard to learn their language, with curious eyes. And, as I think I've mentioned before, one of the first things they'll want to know is where exactly you're from. So prepare to hear this a lot:

🎧 18.1 어디에서 왔어요? [Eodieseo wasseoyo?] Where do you come from?

These words should be familiar to you. Because, let's see…we learned about 어디 in chapter 16, right? And the particle –에서, that means "from," remember? And finally there's the verb 오다, which is "to come." This is all review for you! But what's not review is the conjugation of the verb in this sentence—particularly, this component: 왔.

To understand, it's necessary to tell you that, translated literally, the above sentence in English would be "Where *did* you come from?" not "Where *do* you come from?" Koreans see this as logical because you've already arrived in Korea, so the action of coming is in the past, right? Obviously, what I want to tell you about in this chapter is verb **tenses**.

What *did* you do?

In English, you signify the **past tense** by adding "-d" or "-ed" onto the end of verbs. Well, surprise, surprise—Korean follows the same principle! There's a special conjugative verb and adjective ending to indicate past tense, and it's this: –았– / –었– / –였–. This ending follows conjugation pattern 5, which we learned back in chapter 6 (I told you that chapter was important!). In other words, if the final vowel in the stem is ㅏ or ㅗ, –았– is used; for any other final vowel, you'll need –었–; and 하다 verbs and adjectives take the ending –였– no matter what.

Let's take a look at how we arrived at 왔어요 for "came," shall we? What's the stem of the verb 오다? That's right, 오. Its final vowel is ㅗ, so it's going to take the –았– ending, giving us 오았. But, in this case, 오 + 았 contracts to something shorter and easier to say. Speak 오았 fast and what comes out? Yes, 왔! Now, we need to add the honorific form 1 ending (don't forget your manners!). And this is important—in the case of past-tense verb stems, they always take the –어요 honorific ending, never the –아요 or –여요. And that's how we get 왔어요. A long explanation for a simple question, no?

Now, what if the Korean asking you this question is polite and wants to pay respect to you? To do this, she'd add the **honorific suffix** –(으)시– to the verb stem, right? That gives us a stem of 오시. This changes the rest of our conjugation, because now we have a stem with a final vowel of ㅣ, not ㅗ. So what happens? Uh-huh, we apply the –었– ending in place of –았–. So we have 오시었어요, which contracts into 오셨어요. (Just say 시었 three times fast to understand the contraction.) The honorific question is then:

18.2 어디에서 오셨어요? [Eodieseo oshyeosseoyo?] Where do you come from?

Okay, now that you understand the question inside and out, it's time to answer!

18.3 미국에서 왔어요. [Migugeseo wasseoyo.] I'm from the U.S.

18.4 싱가포르에서 왔어요. [Shinggaporeueseo wasseoyo.] I'm from Singapore.

18.5 홍콩에서 왔어요. [Hongkongeseo wasseoyo.] I'm from Hong Kong.

> 미국 [miguk] U.S., America
> 싱가포르 [shinggaporeu] Singapore
> 홍콩 [hongkong] Hong Kong

Great! So that's a really practical use of the past tense. Want to learn another? We already studied how to say hello to someone in chapter 9: 안녕하세요? But there's an alternate expression of greeting that can go along with that. It's

18.6 밥 먹었어요? [Pap meogeosseoyo?] Did you eat something?

Obviously, the stem 먹 of the verb 먹다 ("to eat") has a final vowel of ㅓ, so it takes the 었어요 past-tense ending. Literally, this translates to "Did you eat (cooked) rice?" But this is just an expression; your new acquaintance doesn't really care to know whether you ate cooked rice, uncooked rice, ramen, or anything else. He just wants to greet you. So instead of screwing up your face and saying "Why do you want to know whether I've eaten cooked rice?", just say:

18.7 네. 규병 씨는 점심 드셨어요? [Ne. Kyubyong ssineun cheomshim teushyeosseoyo?] Yes. Did you (Kyubyong) have lunch?

> 점심 [cheomshim] lunch

Oh, perfect! Your response is going to make 규병 씨 look at you with admiration, because you used the honorific 드시다 instead of the plain 먹다 for "to eat". So you showed respect for 규병 씨. (Remember, saying 씨 after someone's given name is another very common way of being respectful when addressing them.)

This is a good habit to get into, so why don't you memorize this for a greeting to use with new acquaintances?

18.8 안녕하세요, 아침 (점심, 저녁) 드셨어요? [Annyeonghaseyo, achim (cheomshim, cheonyeok) teushyeosseoyo?] Hi, did you have breakfast (lunch, dinner)?

> 아침 [achim] breakfast, morning   저녁 [cheonyeok] dinner, evening

No, you're not a crazy person obsessed with people's diets, you're just being polite!

What *are* you *doing*?

Wow, did you know you just learned the past tense in Korean? In other languages, it can take years to master this element, but I've actually told you nearly all you need to know to speak about the past in Korean. So let's move on to another tense: the **progressive**.

The progressive tense is what you use to describe an action that's currently in progress. For example, I *am explaining* Korean tenses to you, and you *are understanding* me, right!? Well, I think you'll understand this one pretty easily, because it utilizes an ending from conjugation pattern 1, the simplest! To form the progressive tense in Korean, simply add –고 있다 to any verb 🦋 stem. Yup, that's it! So, let's ask your friend what they're doing right now:

🎧 18.9   뭐 하고 있어요? [Mweo hago isseoyo?] What are you doing?

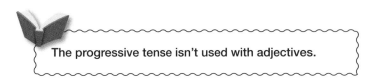

The progressive tense isn't used with adjectives.

See how that works? You just stick –고 onto the stem of the verb 하다 ("to do"), and then conjugate the adjective 있다 accordingly. Of course, if you're addressing a person you don't know well, or someone you need to impress, it's better to use the honorific verb 계시다 instead of 있다:

🎧 18.10   뭐 하고 계세요? [Mweo hago kyeseyo?] What are you doing?

Okay, and your friend will answer with the progressive tense, so you may hear:

🎧 18.11   책 읽고 있어요. [Chaek ilkko isseoyo.] I'm reading a book.

🎧 18.12   텔레비전 보고 있어요. [Telrebijeon pogo isseoyo.] I'm watching TV.

🎧 18.13   음악 듣고 있어요. [Eumak teutgo isseoyo.] I'm listening to music.

🎧 18.14   인터넷 하고 있어요. [Inteonet hago isseoyo.] I'm surfing the Internet.

🎧 18.15   당신 생각하고 있었어요… [Tangshin saenggakago isseosseoyo…] I was thinking about you…

텔레비전 [telrebijeon] TV	듣다 [teutda] to listen
보다 [poda] to watch, to see	인터넷 [inteonet] Internet
음악 [eumak] music	인터넷(을) 하다 to surf the Internet

Oh! It sounds like you guys might be more than just friends, eh? I sense the spark of romance in the air! ^^ But seriously, that last sentence is a little different, isn't it? I think you can figure it out, though. That's right, it's using the **past progressive**. And how does that work? Well, if the present progressive conjugation is V–고 있다, then it makes sense that the past progressive will be V–고 있었다—just use the past tense of 있다, and you've got it!

What *will* you do?

So, what's left in our discussion of Korean tenses? I *am going to let* you guess what tense this *will be*. Okay, enough riddles—I know you know it's the **future** tense!

In English, you express future actions and conditions in two ways: by adding "will" or "shall" in front of a verb, and by saying "going to do." Well, it's only fair that in Korean there are also two ways: using the ending –ㄹ게요 / –을게요, and using the construction –ㄹ / –을 거예요, both of which belong to conjugation pattern 4. However, just as "will," "shall," and "going to do" are not exactly the same, neither are these two endings. Allow me to explain:

🎧 18.16 1. 이따가 숙제를 **할게요**. [Ittaga sukjereul halgeyo.] I promise I'll do my homework later (and if I don't, you can punish me).

🎧 18.17 2. 이따가 숙제를 **할 거예요**. [Ittaga sukjereul hal keoyeyo.] I'm going to do my homework later (but if I don't, I'm not taking any responsibility for my behavior).

> 이따가 [ittaga] later   숙제 [sukje] homework

As you can see, –ㄹ게요 / –을게요 expresses a strong will or **intention** to do something. In fact, it's as if you're making a promise to the listener. For this reason, we often use the adverb 꼭[kkok], meaning "surely" or "at any cost," with this future-tense ending.

On the other hand, –ㄹ / –을 거예요 simply adds the meaning of "in the future" to whatever verb or adjective you're using, without expressing your dedication to living up to your word. This ending is often paired with the adverb 분명히 [punmyeonghi], meaning "definitely," or 아마[ama], "probably."

Let's continue examining the distinctions between the two:

🎧 18.18 다음부터 이를 꼭 닦을게요. [Taeumbuteo ireul kkok takkeulgeyo.] I promise I'll brush my teeth from next time on.

🎧 18.19 다음부터 이를 꼭 닦을 거예요. [Taeumbuteo ireul kkok takkeul keoyeyo.] I'll brush my teeth from next time on.

🎧 18.20 내일은 분명히 비가 올 거예요. [Naeireun punmyeonghi piga ol keoyeyo.] I'm sure it'll rain tomorrow.

🎧 18.21 내일은 아마 비가 올 거예요. [Naeireun ama piga ol keoyeyo.] It'll probably rain tomorrow.

> 다음 [taeum] next time   닦다 [takda] to brush, to clean
> N–부터 [-buteo] from (particle)   내일 [naeil] tomorrow
> 이 [i] tooth   비가 오다 [piga oda] to rain

Okay, let me explain one more useful future-tense expression, which you can employ when you need to avoid making a promise to someone. Of course, you could simply use the ‒ㄹ / ‒을 거예요 ending, but this still implies that you're in agreement with whatever the person wants you to do. Instead, to approximate English **hedging** phrases like "Um…I think…I guess…well…I mean…I'm afraid…," you can utilize the ending ‒ㄹ / ‒을 거 같다. Like the others, this belongs to pattern 4. Watch:

🎧 18.22 저 좀 늦을 거 같아요. [Cheo chom neujeul keo katayo.] I'm afraid I'm going to be a little late.

🎧 18.23 비행기를 놓칠 거 같아요. [Pihaenggireul nochil keo katayo.] It's possible that I'll miss the plane.

좀 [chom] a little	비행기 [pihaenggi] airplane
늦다 [neutda] to be late	놓치다 [nochida] to miss

Hey, 빨리 빨리! You don't want to miss your flight to the next chapter!

Further Vocabulary: Movement

When I say "jump," you say…

서다 [seoda] to stand, to stop
　　EX.: 한 줄로 서 주세요. [Han chulro seo chuseyo.] Stand in line.
앉다 [anda] to sit
　　EX.: 모두 앉아 주세요. [Modu anja chuseyo.] Please everybody sit down.
눕다 [nupda] to lie
　　EX.: 피곤하면 침대에 누우세요. [Pigonhamyeon chimdaee nuuseyo.] If you're tired, lie on the bed.
걷다 [keotda] to walk
　　EX.: 걷는 걸 좋아하세요? [Keonneun keol choahaseyo?] Do you like to walk?
뛰다 [ttwida] to run, to jump
　　EX.: 뛰지 마세요. [Ttwiji maseyo.] Don't run. (Don't jump.)
달리다 [talrida] to run
　　EX.: 여기에서는 달리면 안 돼요. [Yeogieseoneun talrimyeon an twaeyo.] You shouldn't run here.
잡다 [chapda] to hold
　　EX.: 내 손 꽉 잡으세요. [Nae son kkwak chabeuseyo.] Hold my hand tightly.
밀다 [milda] to push
　　EX.: 미세요! [Miseyo!] Push!
당기다 [tanggida] to pull
　　EX.: 당기세요! [Tanggiseyo!] Pull!

당기세요!
Pull!

미세요!
Push!

줄 [chul] line
모두 [modu] everybody
침대 [chimdae] bed
피곤하다 [pigonhada] tired
꽉 [kkwak] tightly

Korean Style: How to multiply your Korean vocabulary

Surely you'll have a basic grasp of Korean and all its different colors and flavors after you finish this book. But why stop there? You're such a dedicated student, I'm sure you'll want to continue learning—more grammar, more culture, more words!

Memorizing vocabulary is a big part of learning any language, but what's the best way to do this? Imagine a Korean friend asks you what the word "extraterrestrial" means. Of course, you might answer, "Oh, you don't need to learn that." Or "Haven't you seen the movie *E.T.*? That's an extraterrestrial!"

But there's a more helpful way of explaining this complicated-looking word, isn't there? You have the prefix "extra-," which means "out, outside." And then the root "terr-" is related to the earth. So put it together and you have something that means "life that exists outside the earth." Perfect! I'm sure your friend will be so happy to have your help, and you'll be able to teach her all kinds of words like "territory" extraordinarily.

Can't this method be applied to Korean as well? Yes! I told you at the beginning of the book that more than two thirds of Korean words are derived from Chinese, remember? There was 국(國), which is used in the names of many countries, and 어(語), which appears in the names of languages. As you can see, by learning a handful of Chinese characters, you can substantially increase your Korean vocabulary!

Let's look at one very useful Chinese character: 외(外), which means "outside," just like the English "extra-." You don't have to memorize the shape itself. Just focus on the meanings that it creates in Korean.

외계인(外界人)
外 outside 界 world 人 people, life →
　　life that exists outside our world → extraterrestrial

외국인(外國人)
外 outside 國 country 人 people, life →
　　people who live outside our country → foreigners

외출(外出)
外 outside 出 come out →
　　coming outside the house → going out, outing

해외(海外)
海 sea 外 outside →
　　outside one's country across the sea → foreign country, overseas

시외(市外)
市 city 外 outside →
　　outside of the city → countryside, outskirts

See how the characters fit together to create meaning? Even though Korean doesn't use characters in this exact way, much of its vocabulary is based on the same principle.

Have You Ever Seen a Korean Movie?

한국 영화 본 적 있어요? [Hanguk yeonghwa pon cheok isseoyo?]
Turning Verbs and Adjectives into Noun Modifiers

One of the great things about studying a new language is that it can give you insight into your native tongue. So let's think about English for a second. In English, when you have an **adjective** modifying a noun, it usually comes in front of the noun. In other words, you say "a beautiful woman," not "a woman beautiful," right? But, on the other hand, consider what happens when you have a **clause** modifying a noun. Where does it go? In front? No! It comes after the noun, as in "a woman who has a beautiful face."

How confusing! I mean, for students learning English, this discrepancy can cause some major trouble, as it's difficult to remember when a modifier comes first and when it comes second. Well, it's my distinct privilege to inform you that you will *not* be facing the same problem when learning Korean. Why? Because in Korean, **modifiers** of all types always appear in the same place—in **front** of the noun. So while Koreans say "a beautiful woman," they also say "who has a beautiful face woman." Haha! Does that look awkward? I bet, but you'll get accustomed to it quickly.

"Wait!" you may be thinking. "Don't Korean adjectives function like verbs? How then can they also work like English adjectives to modify nouns?" Good question! And the answer, as usual, is **conjugative endings**. By applying a special ending, you can turn an adjective into a modifier and then use it to describe a noun. What's nice about this is that, because adjectives and verbs are so similar, the ending for transforming an adjective into a modifier is very close to the one for changing a verb into a modifier. And unlike in English, where you have to use all kinds of different pronouns ("who," "which," "what," "that") to form a modifying clause, in Korean it's just the ending and nothing else. Simple!

Verb and Adjective Modifier Endings			
P.O.S. Tense	Present	Past	Future
Verbs	V-는 (**pattern 2**)	V-ㄴ / 은 (pattern 4)	V-ㄹ / 을 (pattern 4)
Adjectives	A-ㄴ / 은 (pattern 4)	A-ㄴ / 은 (pattern 4)	A-ㄹ / 을 (pattern 4)

As you can clearly see, the only difference between verb and adjective modifier endings comes in the present tense. Those for past and future are exactly the same.

Ready for a little practice? Now, I could come up with new examples to demonstrate these principles, but instead why don't we use the same ones we went over in chapter 6, when we learned about conjugation? No, it's not because I'm lazy! Rather, I want you to review.

Okay, when you want to turn a **verb** into a **present** modifier, simply add the ending -는 onto the stem. Just remember that this is a pattern 2 ending, so for ㄹ verbs you have to drop the final ㄹ.

🎧 19.1 학교에 **가는** 아이 [hakgyoe kaneun ai] a child who *goes* to school

🎧 19.2 즐겁게 **사는** 사람 [cheulgeopge saneun saram] a person who *lives* happily

Good. See how the noun in each clause is being modified by the verb? Pretty easy, I think. But wait! This isn't the same ending that applies to **adjective** modifiers in the **present** tense. So, instead of constructing these…

~~아주 예쁘는 여자~~
~~너무 다는 과자~~

…you need to use the pattern 4 ending – ㄴ / –은, which will give you:

🎧 19.3 아주 **예쁜** 여자 [aju yeppeun yeoja] a very beautiful woman

🎧 19.4 너무 **단** 과자 [neomu tan kwaja] a too sweet cookie

Of course, the final ㄹ of ㄹ adjectives is still dropped according to pattern 4.

And then, this exact same ending is what you use to create both **verb** and **adjective** modifiers in the **past** tense as well. How nice!

🎧 19.5 학교에 **간** 아이 [hakgyoe kan ai] a child who *went* to school

🎧 19.6 즐겁게 **산** 사람 [cheulgeopge san saram] a person who *lived* happily

And for the **future**? Yep, for both **verbs** and **adjectives**, we attach the ending – ㄹ / –을 to the stem. Hey, doesn't this ending look familiar? I should hope so, because we just learned a little about it in the last chapter when we studied two future-tense constructions: – ㄹ / –을 거다 and – ㄹ / –을 거 같다. Remember? Now it all makes perfect sense, right? Well, at the risk of providing *too* much understanding, let's continue with our examples:

🎧 19.7 학교에 **갈** 아이 [hakgyoe kal ai] a child who *is going to go* to school (next year)

🎧 19.8 즐겁게 **살** 사람 [cheulgeopge sal saram] a person who *will live* happily (if you don't bother her ^^)

Okay, as we've discovered briefly in discussing – ㄹ / –을 거다 and – ㄹ / –을 거 같다, these modifier endings can be used to create lots of set phrases and **expressions**. Now, I could tell you all of them…but I'm feeling a bit sleepy today. Why don't we trim it down a bit? How many do you want to know? Just one? Hey, I didn't want to trim it that much! How about five? Well… Maybe we can find a compromise at three. Yeah, three sounds good. You'll thank me later, because these three expressions are actually very frequently used.

Have you ever…?

Um…have you ever asked someone a question beginning with "have you ever"? Yes, I'm sure you have. But now it's my turn to ask you. Ready?

🎧 19.9 한국 영화 본 적 있어요? [Hanguk yeonghwa pon cheok isseoyo?] Have you ever seen a Korean movie?

> 영화 [yeonghwa] movie   적 [cheok] experience

This question is asking about your **past** experience, isn't it? That's why you use the past modifier ending, –ㄴ / –은, with the verb 보다. As a whole, the expression V–ㄴ / 은 적 (이) 있다(없다) means you have had (have not had) the experience of doing something. So, although there's no way for me to know for sure whether or not you've ever seen a Korean movie, I'm going to make the assumption that if you have, it was probably the famous film *Old Boy*, recipient of the Grand Prix at the 2004 Cannes Film Festival.

🎧 19.10 네, 올드보이를 봤어요. [Ne, oldeuboireul pwasseoyo.] Yes, I watched *Old Boy*.

Actually, Korea produces a lot of excellent movies, and watching them is a great way to learn both the language and culture of the country. Next time you're at the video store, bypass all the formulaic Hollywood blockbusters and find the foreign section, where, if you're lucky, you can pick up a Korean masterpiece like *Old Boy*.

Can / can't, I know / I don't know

In English, the verb "can" is used to signify the ability to do something, and of course you can also word this as "to know how to do something." Well, Korean has two ways of saying this as well. And which modifier ending do you think they employ? Hmm…these expressions aren't talking about something you're doing right now, or something you've already done. Rather, they're referring to something you *could* do in the future. So, that's right, we use the **future** modifier, –ㄹ / –을. Here are a couple pertinent questions for you:

🎧 19.11 한국말 할 수 있으세요? [Hangungmal hal su isseuseyo?] Can you speak Korean?

🎧 19.12 한국말 할 줄 아세요? [Hangungmal hal chul aseyo?] Do you know how to speak Korean?

> 수 [su] ability   줄 [chul] means   알다 [alda] to know

The two expressions are these: –ㄹ / –을 수 있다 and –ㄹ / –을 줄 알다, and they roughly translate as "to have the ability to do something" and "to know how to do something," respectively. And just like in English, they both have more or less the same meaning.

And so how would you answer these questions? Of course, you're a Korean superstar, right? But let's be modest. Modesty is very important in Korea.

🎧 19.13 네, 조금요. [Ne, chogeumyo.] Yes, a little bit.

> 조금 [chogeum] a little bit

Or maybe you're not really in the mood to engage in a lengthy Korean conversation, so you want to say you can't speak Korean. How would you express this? Well, the antonym of the adjective 있다 is 없다, and 알다's antonym is 모르다. So simply insert these new words into the expressions above to make 할 수 없다 and 할 줄 모르다.

🎧 19.14 아니요, 할 수 없어요. [Aniyo, hal su eopsseoyo.] No, I can't.

🎧 19.15 아니요, 할 줄 몰라요. [Aniyo, hal chul molrayo.] No, I don't know how to.

> 모르다 [moreuda] to not know

Yes, these expressions are pretty good. But, in fact, there's an even easier way to change a sentence from positive to negative, and it's more frequently used than these two. What is it? Hey, if you ask me, I say it's time to rest. You've learned enough expressions for one day, don't you think? I promise I'll share with you the secret of making negative sentences in Korean in the next chapter. So go take a quick catnap, and I'll see you there!

Further Vocabulary: Dedicated noun modifiers

As we've seen, Korean adjectives function like verbs, and if we want them to modify a noun like English adjectives do, we have to conjugate them with a modifier ending. However, there are a handful of Korean adjectives that were born with the singular fate of modifying nouns. They don't look like ordinary adjectives, and they don't function as verbs like all their brothers and sisters do. How sad.

새 [sae] new
> EX.: 새 옷 [sae ot] new clothes

헌 [heon] old, used
> EX.: 헌 지갑 [heon chigap] old (used) wallet

옛 [yet] old
> EX.: 옛 친구 [yet chingu] an old friend

모든 [modeun] all, every
> EX.: 모든 사람 [modeun saram] everyone

과학적 [kwahakjeok] scientific
> EX.: 과학적 개념 [kwahakjeok kaenyeom] scientific concept

사회적 [sahoejeok] social
> EX.: 인간은 사회적 동물이다. [Inganeun sahoejeok tongmurida.] Human beings are social animals.

옷 [ot] clothes
지갑 [chigap] wallet
개념 [kaenyeom] concept

인간 [ingan] human being
동물 [tongmul] animal

Korean Style: The disaster of misunderstanding the word 시원하다

One day, a foreigner living in Korea went into a bathhouse. While sitting in the steaming waters, he overheard a man remark, 아, 시원하다 [a, shiwonhada], which means "Ah, it's cool!" The foreigner found this very odd, as it was quite hot in the spa. He was almost sure 시원하다 was the adjective for "cold," but he figured he must be mistaken.

After finishing his bath, the foreigner went to a barbershop. The barber leaned his head back into the sink to wash it. But the water was way too hot, so the foreigner said 아, 시원하다! The barber, puzzled, turned the hot water higher. The foreigner's head was now scalding under the flow of steaming water. So he shouted 아, 아, 시원하다! Shrugging his shoulders, the barber switched off the cold tap completely and turned up the hot water as high as it would go. The foreigner's hair was almost burned off!

The word 시원하다 is a little weird, even to Koreans. It means "cool, cold." So to describe the feeling of having your head under a stream of steaming water with 시원하다 is definitely incorrect. But think about this. When you're exhausted from a hard day of work on a cold winter's day, and you go home and take a nice, hot shower, it makes you feel happy and refreshed, right? Well, 시원하다 has this meaning as well, which is how the man in the spa was using it.

Be careful in those bathhouses!

I Couldn't Study So Much
공부를 조금밖에 못 했어요.
[Kongbureul chogeumbakke mot haesseoyo.]
Negations

How are you? Full of energy and ready to learn new things? Excellent! But first, I gave you my word in the last chapter that we'd look more in depth at how to make negations in Korean. Remember? And yes, I always keep my word (except when I don't ^^).

I know you already know some ways of making negations. First of all, there's the negative form of the verb ending –이다, "to be." Wow, yeah, I'm reaching pretty far back for this one, but we went over it in chapter 12, right? That negative form is the independent adjective 아니다. And then, in the same chapter, you learned the negative form of 있다 (also meaning "to be"), which is 없다. Now, that brings us back to the end of the last chapter, when I showed you the expression 할 수 없다, for "I can't." And we also looked at 할 줄 모르다, meaning "I don't know how to." Remember, the verb 모르다 is the opposite of 알다 ("to know").

Okay, but those are set negative phrases, with set meanings. Isn't there a way to turn any phrase from a positive to a negative, you might ask? Well, lucky you—there is! And, even better, it's really easy to learn and use, because it's not a conjugative ending. All you have to do is add the word 안 or 못 before the verb (안 can also be used with adjectives, but 못 can't). That's it!

But why are there two different words you can use? Well, there's actually a difference in meaning between 안 and 못. Allow me to show by example. Say you had been invited to attend your friend's birthday party that took place yesterday, but you didn't go:

🎧 **20.1** 어제 규병 씨의 생일 파티에 갔어요? [Eoje kyubyong ssiui saengil patie kasseoyo?] Did you go to Kyubyong's birthday party yesterday?

🎧 **20.2** 아니요, 안 갔어요. [Aniyo, an kasseoyo.] No, I didn't go (because I hate him and chose not to).

🎧 **20.3** 아니요, 못 갔어요. [Aniyo, mot kasseoyo.] No, I couldn't go (because there was an earthquake, but I really wanted to go).

파티 [pati] party

Don't worry. Earthquakes seldom occur in Korea. ^;^ Anyway, as you can see, 안 applies more to the speaker's **intention** or conscious choice, while 못 is related to **ability**. So, now you can answer our question from the last chapter using 안 or 못.

🎧 20.4 한국말 할 수 있으세요? [Hangungmal hal su isseuseyo?] Can you speak Korean?

🎧 20.5 아뇨, 못 해요. [Anyo, mot haeyo.] No, I can't (I don't have the ability).

> 아뇨 [anyo] no (a shortened form of 아니요)

Hey, you're going to make me cry! I know you can speak Korean!

안 vs. 못: two scenes

Let's get in a little more practice with 안 and 못, shall we? Here are two scenarios to help you learn.

Scene #1: You run into your friend early one morning, and he notices the dark circles around your eyes:

🎧 20.6 어젯밤에 잘 잤어요? [Eojetbame chal chasseoyo?] Did you sleep well last night?

🎧 20.7 아뇨, 잠이 **안** 와서 한숨도 **못** 잤어요. [Anyo, chami an waseo hansumdo mot chasseoyo.]
No, I couldn't sleep a wink because the Sandman didn't come to me.

> 어젯밤 [eojetbam] last night   잠 [cham] sleep
> 잘 [chal] well   한숨 [hansum] a wink (of sleep)
> 자다 [chada] to sleep

In Korean, there's a widely known expression: 잠이 오다 / 잠이 안 오다. It translates literally as "Sleep comes to me" / "Sleep doesn't come to me." But nobody says 잠이 **못** 오다 for the negative version, because no one's actually preventing the Sandman from coming to you. He just chooses not to come. He's a busy guy, I guess. And so you're stuck with no sleep.

On the other hand, 잠을 못 잤어요 is also correct, meaning "I couldn't (didn't have the ability to) sleep." If you use 안 in this expression, saying 잠을 안 잤어요, it implies that you didn't sleep because you just don't like to sleep. But who doesn't like sleep!?

Scene #2: There's an important exam in class today, and you see a classmate approaching you to ask a question:

🎧 20.8 시험 공부 많이 했어요? [Shiheom kongbu mani haesseoyo?] Did you study for the exam?

> 시험 [shiheom] exam, test

There are three possible kinds of answers to this question. Pay close attention as I explain them, but don't worry—there won't be an exam at the end...or will there?

1. 네, 두 시간이나 했어요. [Ne, tu shiganina haesseoyo.] Yes, I did as many as two hours.
   🎧 20.9 (This answer is expressing pride, as if usually you don't study at all! But I'm sure that's not true, is it?)

2. 아니요, 전혀 안 했어요. [Aniyo, cheonhyeo an haesseoyo.] No, I didn't study at all.

🎧 20.10 (Oh, now you're just trying to show off, pretending as if you knew it all already and didn't need to study! Ha! But I bet you actually studied a lot.)

3. 아니요, 바깥이 시끄러워서 조금밖에 못 했어요. [Aniyo, pakkachi shikkeureoweoseo chogeumbakke
* mot haesseoyo.] No, I couldn't study much because it was really noisy outside.

🎧 20.11 (Okay, this is your most strategic answer. Now, if you fail, you have an excuse—you couldn't study! But actually, I bet this is another little white lie and you actually did study a lot. You just don't want to admit it. In fact, I happen to know you live in a very quiet neighborhood!)

두 [tu] two
시간 [shigan] hour
N-(이)나 [(i)na] as much/many as (particle)
전혀 [cheonhyeo] (not) … at all

바깥 [pakkat] outside
시끄럽다 [shikkeureopda] noisy
N-밖에 [bakke] with the exception of
  (particle)

Hey, check it out, you just learned some new **particles**! –(이)나 emphasizes that the amount or extent (the noun it attaches to) is relatively large. Conversely, –밖에 shows that it's small, although literally it has the meaning of "with the exception of." So 조금밖에 못 했어요 can be translated as "I couldn't do it with the exception of a little." But in common usage it carries the meaning of "I couldn't do very much" or "I could do only a little."

Both of these particles are very effective and economic little additions that help express what the speaker is feeling. For instance, if you say 공부를 30 분**이나** 했어요, you're implying that you think 30 minutes is a lot of time to spend studying; change this to 공부를 30 분**밖에** 못 했어요, though, and your meaning becomes the opposite. Interesting, huh?

–지 않다 / 못하다

By now, I bet you're quite surprised at how simple it is to create negatives in Korean. Hey, we take these little victories when we can get them, right? Well, I don't want to crash your party, but there's just one more method of negation construction that I want to go over. Don't think of this as a burden, but rather as a bonus. Are you with me?

So, what we already learned in this chapter was the **short-form** negation, and, as you saw, it didn't involve any new conjugative endings. Well, what's the one thing you can probably guess about its counterpart, the **long-form** negation? Uh-huh, it uses an ending! But really, this isn't so bad, as it belongs to pattern 1. And what's great about pattern 1? Right, it's the simplest, because you can just stick the ending on any old verb or adjective stem without worrying about changes taking place.

Alright, and just like there were two versions of the short-form negation (using 안 and 못), there are, correspondingly, two versions of the long form. Watch and learn:

Meaning	Short-form negation	Long-form negation
do NOT	안 + A/V	A/V–지 않다
can NOT	못 + V	V–지 못하다

It's easy to see that both of the long-form negation endings use –지, which, like I said, gets put right on the end of the stem, no matter what. And then you add 않다 if you want the meaning of conscious **intent**, or the verb 못하다 to signify a lack of **ability**. –지 않다 corresponds to 안…, and –지 못하다 is the same as 못… See?

But, um, why would you ever want to use this long form when the short-form negations are so much easier (admit it though, both are pretty simple!)? Well, the long form is more formal, and it's used a lot in written language. Here's a quick comparison of the short and long forms negating an adjective (remember, adjectives can't be negated with 못 in either short or long forms):

 한국어는 안 어려워요. [Hangugeoneun an eoryeoweoyo.] The Korean language is not difficult.

 한국어는 어렵지 않아요. [Hangugeoneun eoryeopji anayo.] The Korean language is not difficult.

> 어렵다 [eoryeopda] difficult

And here are two sentences that utilize both the 안 and 못 negations, the first in the short form, and the second in the long form:

20.14 몸이 안 좋아서 오늘 회사에 못 갔어요. [Momi an choaseo oneul hoesae mot kasseoyo.] I was sick so I couldn't go to the office today.

20.15 몸이 좋지 않아서 오늘 회사에 가지 못했어요. [Momi chochi anaseo oneul hoesae kaji motaesseoyo.] I was sick so I couldn't go to the office today.

> 몸 [mom] body
> 몸이 좋지 않다 [momi chochi anta] to not feel good
> 회사 [hoesa] office, company

Note that in English when you feel sick, you say *you* don't *feel* good. In Korean, though, your *body is not good.*

Hmm…what's wrong? You have a bad headache and are running a fever? Wow, I feel really bad for you. I suggest that you get some rest now. And then, when you feel better, I suggest that you read the next chapter. Any guesses what we'll be talking about?

Further Vocabulary: Health

Hmm…looks like it's time to go over some health-related vocabulary.

건강하다 [keonganghada] healthy
아프다 [apeuda] sick, painful
낫다 [natda] to be cured, to recover from
걸리다 [keolrida] to get sick
피곤하다 [pigonhada] tired, fatigued
다치다 [tachida] to hurt, to be wounded

병 [pyeong] disease, illness
감기 [kamgi] cold, flu
열 [yeol] fever
기침 [kichim] cough
몸살 [momsal] illness from fatigue

Korean Style: Word relay

Have you ever played this game? You choose a certain category—say, celebrities. And then you and a friend or friends go back and forth naming celebrities. But each name has to start with the same letter that the previous name ended with. For example, Tom Cruise ⟶ Eddie Murphy ⟶ Yasmine Bleeth ⟶ …

There's a similar game in Korean called 끝말잇기 [kkeunmaritgi]. The difference is that instead of relaying the last letter, it's the final syllable of a word that gets carried over. This game is too difficult if you limit it to only one category, so usually you can use any word you want.

For example, 남자 [namja] ("man") ⟶ 자연 [chayeon] ("nature") ⟶ 연습 [yeonseup] ("practice") ⟶ 습관 [seupgwan] ("habit") ⟶ 관광 [kwangwang] ("tour") ⟶ …

One way to change the game would be to limit it to only three-syllable words, or even by relaying the middle syllable of a three-syllable word, like this: 전화기 [cheonhwagi] ("telephone") ⟶ 화장지 [hwajangji] ("tissue") ⟶ 장난감 [changnangam] ("toy") ⟶ …

It's pretty simple, but Koreans like this game a lot. And if you play it, I bet you'll learn lots of new words very quickly. If you do ever have the opportunity to join in, let me tell you the key to victory. There aren't any words in Korean that begin with the syllable 름 [reum]. Because of this, if you can find a word ending with 름, you'll definitely win. Let's see, there's 지름 [chireum] ("diameter"), 여드름 [yeodeureum] ("pimple"), 고드름 [kodeureum] ("icicle"), 여름 [yeoreum] ("summer"), 기름 [kireum] ("oil")…

21

I Should Talk to My Wife First

아내하고 먼저 얘기해야 돼요.
[Anaehago meonjeo yaegihaeya twaeyo.]
Suggestion, Supposition, Obligation, and Prohibition

Ah, I'm glad you've heeded my suggestion and continued on to chapter 21! The themes for today are **propositive** and **imperative** sentences. Hmm, and what do these mean? Well, we've already learned a lot about declarative sentences, which simply state information about something. And we've covered many different ways to make interrogative sentences, which ask about something. So what's left? Stop. Put the book down. Think about my question. (Any ideas? ^^)

That's right, imperative sentences are what you use to give commands to people. And, just like in English, you can form these without stating the subject of the sentence. For example, simply say "Stop" instead of "You, stop" (the subject is always understood as "you," or "you all").

So those are imperatives, which we'll get to later. But what about propositives? What are those? *Let us think* about that… *Shall we* pool our ideas…? Right! Propositive sentences **propose** something. Now, we briefly went over one of these forms long ago back in chapter 6, didn't we? It was the pattern 1 conjugative ending –자, which adds the meaning of "let's" to a verb. But you can't use this ending to make a suggestion to a person you're not close to; in other words, it's a **plain** ending. But don't worry, because there are other, even easier ways of doing this, and one is to simply add 우리 ("we/us") at the beginning of the sentence, like so:

우리 다음 주에 산에 가요. [Uri taeum chue sane kayo.] Let's go hiking next week. (*Lit:* Let us go to the mountains next week.)

우리 같이 공부해요. [Uri kachi kongbuhaeyo.] Let's study together.

주 [chu] week	산 [san] mountain

Using 같이 in addition to 우리 makes the proposition even stronger, so whoever you're talking to will have a hard time turning you down! So, I see you've proposed that we study together more. Okay, I can't help but accept! Let's keep studying as you proposed.

We don't even need to study that one anymore—it's too easy! Actually, it's so easy I feel guilty. I'm supposed to be challenging you to learn new things, right? So now I feel like scaring you with a more complicated propositive form. ^;^ And that would be the verb ending –ㄹ까요? / –을까요?

Hmm…you might be thinking this looks like an interrogative ending. It ends with a question mark after all, right? But wait. Shall we think about this? Shall we figure it out? Yes, these are **questions**, but they're also propositions! In fact, forming your propositive sentences in this way is a softer, more **respectful** way of doing it. And you know how Koreans appreciate respect!

Okay, if you look closely at this ending, you might notice something familiar. It includes the **future** ending – 르 / –을, doesn't it? We've learned a lot about that one recently. And it makes sense that the future ending would be included in this propositive form, because in English we translate it into "*Shall* we...?" "Shall" is the future tense form of "should," so there you have it! As you can see, we're still going to use 우리, and sometimes 같이, in these sentences as well. Now, shall we practice?

우리 다음 주에 산에 갈까요? [Uri taeum chue sane kalkkayo?] Shall we go hiking next week?

우리 같이 공부할까요? [Uri kachi kongbuhalkkayo?] Shall we study together?

우리 같이 영화 볼까요? [Uri kachi yeonghwa polkkayo?] Shall we watch a movie together?

우리 결혼할까요? [Uri kyeolhonhalkkayo?] Shall we get married?

> 결혼하다 [kyeolhonhada] to get married

Oops, I'm sorry...but I'm already married. I can't accept your proposal. ㅠㅠ But if I hadn't gotten married, I'd consider it. (Uh-oh, where's my wife? Please don't show this page of the book to her. ^^)

If I hadn't gotten married...

The word "if" is a useful one. Let's think about a scenario. A friend of yours asks you to lend him a large sum of money, but you don't have it. So you might respond, "Of course I'll lend you the money, if you lend it to me first." ^^ If it weren't for the word "if," you'd have no choice but to lend your money! And nobody wants that. So let's learn how to express the meaning of "if." Of course, this is done through another conjugative tool, in this case the **conditional** or suppositive ending: –(으)면.

내가 결혼을 안 했으면… [Naega kyeolhoneul an haesseumyeon...] If I hadn't gotten married…

–(으)면 belongs to conjugation pattern 3, remember? I know you've seen it before. If the stem of the verb or adjective ends with a consonant, you need to add –으 before 면 for the convenience of pronunciation. In the sentence above, you can see this happen when the ending is added to the past-tense stem of 하다: 했.

Oh, I bet you're still wondering how to say that bit about the money lending, right? Ha, I knew it! Let's look:

돈 있으면 좀 빌려주세요. [Ton iseumyeon chom pilryeojuseyo] If you have money, please lend me some.

좋아요. 먼저 규병 씨가 돈을 빌려주면 저도 빌려드릴게요. [Choayo. Meonjeo kyubyong ssiga toneul pilryeojumyeon cheodo pilryeodeurilgeyo.] Sure. If you (Kyubyong) lend me the money first, I'll lend you some, too.

> 돈 [ton] money
> 빌려주다 [pilryeojuda] to lend
>
> 먼저 [meonjeo] first
> 빌려드리다 [pilryeodeurida] to lend (honorific form of 빌려주다)

In these two sentences, we can see two uses of the conditional ending: 있으면 and 빌려주면. The first is 있 + 으면, while the second is 빌려주 + 면. I can't stress it enough: remember to always pay attention to whether the stem ends in a consonant or a vowel.

Anyway, in my case, before I lend you any money, I really *should* get permission from my banker...my wife.

Should, should not

So how would I express **obligation** to you in Korean, that I "should" or "have to" do something? For those of us who are married or in a serious relationship, this is an important one, right? And, just like relationships can be quite complicated at times, the ending for this one isn't too simple. It follows the rules of pattern 5, the most difficult, and here it is: –아야 / –어야 / –여야. You conjugate the principal verb using this ending, and then add the verb 되다 after it. So the full expression is –아야 / –어야 / –여야 되다. Check it out:

 아내하고 먼저 얘기해야 돼요. [Anaehago meonjeo yaegihaeya twaeyo.] I should talk to my wife first.

얘기하다 [yaegihada] to talk

Remember the rules of **vowel contraction**? That's why, when we add the ending –여야 to the verb stem 얘기하, we get 얘기해야. Likewise, the honorific form 1 ending –어요 attached to the verb stem 되 gives us 돼요.

Okay, and what's the only thing more important than knowing what you *should* do? Right—what you should *not* do! This is an expression of **prohibition**, and actually it's a form of negation. Sound familiar? Of course, following what you learned in the last chapter, you might be tempted to simply turn the verb 되다 into a negative by saying 안 되다. And you'd be correct! But in this case, you don't use the –아야 / –어야 / –여야 ending for the main verb, but rather the conditional –(으)면. So the final product for the prohibitive expression is –(으)면 안 되다.

 학교에 늦으면 안 돼. [Hakgyoe neujeumyeon an twae.] You shouldn't be late for school. (My mom had to tell me this every day.)

 회사에 늦으면 안 돼요. [Hoesae neujeumyeon an twaeyo.] You shouldn't be late for work. (Now, my wife has to tell me this every day.)

늦다 [neutda] to be late

Do, do not

As you can see, I have a problem with being late! But the people in my life have always managed to keep me under control. Of course, sometimes they use "don't" instead of "you should not" when they tell me these things: "Don't be late for school." "Don't be late for work." These are negative commands (**imperatives**).

Again, this relates back to what we studied in the previous chapter. Remember the endings –지 않다 ("do not") and –지 못하다 ("cannot")? Similarly, the formation of a negative imperative is going to employ the ending –지. It's –지 말다. We'll usually conjugate the verb 말다 using the honorific suffix –(으)시. After all, you're telling someone what not to do, so you need to soften it up as much as you can. This gives us a set expression of –지 마세요.

Hmm…what do you tell people not to do?

일을 너무 열심히 하지 마세요. [Ireul neomu yeolshimhi haji maseyo.] Don't work too hard. (All work and no play makes Jack a dull boy.)

담배를 끊지 마세요. [Dambaereul kkeunchi maseyo.] Don't quit smoking. (Think of all those poor employees of tobacco companies who will lose their jobs. ^^)

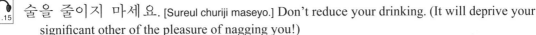

술을 줄이지 마세요. [Sureul churiji maseyo.] Don't reduce your drinking. (It will deprive your significant other of the pleasure of nagging you!)

일 [il] work	끊다 [kkeunta] to quit
너무 [neomu] too (much)	술 [sul] alcohol
열심히 [yeolshimhi] hard	줄이다 [churida] to reduce
담배 [tambae] cigarette	

Hmm…I'm unsure of the quality of advice I'm giving you, but at least you'll remember this expression now. ^^

Phew! That's a lot of **propositives** and **imperatives** we just learned! Shall we review quickly?

1. In Korean, to make a proposal, you can simply add 우리 and 같이 to your sentence, or use the –ㄹ까요? / –을까요? propositive ending.

2. To express the idea of "if," use the conditional ending –(으)면.

3. By conjugating a verb with the –아야 / –어야 / –여야 ending and then adding the verb 돼요, you can tell someone what they "should" do.

4. Conversely, to say "should not," you use the expression –(으)면 안 돼요.

5. And lastly, to create the meaning of "don't," use the expression –지 마세요.

Look at all the versatility you've just added to your repertoire. Slowly but surely, you're building up quite the bag of Korean tricks!

Further Vocabulary: Interjections

What! Have I not taught you interjections yet!? Holy…

어 [eo] ah…
글쎄 [keulsse] well…
음 [eum] um…
저 [cheo] well…, um…
아아 [aa] oh, ah!
아이고 [aigo] oh!, oops!, my goodness!
와 [wa] wow!
아하 [aha] aha!
세상에 [sesange] boy!

Korean Style: Korean proverbs

The more Korean you learn, the more interesting it gets, right? One thing I can teach now that you've progressed so far is Korean proverbs. Because proverbs are supposed to be allegorical, they can be confusing for beginners. Lucky for you, I'm here to explain everything to you. And once you learn how to use these proverbs correctly, your Korean will be considered excellent! Here are a few of the simpler Korean proverbs:

가는 말이 고와야 오는 말도 곱다 [kaneun mari kowaya oneun maldo kopda]
Lit. Talk to others nicely and they will talk to you nicely, too.
This one's easy, right? It's the equivalent of "Do unto others as you would have them do unto you."

가재는 게 편이다 [kajaeneun ke pyeonida]
Lit. Crawfish are on the side of the crab.
Do you know what crawfish and crabs look like? I'm not sure what exact species this proverb is referring to, but the point is they have a similar appearance. So this one means, "People stick up for their own kind."

낮말은 새가 듣고 밤말은 쥐가 듣는다 [nanmareun saega teutgo pammareun chwiga teunneunda]
Lit. Birds may hear you during the day and rats at night.
Yes. These days animals are quite smart, and they can understand your spoken language, even Korean! Be careful of what you say out loud, because "The walls have ears."

뛰는 놈 위에 나는 놈이 있다 [ttwineun nom wie naneun nomi itda]
Lit. When you are running, someone is flying.
This one seems strange to me. After all, humans can't fly, can they? Maybe it's talking about people in a plane. Anway, the meaning is, "There is always someone one step ahead of you."

배보다 배꼽이 더 크다 [paeboda paekkobi teo keuda]
Lit. The belly button is bigger than the belly.
What? This one's funny, right? How can your belly button be bigger than your belly? But hey, stranger things have happened! In this case, we're talking about a case in which "the tail is wagging the dog." In other words, something of an otherwise minor importance has taken over the situation.

CHAPTER

22

Canada Is Larger than the U.S.
미국보다 캐나다가 더 넓어요.
[Migukboda kaenadaga teo neolbeoyo.]
Special Adverbs

As we've discussed before, it's often the little words in a language that are most important. Just think about how many times a day you use the words "the" and "a" in English conversation. Oops, and there's another one too: "and"! That's an essential one, isn't it? Yes, it is, which is why we're going to start out this chapter by covering this and similar words—known in English as conjunctions, or conjunctive adverbs.

Conjunctive adverbs

But what exactly are conjunctive adverbs? You know, it's funny how sometimes native speakers don't know much about the structure of their language. They just speak it! That's one great thing about learning another language: you get to find out things about your own.

There are different kinds of conjunctive adverbs in English, but the simplest are little words like "and," "but," and "so" that **connect** two clauses or two complete sentences. For example, the conjunction "and" lets you turn this:

"I ate two pizzas for lunch. I'll eat one more for dinner."

into this:
"I ate two pizzas for lunch, *and* I'll eat one more for dinner."

Similarly, we have "but," which combines these two:
"I usually eat two servings of spaghetti for breakfast. Today I only ate one."

into a single sentence:
"I usually eat two servings of spaghetti for breakfast, *but* today I only ate one."

And finally, "so" lets us take this:
"I only had ten candy bars today. Now I'm really hungry."

and change it to this:
"I only had ten candy bars today, *so* now I'm really hungry."
Hmm…these sentences are pretty strange, but for some reason *I'm* really hungry all of a sudden!

Anyway, my point is that in English these words can be inserted between two clauses or sentences to connect the ideas and form a new complete sentence. But in Korean it's different. Now, I'm not saying Korean doesn't have conjunctive adverbs—that would make for a pretty short chapter, wouldn't it!? Actually, there do exist individual words for these conjunctions, but when you use them to connect two ideas, they're expressed through...your favorite...**conjugative endings**.

Hey, come on, don't roll your eyes! After all, you should be familiar with this idea, because we've already learned one example, the ending: –아서 / –어서 / –여서. And, as I'm sure you recall, this ending has two meanings: "and then" and "so/therefore." Hmm...are you doubting that you've studied this before? I think you're just in denial. Allow me to refresh your memory with the example sentences we used in chapters 16 and 20.

 이 쪽으로 죽 가서 왼쪽으로 도세요. [I jjogeuro chuk kaseo oenjjogeuro toseyo.] Go straight this way and then turn left.

 몸이 좋지 않아서 오늘 회사에 못 갔어요. [Momi chochi anaseo oneul hoesae mot kasseoyo.] I was sick so I couldn't go to the office today.

Okay, the conjunctive adverbs used here ("and then" and "so/therefore") are expressed by conjugating the verb of the first clause with the ending –아서 / –어서 / –여서. Of course, it's possible to divide each of these sentences into two clauses, in which case the adverbs would be rendered instead as full, **independent** words. This makes for a pretty simplistic way of speaking, but let's check it out anyway.

For "and then," you can say 그러고 나서, while "so/therefore" becomes 그래서, giving us:

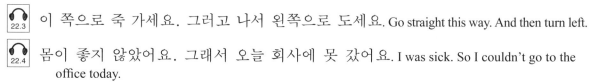

이 쪽으로 죽 가세요. 그러고 나서 왼쪽으로 도세요. Go straight this way. And then turn left.

몸이 좋지 않았어요. 그래서 오늘 회사에 못 갔어요. I was sick. So I couldn't go to the office today.

Does that make sense? Obviously, it sounds smoother to use the conjugative ending, but either way works.

So let's go on to look at two extremely common conjunctive adverbs: "**and**" and "**but**." Conjugating verbs and adjectives to add these meanings is quite easy, because both endings follow pattern 1. The ending for "and" is –고, whereas the one for "but" is –지만. And then, the stand-alone conjunctions are 그리고 and 그렇지만, respectively. Here they are in context:

 저는 낮에 자**고**, 밤에 일어나요. [Cheoneun naje chago, pame ireonayo.] I sleep during the day and wake up at night.

저는 낮에 자요. **그리고** 밤에 일어나요. [Cheoneun naje chayo. Keurigo pame ireonayo.] I sleep during the day. And I wake up at night.

지난달은 바빴**지만**, 이번 달은 한가해요. [Chinandareun pappatjiman, ibeon tareun hangahaeyo.] I was busy last month, but I'm free this month.

지난달은 바빴어요. **그렇지만** 이번 달은 한가해요. [Chinandareun pappasseoyo. Keureochiman ibeon tareun hangahaeyo.] I was busy last month. But I'm free this month.

낮 [nat] day
일어나다 [ireonada] to wake up, get up
지난달 [chinandal] last month
바쁘다 [pappeuda] busy

이번 [ibeon] this (time)
달 [tal] month
한가하다 [hangahada] free

Let's sum this all up with a handy table, shall we?

Meaning	Conjugative ending	Independent conjunctive adverb
and then	-아서 / -어서 / -여서	그러고 나서
so, therefore	-아서 / -어서 / -여서	그래서
and	-고	그리고
but	-지만	그렇지만

Maybe you're wondering why all of the independent conjunctive adverb words begin with 그. This is because they're all derived from the verb 그러다 ("to do so"), or the adjective 그렇다 ("like so"). So, literally, 그러고 나서 means "after doing so," 그래서 means "because of doing so," and 그렇지만 means "despite doing so." Interesting, huh?

Frequency adverbs

There are tons of adverbs in Korean, just like there are in English. But I'm a nice guy, right? So of course I'm not going to introduce all of them in this book. Instead, we're just looking at some of the most special. Keeping that in mind, let me usher in the second type: frequency adverbs.

Frequency adverbs are used to describe **how often** (or, um, frequently ^;^) an action takes place. Can you think of some examples of these? Sure you can! There's "usually," "sometimes," "(not) at all," "often," "always"... And then, can you arrange them in order from the lowest to the highest frequency? I believe you can. Using this order, I'll create some examples for you:

 저는 이번 주에 **전혀** 씻지 않았어요. [Cheoneun ibeon chue cheonhyeo ssitji anasseoyo.] I didn't wash myself this week *at all*.

 저는 **가끔** 샤워를 해요. [Cheoneun kakkeum shyaweoreul haeyo.] I *sometimes* take a shower.

 저는 **보통** 손을 안 씻고 밥을 먹어요. [Cheoneun potong soneul an ssitgo pabeul meogeoyo.] I *usually* eat without washing my hands.

 저는 이 닦는 일을 **자주** 잊어요. [Cheoneun i tangneun ireul chaju ijeoyo.] I *often* forget to brush my teeth.

 저는 머리에서 **항상** 냄새가 나요. [Cheoneun meorieseo hangsang naemsaega nayo.] My hair *always* smells.

전혀 [cheonhyeo] (not) at all
씻다 [ssitda] to wash
가끔 [kakkeum] sometimes
샤워 [shyaweo] shower
샤워(를) 하다 to take a shower
보통 [potong] usually

자주 [chaju] often
잊다 [itda] to forget
항상 [hangsang] always
냄새 [naemsae] smell
냄새가 나다 [naemsaega nada] to smell

저는 머리에서 **항상** 냄새가 나요.
My hair *always* smells.

Stop! Please stop this! Oh, why? Please improve your hygiene, if not for your own health, then for mine!

Phew. Sorry, I'm a little finicky when it comes to cleanliness. Anyway, you get the idea of frequency adverbs, right? Rather than belaboring the point, let's move on to another important category: **comparatives** and **superlatives**.

More, Most

When I was little, I'd often hear this question: "Who do you like more, your mommy or your daddy?" This isn't a very common question in the Western world, but in Korea children are asked this a lot. I always thought it was silly, because it was so easy to answer: "Whoever pays my allowance!" ㅋㅋ.

I doubt you'll get asked this question in Korea, but there are others that follow the same principle. For example, maybe you'll hear this:

[22.14] 미국하고 캐나다 중에 어디가 더 넓어요? [Migukago kaenada chunge eodiga teo neolbeoyo?]
Between the U.S. and Canada, which is larger?

중 [chung] middle	더 [teo] more	넓다 [neolda] large, wide

Hmm…let me see. Actually, I don't know the answer to this one. But frankly, it's not really that important to me. I'm a lot more interested in which is larger, my house or my neighbor's. ^^ So instead of paying attention to the particular meaning of the question, let's focus on the adverb 더, which has the meaning of "**more**." In English, it can be quite confusing to know whether to make a comparative by saying "more" or adding the comparative suffix "-er" to the end of the word. I mean, think about "fun." Is it "more fun," or "funner," I still don't know! In Korean, though, you don't have to worry about that. Just add 더 before any adjective…it even works for verbs, too!

And what about the element 중에 in the sentence? When two choices are being discussed, you put the word 중에 after them to mean "between" or "among." (중 means "middle," but its meaning changes with the particle -에.)

Okay…I've had a little time for some research, so I'll ask again: which one is larger? No idea? Here's the answer:

[22.15] 미국보다 캐나다가 더 넓어요. [Migukboda kaenadaga teo neolbeoyo.] Canada is larger than the U.S.

Interesting, huh? It's tempting to say that the U.S. is bigger, but actually it's Canada that has more land area by just a bit. But what's that particle stuck on the end of the first noun? What could that mean? That's right, it's the equivalent of "**than**"! The particle -보다 goes on the end of the first object being compared, the one that corresponds to the "less" portion of the comparison. And then the word 더 goes directly before the verb or adjective. So remember, …-보다 …더. Got it?

So now you know "more," but what about "**most**"—the superlative? Just as before, you never have to worry about whether you need to include the separate word "most" or tack on "-est" to the end of the word. In Korean, all you need to do is put 제일 before the verb or adjective. So we can say:

[22.16] 어떤 색깔을 제일 좋아하세요? [Eotteon saekkkareul cheil choahaseyo?] What color do you like most?

[22.17] 저는 하얀색을 제일 좋아해요. [Cheoneun hayansaegeul cheil choahaeyo] I like white most.

색깔 [saekkkal] color	하얀색 [hayansaek] white	제일 [cheil] most

Just like 더 is the equivalent of the **comparative** "more" in English, 제일 is the **superlative** "most." See how that works? Easy!

Well, we've spent a lot of time together now…22 chapters' worth, right!? And I can honestly say that I like you *more than* any other language study partner. I'm having the *most* fun guiding you through the world of Korean!

Further Vocabulary: More conjunctive adverbs

Don't stop now! Here are some more handy adverbs to help you put your sentences together.

그러나 [keureona] but, however (used more in writing than in conversation)
하지만 [hajiman] but, however (used in both writing and in conversation)
그러니까 [keureonikka] so   또는 [ttoneun] or
그러므로 [keureomeuro] therefore, accordingly   한편 [hanpyeon] meanwhile
그런데 [keureonde] by the way, however   어쨌든 [eojjaetdeun] anyway

Korean Style: He's an owl.

An owl!? Is there a legend of some sort of owl man in Korea, like the American Batman or Spiderman? Well, anything's possible. There certainly could be a man who was bitten by a strange owl and was given super powers. But not in this case!

If someone says 그 사람 정말로 올빼미예요, they're saying that the person doesn't sleep at night, but during the day instead.

> 정말로 [cheongmalro] really   올빼미 [olppaemi] owl

올빼미 means "owl," and of course you know owls are nocturnal. There's a similar expression in English, isn't there? You can describe someone as a "night owl." But it doesn't stop there, because Koreans frequently use lots of other animal comparisons to describe people. Check out the list:

그 사람 정말로 올빼미예요. [Keu saram cheongmalro olppaemiyeyo.] He/she's a real owl. (He/she is awake at night and asleep during the day.)
그 여자는 여우예요. [Keu yeojaneun yeouyeyo.] She's a fox. (She's sly.) (Careful—this doesn't refer to looks like it does in English!)
남자들은 다 늑대예요. [Namjadeureun ta neukdaeyeyo.] All men are wolves. (Men are no good.)
제 남편은 곰이에요. [Che nampyeoneun komieyo.] My husband is a bear. (My husband is slow-moving.) or, (My husband is insensitive.)

그렇게 많이 먹으면 돼지가 될 거예요.
[Keureoke mani meogeumyeon twaejiga toel keoyeyo.] If you eat so much, you'll become a pig. (If you eat so much, you'll get fat.) (Be careful! This can be quite offensive.)
그 사람은 물 안에서는 완전히 물개예요.
[Keu sarameun mul aneseoneun wanjeonhi mulgaeyeyo.]
He/she is a perfect seal in water. (He/she swims very well.)

Which animal are you?

CHAPTER
23

One, Two, Three...
하나, 둘, 셋... [hana, tul, set]
Counting: Numbers and Counting Units

Remember learning the multiplication tables in elementary school? We all thought it was pretty tough at first, but our teachers made us practice, practice, and practice some more, and eventually we made it! Well, most of us, anyway. ^^ But don't worry if you still have trouble remembering what 9 times 7 is. What I want to talk about in this chapter is much easier—we're going to learn to count!

We've been focused on words so much throughout the book that we've nearly overlooked numbers. But numbers are essential parts of a language, right? After all, if you don't know your numbers, how are you going to ask for the proper change back when you buy a soda, or what will you do when a new friend wants to give you their cell number? Phew—good thing we're learning this now!

But hold on...I have a little bit of bad news first. You know how Korean is simpler than English in some ways but more complex in others? Well, guess which one applies here. That's right, we have some complexity.

In Korean, there are actually **two** number systems. Two!? That's right, two. But why!? The answer is simple: one system is pure Korean, created by Koreans and used since the beginning of the language. The second one comes from Chinese. Remember that both Korean language and society have been strongly influenced by China, so it's really no surprise this other number system was adopted, too.

Unfortunately, the two number systems are not interchangeable. One is used for some things, the other for others. So not only do you have to memorize two different words for each number, but you also have to learn the proper circumstances for using each system! Tough, I know. But hey, I'm here to help, so don't despair! Mastery of these number systems will come quicker than you think, just as your multiplication tables did.

Sino-Korean

As it turns out, the Chinese-influenced (or Sino-Korean) numbers are a little easier and more systematic. So let's tackle those first. Ready? 3, 2, 1...begin!

0: 영 [yeong] *or* 공 [kong]
1: 일 [il]
2: 이 [i]
3: 삼 [sam]
4: 사 [sa]
5: 오 [o]
6: 육 [yuk]
7: 칠 [chil]
8: 팔 [pal]
9: 구 [ku]
10: 십 [ship]

If you've studied other East Asian languages, like Japanese, you might notice these are quite similar to the counting systems in those languages. Why's that? Well, Korea isn't the only culture China has affected!

But, hmm...did you notice something strange in this list? Yeah, why are there two different ways to say 0? Actually, in almost all cases 영 is the correct form to use. But for some reason, when people are giving out their telephone number, they prefer to say 공 instead. Here, let me give you an example using my cell number. Just... uh...don't try to call me. ^;^

010-1234-5678

How would you say this number? That's right: 공일공, 일이삼사, 오육칠팔. Notice that for telephone numbers you say each number **individually**. I know in English you like to get fancy and say "twelve" or "fifty-six, seventy-eight," but in Korea we don't do that. Just keep it simple! The same goes for numbers that are repeated, like this: 007. How do you say that? Yes, it's 공공칠 [konggongchil]. There's no "double-oh" here, got it?!

Okay, so far so good. Are you ready for more? How about 11 through 20? This is where that simplicity I promised comes in. Notice that 11 through 19 are exactly the same as 1 through 9, only they have 십, the word for 10, in front of them. Even though this is the opposite of English—we say "seven-teen," not "ten-seven"—it's still quite logical and makes learning Sino-Korean numbers a breeze. Actually, I like this better than the English system, but of course, I'm biased. ^^

🎧 23.2

11: 십일 [shibil]
12: 십이 [shibi]
13: 십삼 [shipsam]
14: 십사 [shipsa]
15: 십오 [shibo]
16: 십육 [shimyuk]
17: 십칠 [shipchil]
18: 십팔 [shippal]
19: 십구 [shipgu]
20: 이십 [iship]

Look at 20. It's just 2 (이) + 10 (십)! How easy can you get? And, moving on, the simplicity continues:

🎧 23.3

21: 이십일 [ishibil]
22: 이십이 [ishibi]
23: 이십삼 [ishipsam]
24: 이십사 [ishipsa]
25: 이십오 [ishibo]
26: 이십육 [ishimyuk]
27: 이십칠 [ishipchil]
28: 이십팔 [ishippal]
29: 이십구 [isipgu]

I don't even need to explain what's going on here, do I? So let's keep going:

30: 삼십 [samship]
40: 사십 [saship]
50: 오십 [oship]
60: 육십 [yukship]
70: 칠십 [chilship]
80: 팔십 [palship]
90: 구십 [kuship]

No, don't stop there!

100: 백 [paek]
1,000: 천 [cheon]
10,000: 만 [man]
100,000: 십만 [shimman]
1,000,000: 백만 [paengman]
10,000,000: 천만 [cheonman]
100,000,000: (일)억 [(il)eok]

Wow! "Why would I ever need to count so high?" you may be asking. But remember, it takes about 1,000 units of the Korean currency, the won, to equal 1 U.S. dollar. So, when money's involved, things can add up fast.

Now, you may have noticed above that Sino-Korean has a totally separate name for the number 10,000. It's not just 10 (십) + 1,000 (천), but rather 만. In English counting, you place a comma after every three digits, right? But Sino-Korean numbers were originally broken up into units of **four** digits instead of just three. This can create some confusion in modern times, as the three-digit units have come to be commonly used. There are some in Korea who advocate switching back to four-digit increments, but this isn't likely to happen. However, for the purpose of our understanding, let's see what that would look like:

100: 백
1000: 천
1,0000: 만
10,0000: 십만
100,0000: 백만
1000,0000: 천만
1,0000,0000: (일)억

The number names make a bit more sense when you look at them this way, don't they?

I want to mention one more thing about Sino-Korean numbers. In English, we always pronounce 100 as "one hundred," never simply "hundred." But with Sino-Korean numbers, it's more common to omit the "one" when it comes in front of 100 (백), 1,000 (천), or 10,000 (만).

So 132 is not 일백삼십이, but 백삼십이. 1,567 is not 일천오백육십칠, but 천오백육십칠. And 13,982 is not 일만삼천구백팔십이, but rather 만삼천구백팔십이. For 100,000,000 (억), though, you need the 일.

Pure Korean

Great! Halfway done. It's time to take on the pure Korean numbers, which aren't quite as easy as the Sino-Korean, but still relatively simple. There's no pure-Korean word for 0, so we'll start with 1 through 10:

1: 하나 [hana]
2: 둘 [tul]
3: 셋 [set]
4: 넷 [net]
5: 다섯 [taseot]
6: 여섯 [yeoseot]
7: 일곱 [ilgop]
8: 여덟 [yeodeol]
9: 아홉 [ahop]
10: 열 [yeol]

Nope, these shouldn't remind you of any other language. They're pure Korean!

Lucky for you, 11 through 19 are formed using the same pattern as the Sino-Korean numbers (e.g., 10 + 1). So we have:

11: 열하나 [yeolhana]
12: 열둘 [yeoldul]
13: 열셋 [yeolset]
14: 열넷 [yeolnet]
15: 열다섯 [yeoldaseot]
16: 열여섯 [yeolyeoseot]
17: 열일곱 [yeolilgop]
18: 열여덟 [yeolyeodeol]
19: 열아홉 [yeolahop]

And now, what about 20? Will it be 둘열? Oh, I wish it were that easy, but that's wrong! Koreans have another unique name for 20: 스물. Likewise, 30 is not 셋열, but 서른. Check it out:

20: 스물 [seumul]
21: 스물하나 [seumulhana]
22: 스물둘 [seumuldul]
...
30: 서른 [seoreun]
40: 마흔 [maheun]
50: 쉰 [shwin]
60: 예순 [yesun]
70: 일흔 [ilheun]
80: 여든 [yeodeun]
90: 아흔 [aheun]

That's it! Just as there's no pure-Korean word for 0, there aren't any for anything higher than 99. Instead, the Sino-Korean terms are always used for these.

Want to hear something funny? Koreans have these two counting systems, but the truth is many of them find it awkward to learn so many different number names, especially those in the younger generation. What you'll find is that the majority of people only use pure-Korean numbers up to 19 and then switch over to Sino-Korean because they're easier, even in cases when the pure Korean is called for! So, even if you only feel like learning the first 19 pure-Korean numbers, chances are you'll be just fine.

Counting units

Okay, we can't end our discussion of numbers and counting without an explanation of counting units. And what are these? Well, in English, when you want to tell someone how much money you have in your pocket, you don't just say "I have 32." You have to specify what you're talking about: "I have 32 *dollars*." This is a **counting unit**, and Korean is full of special words that function as counting units for different things. And, as you could probably guess, some are used only with Sino-Korean numbers and others only with pure-Korean.

Sino-Korean counting units mainly deal with time, and here are some important ones:

23.9 년 [nyeon]: years

23.10 월 [weol]: months of the year

23.11 일 [il]: days of the month

23.12 분 [pun]: minutes

23.13 초 [cho]: seconds

Don't worry about these now, because you'll get very familiar with them in chapters 25 and 26.

Pure-Korean counting units, on the other hand, are numerous and varied. What's more, when you use a counting unit with pure-Korean numbers 1 through 4, the number names **contract** a little bit. Confusing? Here's what I mean:

Number	Original name	With a counting unit
1	하나	한 [han]
2	둘	두 [tu]
3	셋	세 [se]
4	넷	네 [ne]

Naturally, this applies for 11 through 14 as well:

Number	Original name	With a counting unit
11	열하나	열한 [yeolhan]
12	열둘	열두 [yeoldu]
13	열셋	열세 [yeolse]
14	열넷	열네 [yeolne]

There's no need to learn all the counting units right this instant, but let me just show you some of the most common so you can get an idea of what I'm talking about.

When you count people, you put 사람 [saram] or 명 [myeong] after the number. This would give you:

3 [세]사람, 4 [네]명, ...

Of course, to be respectful you should use the honorific form of "person" instead, which is 분 [pun]. This creates:

3 [세]분, 4 [네]분, ...

For counting generic items, the unit 개 [kae] is used. With 개, however, you need to specify what it is you're counting. So:

사탕 10 [열]개 ("ten candies")

의자 11 [열 한]개 ("eleven chairs")

> 사탕 [satang] candy　　　　의자 [uija] chair

That's it! Have a look at the *Further Vocabulary* section for more information on pure-Korean counting units.

When I count to 3, you'll be finished with this chapter. 하나, 둘, 셋...

Further Vocabulary: Counting units

Counting units used with pure-Korean numbers:

Counting unit	Type of item	Example
마리 [mari]	animals	곰 3 [세]마리 ("three bears")
그루 [keuru]	trees	소나무 4 [네]그루 ("four pines")
대 [tae]	cars	차 10 [열]대 ("ten cars")
벌 [peol]	pairs, sets	청바지 2 [두]벌 ("two pairs of jeans")
권 [kweon]	volumes, books	책 7 [일곱]권 ("seven books")
번 [peon]	times	11 [열 한]번 ("eleven times")
병 [pyeong]	bottles	맥주 1 [한]병 ("one bottle of beer")
잔 [chan]	glasses, cups	물 5 [다섯]잔 ("five cups of water")
살 [sal]	years of age	12 [열 두]살 ("twelve years old")
시간 [shigan]	hours	6 [여섯]시간 ("six hours")
시 [shi]	o'clock	9 [아홉]시 ("nine o'clock")
장 [chang]	sheets	종이 15 [열 다섯]장 ("fifteen sheets of paper")
켤레 [kyeolre]	pairs of shoes	구두 8 [여덟]켤레 ("eight pairs of shoes")

소나무 4[네]그루
Four pines

Korean Style: The three-six-nine game

Everyone likes a good, fun group game, right? This one's particularly popular in orientation sessions and team-building seminars, as well as at most local bars on a weekend night. If you spend more than a couple weeks in Korea, I'm almost positive you'll play this at least once. So you'd better practice now! And, as it turns out, this game is perfect for learning your numbers. It's called the 3-6-9 [삼육구] 게임 (three-six-nine game).

Okay, first get yourself a group of people—size doesn't matter, but the more the merrier—and circle round. The basic principle of the game is actually quite simple. Going in a circle and taking turns, each person says a Sino-Korean number in order starting from 1. Only, when you get to a number that contains a 3, 6, or 9, you have to clap your hands instead of speaking the number. If you clap your hands when you're not supposed to, or you say the number when you're supposed to clap, you get a penalty. Let's look at how the game starts off:

1 [일], 2 [이], 👏, 4 [사], 5 [오], 👏, 7 [칠], 8 [팔], 👏, 10 [십], 11 [십일], 12 [십이], 👏, 14 [십사], 15 [십오], 👏, 17 [십칠], 18 [십팔], 👏, 20 [이십], 21 [이십일], 22 [이십이], 👏, 24 [이십사], 25 [이십오], 👏, 27 [이십칠], 28 [이십팔], 👏

Pretty easy, right? But what happens when you get to 30!? Ah! All the numbers have 3s in them!

👏, 👏, 👏, 👏👏, 👏, 👏, 👏👏, 👏, 👏, 👏👏, 40 [사십], 41 [사십일], 42 [사십이], 👏, 44 [사십사], 45 [사십오], 👏, 47 [사십칠], 48 [사십팔], 👏, 50 [오십], 51 [오십일], 52 [오십이], 👏, 54 [오십사], 55 [오십오], 👏, 57 [오십칠], 58 [오십팔], 👏

33, 36, and 39 are the worst, because you have to clap twice! Yikes!

The second crisis comes when you hit the 60s.

👏, 👏, 👏, 👏👏, 👏, 👏, 👏👏, 👏, 👏, 👏👏, 70 [칠십]…

Well, what do you think? Does it still seem a little too easy to be fun? Just remember—a lot of times you'll be playing this after knocking back a pint or two of Cass or OB. And also, if you make a mistake, the rest of your group gets to decide your punishment! One thing's for sure: after a few rounds of the 3-6-9 game, you'll know your numbers!

CHAPTER
24

How Much Is This?
이거 얼마예요? [Igeo eolmayeyo?]
How to Shop

Korean cities like Seoul and Busan are bustling metropolises where you can find all kinds of people doing and selling all kinds of things. 명동, Seoul's upscale shopping district, and 남대문시장, it's largest traditional market, are two popular spots for foreigners to visit, both to shop and simply to watch the action.

If your sole purpose for going is the latter, well then you can just skip this chapter! ^;^ But if you're ever planning on buying something here or elsewhere in the country, you're going to need to learn some key shopping expressions, right? Right. We'll start out with something easy. How do you say "shopping" in Korean? Hey, guess what? It's just 쇼핑!

So, you've been 쇼핑 around, and you've finally found something you want to buy. Most likely, the store clerk has already spotted you and will come over to say:

🎧 24.1 뭘 도와 드릴까요? [Mweol towa teurilkkayo?] May I help with anything?

뭘 [mweol] what (shortened form of 무엇을)   돕다 [topda] to help
V-아 / 어 / 여 주다 / 드리다 [-a/eo/yeo chuda/teurida] to do something for someone

---

뭘 도와 드릴까요?
May I help with anything?

드리다 (honorific) and 주다 (plain) both mean "to give," but when either of them is used after the verb ending –아 / –어 / –여, it makes whatever you're saying sound extra polite. The clerk wants to be as polite as possible, of course, so he's not going to say 뭘 도울까요? or 뭘 도와 줄까요?, but rather 뭘 도와 드릴까요? I'm sure you recognize the **propositive** ending –ㄹ까요? / –을까요?, right?

Likewise, this form can make a **command** sound nicer. So if you do in fact need the clerk's help, don't say 나를 도와요. Nobody's going to want to help you if that's what they hear. Instead, you should say 저를 도와 주세요, looking as helpless as possible.

By the way, what are you hoping to buy? A 핸드폰 ("cell phone")? A 시계 ("watch")? Or are you just window shopping? In Korean, people use the term 아이 쇼핑 ("eye shopping") when they're simply looking around without anything specific in mind. Don't think they're actually shopping for eyes! But if that's what you're doing, then how would you tell the clerk, "I'm just looking around so I don't need your help. If you'll only leave me alone I might buy all the things in this shop!"? Basically, like this:

🎧 **24.2** 괜찮아요. 그냥 구경하고 있어요. [Kwaenchanayo. Keunyang kugyeonghago isseoyo.] I'm okay. I'm just looking around.

> 그냥 [keunyang] just   구경하다 [kugyeonghada] to look around

Very nice! Upon hearing this, the clerk will retreat to wherever he was sitting before, defeated by your expert Korean. But, oops…wait! You've just found some clothes you love and you really want to try them on. Hurry, catch him before he sits down and ask:

🎧 **24.3** 이 옷 입어 봐도 돼요? [I ot ibeo pwado twaeyo?] May I try on these clothes?

> 옷 [ot] clothes   입다 [ipda] to wear
> V-아 / 어 / 여 보다 [-a/eo/yeo poda] to try

Ordinarily, the verb 보다 means "to see." But just as we learned above, conjugating a verb with the ending –아 / –어 / –여 and then adding 보다 changes its meaning. It now signifies "to give something a try."

But there's actually a second expression being used in the sentence above: –아도 / –어도 / –여도 되다. 되다 is the verb for "to become," remember? And guess what? That's right, in this case it has nothing to do with "becoming," but rather it's how you ask **permission** to do something. (Incidentally, the expressions –아야 / –어야 / –여야 되다 (for obligation) and –(으)면 안 되다 (for prohibition), which we learned in chapter 21, use the verb 되다 as well.)

So, using a combination of the two expressions we just covered, the final product is 이 옷 입어 봐도 돼요? 봐도 is the contracted form of 보아도, and 돼요 is the contracted form of 되어요. Make sense?

This is a very polite expression, and it's important to use it while shopping. The customer is king, of course, but you still need to ask permission nicely to try something on. After all, they're not your clothes yet; they're still the shop owner's! But once you honor him with your polite speech, he's sure to respond:

🎧 **24.4** 네. 입어 보세요. [Ne. Ibeo poseyo.] Sure. Try them on.

Next, you'll be ushered into a tiny room where you can put on the clothes and…poof! You'll be transformed into a different person. Your clerk will no doubt have some flattering things to say about your new look, eyeing that money burning a hole in your pocket. But remember, there's no hurry. We have time for some serious negotiation here. First, ask the **price**:

🎧 **24.5** 이거 (가격이) 얼마예요? [Igeo (kagyeogi) eolmayeyo?] How much is this?

> 이거 [igeo] this (shortened form of 이것)

가격 is another word for "price" in Korean, but you can usually omit it. The clerk knows exactly what you're talking about. When you inquire about a price, the key is the noun 얼마, meaning "how much" or "what."

Right, and now the moment of truth:

🎧 24.6 만 원이에요. [Man weonieyo.]

You remember 원, right? It's the Korean currency. Good. And then how much is 만? No? Can't remember? Okay, I give you permission to flip back to the previous chapter and find out. Or, better yet, let's figure it out here.

Keep in mind, the origin of Sino-Korean number names is based on **four** digits separated by commas, not just three. So 10 is 십, 100 is 백, 1,000 is 천, and 10,000 is…십천? No! 10,000 has its own name, rather than being a combination of 10 + 1,000. And that name is 만, of course.

Now, you've been given a price of 만 원, but how much is that really? If you're not familiar with the value of the Korean currency, it might sound like a lot, right? Well, here's a good guideline for remembering the worth of the won. As of 2009, a Big Mac costs about 3,300 원. In that case, 만 원 is just enough to give yourself a heart attack by eating three burgers! Wow!

So, do you think those jeans you just tried on are worth three Big Macs? If not, then you're in luck, because Korea is by and large a **haggling** society. You can't do this in a department store, where the salespeople will look down their noses at you if you try to ask for a discount, but in traditional markets, it's quite appropriate to put your bargaining skills to use.

Your clerk has suggested 만 원 for this pair of designer jeans. Even if you think this is already the best deal in the world, you can still try to whittle it down by saying:

🎧 24.7 너무 비싸요. [Neomu pissayo.] It's too expensive.

> 비싸다 [pissada] expensive

Ah, let the haggling begin. Don't let up now! You have to continue your attack. Instead of just saying "it's too expensive," you have to ask him to discount the price for you:

🎧 24.8 깎아 주세요. [Kkakka chuseyo.] Please give me a discount.

The verb 깎다, in a general sense, means "to cut" (as in a carrot, or one's hair), but it's also used for "to discount." And, as you can see, you're using the expression –아 / –어 / –여 주다 that we learned above, both politely and desperately asking the favor of a lower price.

And what happens next? Who can say? Whether or not you'll get a discount depends on the clerk, as well as how expertly you can use your Korean. But if you succeed and he asks you afterwards, "Where the heck did you learn this practical, cut-throat Korean?" don't forget to say, "Why, from *Korean for Beginners*, of course!"

Further Vocabulary: Shopping

Ah, the joys of the Korean market. Here are some more words to help you make your visit there a worthwhile one.

사다 [sada] to buy
팔다 [palda] to sell
돈 [don] money
내다 [naeda] to pay, give
값 [kap] price

싸다 [ssada] cheap, inexpensive
비싸다 [pissada] expensive, costly
입다 [ipda] to put on, wear
벗다 [peotda] to take off, undress

Korean Style: Korean euphemisms

My wife has an interesting habit. Maybe you know someone who's the same way. When she goes shopping for clothes, she likes to try on practically everything in the store, but she hardly ever finds something she likes enough to buy. As she's leaving, the clerk will ask her if there's anything she'd like to purchase, but she just says 다음에 살게요 ("I'll buy something next time."). Of course, she won't. But she doesn't want to hurt the shopkeeper's feelings by telling him "I don't like your clothes."

In English, we call this a white lie, right? White lies are little untruths we tell people in order to spare them unnecessary pain. For instance, you tell your sister she has a nice singing voice even though she sounds like a dying cat. Or you might reassure your friend that his new haircut doesn't look that bad, when all you really want to do is point and laugh. Another term for a white lie is a euphemism.

Euphemisms and other indirect, polite forms of speech have developed in Korean, too. And, unlike the Korean proverbs we learned a little while back, these are pretty easy to understand. See for yourself:

아버지는 제가 세 살 때 하늘 나라로 가셨어요. *Lit.* My father went away to heaven when I was three.
아버지는 제가 세 살 때 돌아가셨어요. *Lit.* My father returned when I was three.
아버지는 제가 세 살 때 죽었어요. My father died when I was three.

때 [ttae] time
하늘 [haneul] sky, heaven
나라 [nara] country, nation

돌아가다 [toragada] to return
죽다 [chukda] to die

Just like in English, Koreans sometimes use softer speech like this when they're talking about death, as saying the word directly can be taken as harsh or insensitive in some instances.

Here's another example:

화장실에 갔다 올게. Let me go to restroom.

In English, we say "restroom" in place of "toilet" to be polite, even though it's not actually a room for resting. Similarly, Koreans say 화장실, which literally means a place where people put on makeup, despite the fact that men (well, most men ^^) don't use it for that purpose.

And finally, compare these sentences:

운전 면허 시험에 미끄러졌어요. *Lit.* I slipped the driver's license test.
운전 면허 시험에서 미역국을 먹었어요. *Lit.* I seaweed soup-ed the driver's license test.
운전 면허 시험에 떨어졌어요. I failed the driver's license test.

> 운전 [unjeon] driving
> 면허 [myeonheo] license
> 미끄러지다 [mikkeureojida] to slip
>
> 미역국 [miyeokguk] seaweed soup
> 떨어지다 [tteoreojida] to fail

Wow, these are pretty strange, aren't they? I mean, using "to slip" in place of "to fail" makes a little bit of sense, but what's with the seaweed soup? Well, if you've ever had the pleasure of eating this dish, you'll know that the seaweed is quite slippery. Hence, it's sometimes used as a euphemism for "to fail" in the same way "to slip" is!

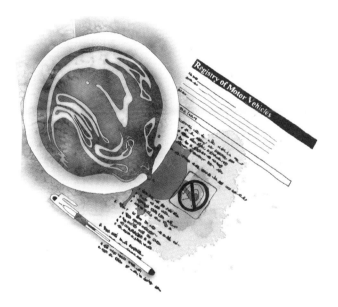

25

What Time Is It?

지금 몇 시예요? [Chigeum myeot shiyeyo?]
Asking and Telling Time and How Many

"Excuse me, do you have the time?"

What a useful question this is, especially if you're like me and don't typically wear a watch. We should probably learn how to ask for this information before the book comes to an end, wouldn't you agree?

So, to ask "what" time it is, you need a word for "what," don't you? We've looked at this issue a little bit already...waaaaaay back in chapter 11. There was the basic form of the word, 무엇, and then its **contracted** spoken form, 뭐. Remember? Of course you do.

In this case, though, we need a modifier version of "what," because it's going to be interacting with the word "time." Usually, when you want to use 무엇 as a modifier, you'll say 무슨 [museun]. And the word for "time" is 시간 [shigan]. Following this, it would be logical to construct the question as 무슨 시간이에요? Unfortunately, it would also be wrong.

That's because, when the noun you're modifying is related to numbers, you need to use a different form of "what": 몇. And instead of literally saying "time" in this question as we do in English, Koreans insert 시 [shi], which as we learned in chapter 23 is the counting unit for "hour," or "o'clock." So, are you finally ready to see the end result? I'd say so. Let's ask the time in Korean:

 지금 몇 시예요? [Chigeum myeot shiyeyo?] What time is it now?

Okay, great! And now, after that long explanation, I have some good news about the kinds of answers you'll get to this question. Think about how many ways there are of saying the time 3:45 in English: "three forty-five," "forty-five past three," "quarter till four,"... Look at all those structures and prepositions. Learning these correctly is a big challenge for non-native speakers.

Lucky for you, though, telling time in Korean is much simpler. First, there are no separate words for "o'clock" or "quarter." You use 시 for the first and the number 15 for the next. Second, each number you say will be followed by either 시 ("hour"), 분 ("minute"), or 초 ("second"), so there won't be any confusion. Third, the time is always given in order from **longest** to **shortest**—in other words, hour-minute-second. You can forget about expressions such as "ten till two" and "half past three." And fourth...well this part isn't actually that simple, but it's not hard either. You have to use **pure-Korean** numbers with 시, but **Sino-Korean** numbers for 분 and 초.

Now you know the basics, so let's practice. It's six o'clock. Quick—what do you say?

여섯 시예요. [Yeoseot shiyeyo.]

여섯 시예요.
It's 6:00.

Very good! Oh, but wait…how does the listener know if it's a.m. or p.m.? Well, they could just stick their head out the window, for one thing. ^;^ But, if you're someone who's obsessed with identifying the time exactly, just add 오전 ("a.m."), 오후 ("p.m."), 아침 ("in the morning"), 저녁 ("in the evening"), or 밤 ("at night") before the time, depending on what meaning you want. So,

25.3 오후 여섯 시예요. [Ohu yeoseot shiyeyo.] It's six o'clock p.m.

25.4 아침 여섯 시예요. [Achim yeoseot shiyeyo.] It's six o'clock in the morning.

25.5 저녁 여섯 시예요. [Cheonyeok yeoseot shiyeyo.] It's six o'clock in the evening.

Hmm…that took a few minutes to explain. Now it's ten past six, so how would you say this? Hey, I told you, banish the thought of "past" from your mind. All you have to say is "six ten":

25.6 여섯 시 십 분이에요. [Yeoseot shi ship punieyo.]

And remember, this is the only tricky part: don't say 육 시 십 분이에요, or 여섯 시 열 분이에요. It's pure Korean for 시, Sino-Korean for 분.

Okay, pop quiz: it's 10:15 at night.

25.7 밤 열 시 십오 분이에요. [Pam yeol shi shibo punieyo.]

As I said, there's no word for "quarter" in Korean. 십오 (15) is all you need.

Half, to
Okay, so maybe I've simplified the idea of telling time just a bit. It's true that there's no word for "quarter," but there does happen to be one for "half," and it's 반 [pan]. In fact, it's pretty commonly used in place of 30. Only, when you say it, you don't need to attach 분. So it's 삼십 분 or 반. Oops, how the time is flying! It's already 7:30:

25.8 일곱 시 삼십 분, or **25.9** 일곱 시 반,

but not 일곱 시 반 분.

And finally, there's an expression for "to," as in "five to eleven." However, you still follow the order of hour-minute when you say this, and you use a word not for "to," but for "before": 전 [cheon]. So, how do you say five to eleven?

25.10 열한 시 오 분 전이에요. [Yeolhan shi o pun cheonieyo.] It's five to eleven.

Great! That's all you need to know about telling time. Naturally, you should be able to give me all these times in Korean:

3:10 p.m.
5:30 a.m.
12:45
8:55

Possible answers:

 3:10 p.m.: 오후 세 시 십 분

5:30 a.m.: 오전 다섯 시 삼십 분 or 오전 다섯 시 반

12:45: 열두 시 사십오 분

8:55: 여덟 시 오십오 분 or 아홉 시 오 분 전

Now you are the master of the clock!

몇, 얼마나

I realize it's late, but before we go I want to show you another use for the modifier 몇. It's good for asking other things besides the time, such as "**how many**" of something there are. To do this, you insert 몇 between a noun and its counting unit. Hey, this is the perfect opportunity to show off what you studied in chapter 23, right?

어제 책 몇 권 샀어요? [Eoje chaek myeot kweon sasseoyo?] How many books did you buy yesterday?

사과 몇 개 먹었어요? [Sagwa myeot kae meogeosseoyo?] How many apples did you eat?

서울에서 부산까지 KTX (케이티엑스)로 몇 시간 걸려요? [Seoureseo pusankkaji KTX(keitiekseu)ro myeot shigan keolryeoyo?] How many hours is it from Seoul to Busan by KTX?

권 [kweon] book, volume (counting unit)   사과 [sagwa] apple
사다 [sada] to buy   걸리다 [keolrida] to take, last (time)

If you run into a situation where for some reason you can't remember which counting unit to use, don't despair. Instead, you can substitute the word **얼마나**. This should look familiar, right? In the last chapter, we learned the noun 얼마, which is used for asking the price of something. 얼마나 is an **adverb** form of 얼마, and you can whip it out when asking the number of something. So, if in our previous sentence you somehow couldn't remember that 시간 was the counting unit for "hour," you could say this instead:

서울에서 부산까지 KTX (케이티엑스)로 얼마나 걸려요? How long is it from Seoul to Busan by KTX?

KTX is the Korea Train Express, which opened in 2004. Before the KTX, the fastest train available was called 새마을 [saemaeul], and it took around four and a half hours to travel from Seoul to Busan. So what about the KTX?

🎧 세 시간 정도 걸려요. [Se shigan cheongdo keolryeoyo.] It takes about three hours.
25.19

> 정도 [cheongdo] around, approximately

Notice how you still use the **pure-Korean** numbers with 시간, just like you did with 시. And if you wanted to tack on minutes to this time, you'd need to express them with the **Sino-Korean** system.

Wow, three hours, huh? So if you brought your portable DVD player on the train and started watching *Gone with the Wind* as it pulled out of Seoul, you'd arrive in Busan before catching the famous closing line of Scarlett O'Hara: "Tomorrow is another day."

Tomorrow is another day.

Further Vocabulary: Approximations

Sometimes, we can't be exactly sure of what we're talking about. Even I suffer from this! When I do, I use these words.

쯤 [jjeum] degree, or so
적어도 [cheogeodo] at least
약 [yak] about, approximately

대략 [taeryak] approximately, roughly
대충 [taechung] roughly, approximately

EX.:   I usually have lunch at about twelve o'clock.
저는 보통 열두 시쯤에 점심을 먹어요.
저는 보통 열두 시 정도에 점심을 먹어요.
저는 약[대략, 대충] 열두 시에 점심을 먹어요.

Korean Style: A two-year-old newborn!? Only in Korea!

One thing foreigners are always taken aback by when they first arrive in Korea is how often they hear this question:

나이가 어떻게 되세요? [Naiga eotteoke toeseyo?] How old are you?

Even people you've just met will ask you this, but remember that in Korean society this isn't rude at all. Koreans consider age to be another part of basic personal information along with your name, hometown, astrological sign, etc. Instead of being offended, take their interest in your age as an expression of friendship.

But answering the question could be more complicated than you think. A typical response might go something like this:

우리나라 나이로는 열 살이고 만으로는 아홉 살이에요. [Urinara naironeun yeol sarigo maneuroneun ahop sarieyo.] I'm ten in Korean age and nine in Western age.

Huh? Korean age and Western age? What's the difference? How can a person have any other age than the one that counts years from the day they were born? Well, in Korea, we begin to calculate a person's age while they're still inside their mother's womb. Then, the day after a Korean is born, he or she is automatically promoted to 1 year old!

After that, we all add on a year at the beginning of each new year, not on our particular birthdays. So obviously, a person's Korean age is always going to be at least a year more than their Western age. But sometimes, it's nearly two years more! For example, if a baby is born on December 31, it will magically turn 2 years old on January 1—one year for being born, and one for the passing of the new year! Strange, huh?

Another common way of answering the age question is to say something like this:

저는 빠른 79예요. [Cheoneun ppareun chilguyeyo.] I was born in early '79.

Hmm…why would someone need to emphasize that they were born early in the year? Well, this distinction is made because of Korea's school system. In Korea, the school year begins in March, and any child who has turned 7 (in Western age) by this time is eligible to enter the system. So, someone born on February 28 can begin school this year, while her friend who was born on March 2 has to stay home and play with his mother for another year, because in Western years he's still 6, not 7. Even though according to Korean age both children are 8, these school system rules separate them into different grades.

This is why when Koreans tell you how old they are, they might add the word 빠른 in front of the year they were born. 빠른 means they were born in January or February of that year, signifying that they're a grade ahead of everyone else who was born in the same year.

Wow, and you thought age was a relatively simple subject. Not in Korea!

CHAPTER
26

Today Is August 15

오늘은 8월 15일이에요. [Oneureun parweol shibo irieyo.]

Days, Dates, and Seasons

In Korea, as in most Western countries, people with office jobs work Monday through Friday and have Saturday and Sunday off. So for many people, Friday evening is a happy time. If you're hoping to ask someone out on a date in Korea, plan a Friday night engagement and you're likely to hear "yes." But before you can do that, you need a firm grasp on how Koreans refer to the days of the week.

First we have the relative terms used to indicate days: 오늘 [oneul] ("today"), 어제 [eoje] ("yesterday"), and 내일 [naeil] ("tomorrow"). Not too hard. And then what about going a little further into the past and future? We do this in English by saying "the day before yesterday" and "the day after tomorrow," but Korean has original words for each of these: 그저께 [keujeokke] and 모레 [more], respectively. So a five-day timeline looks like this:

13 thursday	14 friday	15 saturday	16 sunday	17 monday
26.1	26.2	26.3	26.4	26.5
그저께	어제	오늘	내일	모레
day before yesterday	yesterday	today	tomorrow	day after tomorrow

So let's say, for you fellows out there, that you meet a beautiful Korean girl at a cafe. You're so blown away by her beauty that you can't even remember what day of the week it is! Wow! You'd better ask her. Let's see. Well, the Korean word 요일 [yoil] has the meaning of "day of the week." So what word do you use to ask "what" day of the week it is? 몇? No, remember 몇 is only used to ask about things that are number-related. Come on, I mentioned the correct answer briefly last chapter. Hurry! She's losing interest…yes! 무슨 is the one.

> 26.6 오늘 무슨 요일이에요? [Oneul museun yoirieyo?] What day of the week is it?

Okay, even though this is a pretty silly question, I'm sure she'll answer you kindly because she's a nice person. Uh-oh, but if you don't understand what she says, how are you going to keep the conversation going!? We'd better learn how to say all the days of the week, and fast. Here we go!

Monday: 월요일 [weoryoil]

 Tuesday: 화요일 [hwayoil]

 Wednesday: 수요일 [suyoil]

 Thursday: 목요일 [mogyoil]

 Friday: 금요일 [keumyoil]

 Saturday: 토요일 [toyoil]

 Sunday: 일요일 [iryoil]

Notice how all these names include a unique first syllable followed by the word for "day of the week." Very simple and practical, don't you think? But don't let me interrupt—she's answering:

 목요일이에요. [Mogyoirieyo.] It's Thursday.

Okay, this is great, but you don't want to stand around practicing saying the days of the week in Korean with this girl, do you? Come on. Go ahead and ask her if she's busy Friday night:

 내일 저녁에 시간 있으세요? [Naeil cheonyeoge shigan isseuseyo?] Do you have any time
    tomorrow night?

> 시간(이) 있다 [shigan(i) itda] to have time

Nice job! I hope you get to hang out and talk world peace and interpret each other's dreams through a psychoanalytical perspective. ^^ Or, of course, she could say this:

 내일은 약속이 있어요. [Naeireun yaksogi isseoyo.] I have a prior engagement tomorrow.

> 약속 [yaksok] appointment, engagement

Bummer.

Spring, summer, fall, winter

Different places in the world experience different seasons. I mean, if you live somewhere along the equator in Ecuador or Kenya or Indonesia, you might just have one: hot! But Korea has four distinct seasons: 봄 [pom] ("spring"), 여름 [yeoreum] ("summer"), 가을 [kaeul] ("fall"), and 겨울 [kyeoul] ("winter"). If you ask me, spring and fall in Korea are absolutely perfect! They're so lovely. Traditionally, spring lasts from April through June, and fall comes in October and November. But there's always some confusion regarding the exact dates, because year after year the seasons seem to change slightly, maybe because of global warming. And unfortunately, the seasons that get shortened are 봄 and 가을.

Anyway, I'll stop talking about my favorite seasons so you can practice using what we just learned about the modifier 무슨 to ask what season it is in Korea:

🎧 26.17 한국은 지금 무슨 계절이에요? [Hangugeun chigeum museun kyejeorieyo?] What season is it now in Korea?

> 계절 [kyejeol] season

This question shouldn't be too hard to answer. Unless you're in the Southern Hemisphere (or along the equator, as I said), the season in Korea should be roughly the same as where you are. But, even if you're sitting in the heat of summer or the freezing cold of winter, let's imagine we're in Korea enjoying the beautiful spring and fall.

🎧 26.18 봄이에요. [Pomieyo.] It's spring.

🎧 26.19 가을이에요. [Kaeurieyo.] It's fall.

Days, months, years

In America, you list dates in something of a strange order, I think. It's often month, day, then year. For many other parts of the world, it goes from smallest to largest: day, month, year. Well forget all that, because Korean is totally different. It gives dates from the **largest** unit to the **smallest** one: year, month, day. Just like we learned with time (hour, minute, second) in the last chapter, right?

This might be a little tricky to remember for English speakers, but I have great news. Korean has no long and strange month names to memorize like English does! All you have to do is put a **Sino-Korean** number in front of the word 월 [weol] ("month"). Wow, how easy! And the same goes for years and days. Just use the proper Sino-Korean number and follow it with 년 [nyeon] ("year") or 일 [il] ("day of the month"). This is so simple, I bet you can do it right now:

🎧 26.20 오늘은 이천십 년, 오 월, 십삼 일이에요. [Oneureun icheonship nyeon, o weol, shipsam irieyo.] Today is May 13, 2010.

Oh, it's the 13th of the month? I wonder what day of the week it is.

🎧 26.21 무슨 요일이에요? [Museun yoirieyo?] What day of the week is it?

🎧 26.22 금요일이에요. [Keumyoirieyo.] It's Friday.

Yikes! Today is Friday the 13th! But wait, before you start knocking on wood and throwing salt over your shoulder, consider this: 13 isn't an unlucky number in Korea. No, the number to watch out for in Korea is even worse, because it's so much more common. It's 4! But why would the number 4 be considered unlucky? Well, it's because the pronunciation of four, 사, is the same as the pronunciation of the Chinese character meaning "death." Pretty scary, huh?

Okay, enough about that. Let's move on to talk about a happier day:

🎧 26.23   오늘은 팔월 십오 일이에요. [Oneureun parweol shibo irieyo.] Today is August 15.

What, you don't think August 15th is special? Well, to Koreans it's very important, because August 15, 1945, is the day we regained our independence from Japan. Remember, as I told you at the very beginning of this book, Korea's history is very important to understanding the culture of the modern country.

How about this one:

🎧 26.24   오늘은 구월 이십팔 일이에요. [Oneureun kuweol ishippal irieyo.] Today is September 28.

September 28th…another national holiday? Not really, but it should be. It's my birthday! So, as I'm fond of reminding people:

🎧 26.25   그 날은 제 생일이에요. [Keu nareun che saengirieyo.] That day is my birthday.

> 날 [nal] day

Do you want to congratulate me? If so, you can say:

🎧 26.26   축하해요! [Chukahaeyo!] Congratulations!

고맙습니다. Shall we celebrate? I think so, because once we get to the next chapter, there will be real cause for a party—your graduation party!

Further Vocabulary: Daily words

A few more words on the theme of days and dates:

일주일 [iljuil] a week, one week
주말 [chumal] weekend
휴일 [hyuil] holiday

공휴일 [konghyuil] national holiday
평일 [pyeongil] weekday

Korean Style: Which receives deliveries first: floor 2 or basement level 2?

Because the number 4 is considered unlucky in Korea, in many buildings the fourth floor will be symbolized with an "F" standing for the English "four" instead of the actual number. But actually, what you consider to be the fourth floor in your country might not be the same level as the one in Korea. I mean, different countries have different ways of counting floors. Some count starting with the ground level as #1, while others consider the floor directly *above* ground level to be the first one. Korea follows the first rule. So 1 [일]층 is ground level, 2 [이]층 is the next one up, and so on.

Here's a riddle for thinking about the structure of Korean buildings:

Two Koreans who live in the same building call a Chinese restaurant at exactly the same time to order some noodles for delivery. One of them is on the 2nd floor, while the other is on the 2nd basement level. Who will get their delivery first?

Consider what's going through the mind of the Chinese deliveryperson. She's standing on the ground level, floor 1. To get to floor 2, she has to go up one flight of stairs. But to get to basement level 2, she'll need to go down two flights of stairs. So, who's going to get their food first?

I Wish You Would Come Back to Korea Someday

할 씨가 언젠가 한국에 다시 왔으면 좋겠어요.
[Hal ssiga eonjenga hanguge tashi wasseumyeon chokesseoyo.]

Wanting and Wishing

Well, it's almost time to head back to your country now. I mean metaphorically—the book's almost over! Of course, you can physically stay in Korea as long as you want. ^^

So, what would you want to do if you were really leaving Korea? You'd probably want to head to 인사동 to pick up some last-minute traditional souvenirs. Or you might wish for one last night on the town with your friends. Oh, and you'll probably want to pack your luggage. So…what do you *want* to do? Yes, I agree. Let's learn how to express what you want.

Want to…

It's pretty easy to say what you want in English, isn't it? I mean, you just use the verb "want" and then add the infinitive of whatever action you want to do. Well, this must be a universal thing, because expressing wants in Korean is really easy, too!

In this case, the word for "want" is 싶다 [shipda]. (Don't be fooled—it's not a verb as in English, but actually an adjective!) Okay, then we have to connect this to the action verb we want to do. That's done with the ending –고, which belongs to good ole pattern 1. So, what you get is V–고 싶다. The only important thing to remember here is that this construction only works when what you want is a **verb**. You can't use the word 싶다 with a noun, as in the English sentence "I want candy." Instead, in Korean this would have to be "I want to eat candy" (사탕을 먹고 싶어요. [Satangeul meokgo shipeoyo.])

So let's start with a very general but important question:

 뭐 하고 싶으세요? [Mweo hago shipeuseyo?] What do you want to do?

And now, let's answer:

 우리나라 친구들한테 줄 선물을 사고 싶어요. [Urinara chingudeulhante chul seonmureul sago shipeoyo.] I want to buy gifts to give my friends in my country.

 아는 분들한테 작별 인사를 하고 싶어요. [Aneun bundeulhante chakbyeol insareul hago shipeoyo.] I want to say goodbye to people I know.

짐을 싸고 싶어요. [Chimeul ssago shipeoyo.] I want to pack my luggage.

선물 [seonmul] present, gift
작별 [chakbyeol] farewell
인사 [insa] greeting, salutation

짐 [chim] luggage
싸다 [ssada] to pack

Yes, you'd better start packing. Don't forget to take your Korean book and notes with you!

Don't want to, hate doing…

Are you happy to finally be heading home? Of course you are. But at the same time, you don't want to have to say goodbye to all your friends, do you? Goodbyes are always hard. But hey, why don't you express to your friends how difficult it is to leave them? I'm sure they'll appreciate it.

You need to learn how to say you don't want to leave, or that you hate saying goodbye. Let's start with the first of these. It's a **negation**, right? And I'm sure you remember that there are two ways to make a negative sentence in Korean. Look:

🎧 27.5 안 떠나고 싶어요. [An tteonago shipeoyo.] I don't want to leave.

🎧 27.6 떠나고 싶지 않아요. [Tteonago shipji anayo.] I don't want to leave.

떠나다 [tteonada] to leave

That's right! You can either add 안 before the verb to create the **short**-form negation, or go the **longer** route and use the expression V-고 싶지 않다. But what if you're *really* upset about having to go? You can express yourself in stronger terms by saying you hate doing something:

🎧 27.7 헤어지기 싫어요. [Heeojigi shireoyo.] I hate parting.

헤어지다 [heeojida] to part　　　　싫다 [shilta] hateful

I know, I know. It's very hard to leave, isn't it? But you still have to concentrate for just a little bit longer so we can examine this sentence. Unlike 싶다, 싫다 doesn't come after the ending -고, but rather -기. Are you familiar with this pattern 1 ending? I hope so. This is the ending that turns verbs or adjectives into nouns, just like adding "-ing" to a verb in English, remember? Very useful! 헤어지다 is a verb that means "to part," but in this sentence it's changed into 헤어지기, meaning "parting." As you can see, the verb 싫다 is used with **nouns** that you hate. They don't even have to be verbs that you turn into nouns either—real nouns work too! All you have to do is add the subject particle to them. Check it out:

🎧 27.8 저는 이별이 싫어요. [Cheoneun ibyeori shireoyo.] I hate farewells.

이별 [ibyeol] farewell, parting

Yeah, me too.

I wish...

There's a Korean saying: "Those who meet must part." Yep. It's true in any language. But the real meaning of this saying is that you don't need to be sad on account of parting. It happens to everyone, and you always have the possibility of meeting again.

Yet, this is little consolation when you're leaving friends. All the Koreans you've met during your stay will be so sad to see you go, because Koreans are known for being very passionate and open with their emotions. Your friends will probably say to you, "I wish we could see each other again." Or, "I wish you would come back to Korea someday." So, to make sure you don't miss these important words of parting, let's learn some expressions dealing with wishes.

In English, when you talk about a wish that hasn't been fulfilled yet, you use the past tense: "I wish I *had* a million dollars…" If I *were* a bird…" Why is this? No one knows. But, coincidentally, it works the same way in Korean.

Verbs you're wishing about are conjugated in the past tense and then given the conditional ending "if." You remember this one, don't you? Yes, it's -(으)면. And finally, the word for "to wish," 좋겠다, comes at the end. So in total you have the expression -았으면 / -었으면 / -였으면 좋겠다. I bet you wish to see some examples:

 우리가 다시 볼 수 있었으면 좋겠어요. [Uriga tashi pol su isseosseumyeon chokesseoyo.] I wish we could see each other again.

 할 씨가 언젠가 한국에 다시 왔으면 좋겠어요. [Hal ssiga eonjenga hanguge tashi wasseumyeon chokesseoyo.] I wish you (Hal) would come back to Korea someday.

> 다시 [tashi] again   언젠가 [eonjenga] someday

My sentiments exactly.

The big goodbye

I can't believe how far you've come in 27 short chapters! You've successfully journeyed through the world of Korean language, and with only little old me to guide you. I hope that you've enjoyed my company as much as I've enjoyed yours, and that I've been able to open your eyes to what makes Koreans, their culture, and their language tick. With the knowledge you've gained from this book, you're ready for anything. Don't hesitate to dive in and use it!

You know I hate goodbyes, so I only have one thing left to say:

 보고 싶을 거예요! [Pogo shipeul keoyeyo.] I'll be missing you!

보고 싶을 거예요!
I'll be missing you!

Further Vocabulary: Korean national holidays

I know you're sad, but here are some reasons to celebrate.

설날 [seolral] New Year's Day
삼일절 [samiljeol] 3.1. (Independence Declaration Day, March 1)
어린이날 [eorininal] Children's Day (May 5)
광복절 [kwangbokjeol] National Liberation Day (August 15)
추석 [chuseok] Korean Thanksgiving Day (August 15 in the lunar calendar)
개천절 [kaecheonjeol] National Foundation Day of Korea (October 3)
크리스마스 [keuriseumaseu] Christmas

Korean Style: Crossword puzzle

You're going to need something to pass the time on that long plane ride back to your home country. Do you enjoy crossword puzzles? Me too. When I was little, my dad and I would buy a crossword puzzle book every weekend and solve the puzzles together. That's probably where my love of languages came from. If you feel similarly, then I recommend taking on the challenge of a Korean crossword puzzle. You may think it's difficult…and you'd be right. In fact, most Korean crosswords are too hard for the average Korean. But don't worry, because I've prepared a special one for you, using only words you've learned in this book. A great chance for review, wouldn't you agree? Okay, are you ready? Go!

Across

2. honorific of 자다 ("to sleep")
4. generally, usually
6. friends
8. what you've been learning ("Korean language")
10. most
12. Sino-Korean for thirty-two
14. ramen

Down

1. very, so
3. what (kind of)
4. to see, or to try, or the particle meaning "than"
5. who
7. the modifier form of the pure-Korean word for "eleven"
9. yesterday
11. Japan
13. the particle meaning "to be called"

(See page 159 for answers.)

Appendix: Grammar Terms

English	Korean	Meaning	Example
adjective	형용사	a modifying part of speech, typically helping to describe a noun	The squid tastes **delicious**. 오징어가 **맛있어요**.
adverb	부사	a modifying part of speech, typically used to give information on how an action (verb) is carried out	I **quickly** ate my squid. 나는 오징어를 **빨리** 먹었다.
article	관사	in English, a short word that helps identify a noun; these do not exist in Korean	See **the** squid swimming in the tank? 수조에서 헤엄치는 오징어 보여요?
aspiration	격음	a pronunciation technique in which a puff of air is released along with the sound(s)	The characters ㅋ and ㅍ are aspirated. ㅋ과 ㅍ은 격음이에요.
batchim	받침	in Korean, a consonant that appears in the third position of a syllable; often, special pronunciation rules are associated with them	How do you pronounce the *batchim* ㅍ? 받침 ㅍ은 어떻게 발음해요?
comparative	비교급	a grammatical tool to show a comparison between two things; affects adjectives and adverbs	My squid is **more** delicious **than** yours. 내 오징어가 네 거**보다** **더** 맛있어.
conjugation	활용	rules governing how verb forms are created to show grammatical features like person and tense	How do you conjugate the verb "to walk" in the present tense? 현재 시제에서 동사 "걷다"는 어떻게 활용해요?
conjunctive adverbs	접속 부사	words that connect two different clauses or sentences to show the meaning between them; usually referred to in English as "conjunctions"	I ordered a lot of squid, **but** I couldn't eat all of it. 오징어를 많이 주문했**지만** 다 못 먹었어요. *OR* 오징어를 많이 주문했어요. **그렇지만** 다 못 먹었어요.

English	Korean	Meaning	Example
consonant	자음	a letter or character representing a consonant sound (as opposed to a vowel)	The letter "b" is the first consonant in the English alphabet. "b"는 영어 알파벳의 첫 번째 자음이에요.
contraction	축약	the shortening and joining of two words or sounds to make their pronunciation easier	I simply cannot → **can't** get enough of this delicious squid. 이 오징어는 아무리 많이 먹어도 맛있어요.
declarative (indicative)	평서문	a type of sentence that states information	I love squid. 저는 오징어를 좋아해요.
demonstrative pronoun	지시대명사	a word that singles out or points to a noun	You eat **this** squid, and I'll eat **that** one. 네가 **이** 오징어를 먹으면 나는 **그** 오징어를 먹을게.
diphthong	이중 모음	the combination of two or more vowel sounds to create one new one	The vowel sound in "boy" is [o] + [i], a diphthong. "boy"의 모음은 [o]와 [i]가 결합된 이중 모음이에요.
ending	어미	a set pattern attached to the stem of a verb in order to create meaning through conjugation	Most verbs in English are conjugated into the past tense with the ending **-ed**. 영어에서 대부분의 동사는 과거 시제에서 어미 **-ed** 형태로 활용해요.
future	미래 (시제)	a verb tense indicating something that hasn't happened yet	I **will finish** my plate of squid. 제 오징어를 다 **먹을 거예요.**
homonym	동음이의어	a word with the same spelling and sound as another but a different meaning	"Band" (e.g., a rock band) and "band" (e.g., a rubber band) are homonyms. "록 밴드"의 "밴드"와 "고무 밴드"의 "밴드"는 동음이의어예요.
homophone	동음이형어	a word with the same sound as another but a different spelling and meaning	"Bare" and "bear" are homophones. "bare"와 "bear"는 동음이형어예요.

English	Korean	Meaning	Example
honorific	높임말	verb conjugations and special words used in Korean to show respect to the person you're talking to and/or about	You don't need to use honorifics when talking to your squid. 오징어에 대해 말할 때 높임말을 쓸 필요는 없어요.
imperative	명령문	a type of sentence that gives a command	Love your squid! 오징어를 좋아하세요!
infinitive	동사 원형	the most basic, unconjugated form of a verb	Infinitives in English are signified by the word "to" and in Korean by the ending –다. 부정사란 영어에서는 "to" 와 함께 쓰인 단어, 한국어에서는 어미 –다로 끝나는 단어를 말해요.
inquisitive (interrogative)	의문문	a type of sentence that poses a question	Do you love squid? 오징어를 좋아하세요?
modifier	수식어	a word or other grammatical element that describes or qualifies another	Adjectives and adverbs are considered modifiers in English. 형용사와 부사는 영어에서 수식어예요.
noun	명사	a part of speech representing people, places, and other physical and abstract objects	I'd like more **squid**, please. **오징어** 좀 더 주세요.
object	목적어	a noun that receives the action in a sentence	We ate **squid**. 우리는 **오징어를** 먹었어요.
omission	생략	the removal of sentence elements that are unnecessary because they are already understood	It's okay to omit the subject of a Korean sentence if it can be understood from the context. 한국어에서 문맥을 통해 이해할 수 있을 때는 주어를 생략해도 괜찮아요.
particle	조사	a Korean grammar element, usually attached to nouns, that adds meaning to and/or signifies the grammatical function of a word	The object particle –을 / –를 signifies that a noun is an object. 목적격 조사 "–을 / –를" 은 그 명사가 목적어임을 나타내요.

English	Korean	Meaning	Example
past	과거 (시제)	a verb tense indicating something that has already happened	I **finished** my plate of squid. 저는 제 오징어를 다 **먹었어요**.
personal pronoun	인칭 대명사	a word that singles out or points to a person	**I** will eat **my** squid, and **you** eat **yours**. **저는** 제 오징어를 먹을게요. **당신은 당신** 오징어를 드세요.
plain	반말	verb conjugations and words used when you don't need to show respect to the person you're talking to and/or about	You can use plain forms when talking to your squid. 오징어에 대해 말할 때는 반말을 쓰면 돼요.
possessive	소유격	word forms that indicate ownership of something	The leftover squid is Hal**'s**, not **mine**. 남은 오징어는 제 거가 아니고 할 거예요.
predicate	서술어	the second part of a simple sentence, used in this book to describe how two nouns or a noun and an adjective are linked by the verb "to be"	Squid **is delicious**. 오징어는 **맛있어요**.
preposition	전치사	in English, words used in conjunction with nouns to add meaning; in Korean, particles perform this role	Let's eat squid **at** the restaurant **on** the corner. 우리 저 모퉁이**에** 있는 식당**에서** 오징어를 먹어요.
present	현재	a verb tense indicating something ongoing or habitual	I always **finish** my plate of squid. 저는 항상 제 오징어를 다 **먹어요**.
progressive	진행형	a verb tense indicating something in the process of occurring	I **am eating** squid right now. 저는 지금 오징어를 **먹고 있어요**.
propositive	청유문	a type of sentence that makes a suggestion or proposal	**Let's** eat some squid. 오징어를 **먹자**.
stem	어간	the base of a verb that doesn't change and onto which conjugative endings are added	The stem of the verb "to love" is "lov-." 동사 "to love"의 어간은 "lov-"예요.

English	Korean	Meaning	Example
subject	주어	a noun that performs the action in a sentence	**We** ate squid. **우리는** 오징어를 먹었어요.
suffix	접미사	an element added to the end of words or verb stems to create meaning	In Korean, the honorific suffix is -(으)시. 한국어에서 "-(으)시"는 높임의 접미사예요.
superlative	최상급	a grammatical tool to show that something is the "best" or "most" out of a group of three or more things; affects adjectives and adverbs	My squid is **the most** delicious. 제 오징어가 **제일** 맛있어요.
tense	시제	a conjugative tool that shows the timeframe in which an action (verb) takes place	I wrote a sentence in the past tense. 저는 이 문장을 과거 시제로 썼어요.
verb	동사	a part of speech representing the action taking place in the sentence	I **eat** squid all the time. 저는 늘 오징어를 **먹어요**.
vowel	모음	a letter or character representing a vowel sound (as opposed to a consonant)	The letter "a" is the first vowel in the English alphabet. "a"는 영어 알파벳의 첫 모음이에요.

Korean-English Glossary

abeoji (아버지) father, dad

achim (아침) breakfast (n.), morning

adeul (아들) son

agassi (아가씨) miss (title)

ai (아이) child

ajeossi (아저씨) sir

aju (아주) very, so

ajumeoni (아주머니) madam

ajumma (아줌마) madam

alda (알다) know (v.)

an (안) inside (n.), do not

anae (아내) wife

anda (앉다) sit (v.)

aniyo (아니요) no

annyeonghaseyo (안녕하세요) hello (lit., How are you?)

annyeonghi (안녕히) peacefully

annyeonghi kaseyo (안녕히 가세요) goodbye (to someone leaving)

annyeonghi kyeseyo (안녕히 계세요) goodbye (to someone staying)

anta (앉다) not (negation)

anyo (아뇨) no

ap (앞) front (n.)

apateu (아파트) apartment

apeuda (아프다) sick (adj.), painful (adj.)

appa (아빠) dad

arae (아래) lower

bulgogi (불고기) Korean barbecue

cha (차) tea

chada (자다) sleep (v.)

chaek (책) book (n.)

chaemieopda (재미없다) boring (adj.), dull (adj.)

chaemiitda (재미있다) fun (adj.),

funny (adj.), interesting (adj.)

chajeongeo (자전거) bicycle

chaju (자주) often

chakbyeol (작별) farewell (n.)

chakda (작다) small (adj.)

chal (잘) well (adv.)

chalhada do well (v.)

cham (잠) sleep (n.)

cham (참) very, so

chamae (자매) sister

changmun (창문) window

changnangam (장난감) toy (n.)

chapda (잡다) catch (v.), hold (v.)

che (제) my (honorific of 내)

chebal (제발) please

cheil (제일) most (superlative)

cheo (저) I (honorific of 나), that (far away)

cheoeum (처음) first (time)

cheogeodo (적어도) at least

cheogeot (저것) that (far away)

cheogi (저기) over there (far away)

cheohui (저희) we (honorific of 우리)

cheok (적) experience (n.)

cheomshim (점심) lunch

cheongbaji (청바지) jeans

cheongdo (정도) approximately

cheongmalro (정말로) really

cheonhwagi (전화기) telephone (n.)

cheonhyeo (전혀) (not) at all

cheonyeok (저녁) dinner, evening

cheulgeopda (즐겁다) pleasant (adj.), happy (adj.)

cheulgeopge (즐겁게) happily

cheung (층) floor (story)

chigap (지갑) wallet

chigeop (직업) job, occupation

chigeum (지금) now

chihacheol (지하철) subway

chim (짐) luggage

chimdae (침대) bed

chinaeda (지내다) live (v.)

chinandal (지난달) last month

chingu (친구) friend

chip (집) house, home

choahada (좋아하다) like (v.)

chogeum (조금) a little (bit)

chom (좀) a little, please

chopda (좁다) narrow (adj.)

chota (좋다) good (adj.)

chu (주) week

chuda (주다) give (v.)

chuk (죽) soup, straight (direction)

chukda (죽다) die (v.)

chul (줄) line (n.), means (n.)

chumal (주말) weekend

chumushida (주무시다) sleep (v.) (honorific of 자다)

chung (중) middle

chupda (춥다) cold (adj.)

churida (줄이다) reduce (v.)

chuseok (추석) Korean Thanksgiving

chuwi (추위) cold (n.)

eodi (어디) where

eoje (어제) yesterday

eojetbam (어젯밤) last night

eojjaetdeun (어쨌든) anyway

eolda (얼다) frozen (adj.)

eolgul (얼굴) face (n.)

eolma (얼마) how much, what

eomeoni (어머니) mother

eomma (엄마) mom

eoneo (언어) language

eonje (언제) when

eonjenga (언젠가) someday

eoreun (어른) adult

eoryeopda (어렵다) difficult (adj.)

eotteoke (어떻게) how

eotteota (어떻다) how (adj.)

eumak (음악) music

eumshik (음식) food

eumshikjeom (음식점) restaurant

hada (하다) do (v.)

haendeul (핸들) steering wheel

haendeupon (핸드폰) cell phone

haengbok (행복) happiness

haengbokada (행복하다) happy (adj.)

hakgyo (학교) school (n.)

halmeoni (할머니) grandmother

haneul (하늘) sky, heaven

hangahada (한가하다) free (available) (adj.)

hangeul (한글) the Korean writing system

hangsang (항상) always

hangugeo (한국어) Korean language

hanguk (한국) Korea

hanpyeon (한편) meanwhile

harabeoji (할아버지) grandfather

hayansaek (하얀색) white (the color)

hayata (하얗다) white (adj.)

heeojida (헤어지다) part (v.)

helseu (헬스) fitness

heon (헌) old, used

heori (허리) waist

heurida (흐리다) cloudy (adj.)

hoesa (회사) company, office

hwajangji (화장지) tissue (Kleenex)

hwajangshil (화장실) restroom

hwanada (화나다) get angry (v.)

hyeongje (형제) brother, sibling

hyuil (휴일) holiday

hyujitong (휴지통) wastebasket

i (이) tooth, this

ibeon (이번) this (time)

ibyeol (이별) farewell (n.)

igeot/igeo (이것 / 이거) this

ikda (읽다) read (v.)

il (일) work (n.), job

immat (입맛) appetite

ingan (인간) human being

insa (인사) greeting (n.)

inteonet (인터넷) Internet

ip (입) mouth (n.)

ipda (입다) wear (v.)

ireonada (일어나다) wake up (v.), get up (v.)

ireum (이름) name (n.)

itda (있다) exist (v.)

itda (잊다) forget (v.)

ittaga (이따가) later

jjada (짜다) salty (adj.)

jjajeungseureopda (짜증스럽다) irritated (adj.)

jjalda (짧다) short (adj.)

jjeum (쯤) approximately

jjigae (찌개) stew (n.)

jjireuda (찌르다) prick (v.)

kabang (가방) bag (n.)

kabyeopda (가볍다) light (in weight) (adj.)

kachi (같이) together

kada (가다) go (v.)

kaenyeom (개념) concept

kaeul (가을) fall (autumn)

kagyeok (가격) price (n.)

kajok (가족) family

kakkapda (가깝다) close (adj.), near (adj.)

kakkeum (가끔) sometimes

kalbitang (갈비탕) beef-rib soup

kamgi (감기) cold (n.), flu

kamsahamnida (감사합니다) thank you

kanhosa (간호사) nurse (n.)

kap (값) price (n.)

karae (가래) phlegm

kare (카레) curry

kaseum (가슴) chest

kasu (가수) singer

keikeu (케이크) cake

keolrida (걸리다) get sick (v.), last (time duration) (v.)

keomda (검다) black (adj.)

keonganghada (건강하다) healthy (adj.)

keonmul (건물) building

keonning (컨닝) cheating (n.)

keopi (커피) coffee

keori (거리) distance

keotda (걷다) walk (v.)

keu (그) that (nearby)

keuda (크다) big (adj.)

keugeot (그것) that (nearby)

keugi (크기) size (n.)

keujeokke (그저께) day before yesterday

keunyang (그냥) just (adv.)

keuraeseo (그래서) so, therefore

keureochiman (그렇지만) but

keureoke (그렇게) so (like this/that)

keurigo (그리고) and

keuriseumaseu (크리스마스) Christmas

kibun (기분) feelings, mood

kichim (기침) cough (n.)

kilda (길다) long (adj.)

kimbap (김밥) rice rolled in dried laver

kipda (깊다) deep (adj.)

kipi (깊이) depth

kippeuda (기쁘다) glad (adj.), happy (adj.)

kireum (기름) oil (n.)

kiri (길이) length

kkakada (깎다) cut (v.), discount (v.)

kkeulda (끌다) draw (v.)

kkeunta (끊다) quit (v.)

kkeut (끝) end (n.)

kkori (꼬리) tail (n.)

kkuda (꾸다) dream (v.)

kkul (꿀) honey

kkum (꿈) dream (n.)

kkwak (꽉) tightly

ko (코) nose

kochu (고추) hot pepper

koeropda (괴롭다) pained (adj.), distressed (adj.)

komapseumnida (고맙습니다) thank you

kong (공) ball

kong (콩) bean

kongbu (공부) studying (n.)

kongbuhada (공부하다) study (v.)

konghyuil (공휴일) national holiday

konsenteu (콘센트) outlet, socket

koyangi (고양이) cat

kugyeonghada (구경하다) look around (v.)

kuk (국) soup

kul (굴) oyster

kunin (군인) soldier

kwaja (과자) cookie

kwangwang (관광) tour (n.)

kwi (귀) ear

kwichanta (귀찮다) troublesome (adj.), tiresome (adj.)

kyejeol (계절) season (n.)

kyeolhonhada (결혼하다) get married (v.)

kyeongchal (경찰) police

kyeoul (겨울) winter

kyeshida (계시다) exist (v.) (honorific of 있다)

kyoshil (교실) classroom

madang (마당) yard, garden (n.)

madeopda (맛없다) bad (adj.)

maepda (맵다) spicy (adj.)

maeum (마음) heart, mind

makda (맑다) clear (sunny) (adj.)

mal (말) speech

malhada (말하다) talk (v.)

malsseum (말씀) speech (honorific of 말)

malsseumhashida (말씀하시다) talk (v.) (honorific of 말하다)

mani (많이) much

mannada (만나다) meet (v.)

manta (많다) plenty (adj.)

mashida (마시다) drink (v.)

mashitda (맛있다) delicious (adj.)

mat (맛) taste (n.), flavor

meokda (먹다) eat (v.)

meolda (멀다) distant (adj.)

meonjeo (먼저) first

meori (머리) head, hair, brain

meotjida (멋지다) handsome (adj.)

miguk (미국) USA

mikkeureojida (미끄러지다) slip (v.)

milda (밀다) push (v.)

mitda (믿다) trust (v.), believe (v.)

miyeokguk (미역국) seaweed soup

modeun (모든) all, every

modu (모두) everybody

mok (목) neck, throat

mom (몸) body

more (모레) day after tomorrow

moreuda (모르다) not know (v.)

mot (못) (can)not

moyang (모양) shape (n.)

mueot (무엇) what

muge (무게) weight

mugeopda (무겁다) heavy (adj.)

munje (문제) problem

mutda (묻다) ask (v.)

myeoneuri (며느리) daughter-in-law

myeonheo (면허) license (n.)

na (나) I (plain)

nae (내) my (plain)

naeda (내다) pay (v.)

naeil (내일) tomorrow

naemsae (냄새) smell (n.)

nai (나이) age (n.)

nal (날) day

nalssi (날씨) weather (n.)

namdongsaeng (남동생) brother (younger)

namja (남자) man

namjjok (남쪽) south

nampyeon (남편) husband

nara (나라) country, land (n.)

nat (낮) day

nat (낯) face (n.)

natda (낫다) recover (v.)

ne (네) yes, your (plain)

neo (너) you (plain)

neohui (너희) you all (plain)

neolbi (넓이) area (extent)

neolda (넓다) large (adj.)

neomu (너무) too (much)

neutda (늦다) late (adj.)

nochida (놓치다) miss (v.)

nopda (높다) high (adj.)

norae (노래) song

noteu (노트) notebook

noteubuk (노트북) laptop

nugu (누구) who

nun (눈) eye (n.), snow (n.)

nupda (눕다) lie (down) (v.)

oda (오다) come (v.)

oeguk (외국) foreign country

oenjjok (왼쪽) left (direction)

oi (오이) cucumber

ojingeo (오징어) squid

olppaemi (올빼미) owl

oneul (오늘) today

oppa (오빠) brother

ot (옷) clothes

paengmireo (백미러) rearview mirror

paeuda (배우다) learn (v.)

paji (바지) pants

pakkat (바깥) outside (n.)

pal (발) foot

pal (팔) arm

palda (팔다) sell (v.)

panchan (반찬) side dish

pang (방) room (n.)

pangapta (반갑다) glad (adj.)

pap (밥) steamed rice

pappeuda (바쁘다) busy (adj.)

pati (파티) party (n.)

peongeori (벙어리) mute (n.)

peotda (벗다) undress (v.)

pi (비) rain (n.)

pibimbap (비빔밥) a rice bowl with assorted ingredients

pibu (피부) skin (n.)

pigonhada (피곤하다) tired (adj.)

pihaenggi (비행기) airplane

pilryeodeurida (빌려드리다) lend (v.) (honorific of 빌려주다)

pilryeojuda (빌려주다) lend (v.)

pissada (비싸다) expensive (adj.)

poda (보다) see (v.), watch (v.), meet (v.)

podo (포도) grape

poepda (뵙다) see (v.), meet (v.) (honorific of 보다)

pokkeumbap (볶음밥) fried rice

polpen (볼펜) ballpoint pen

pom (봄) spring (the season)

potong (보통) usually

ppalrae (빨래) laundry

ppalri (빨리) hurry (n.)

ppang (빵) bread (n.)

ppareuda (빠르다) fast (adj.)

pukjjok (북쪽) north

pumonim (부모님) parents

punwigi (분위기) atmosphere (ambience)

pyeol (별) star (n.)

pyeong (병) illness, disease

pyeongil (평일) weekday

pyeonhada (편하다) comfortable (adj.)

ramyeon (라면) instant noodles

sada (사다) buy (v.)

sadari (사다리) ladder

sae (새) new

saekkkal (색깔) color (n.)

saenggak (생각) thought

saenggakada (생각하다) think (v.)

saengil (생일) birthday

sagwa (사과) apple

sahoejeok (사회적) social

saja (사자) lion

sajin (사진) photo

salda (살다) live (v.)

sam (삶) life

samgyetang (삼계탕) chicken soup with ginseng and various ingredients

san (산) mountain

sarajida (사라지다) disappear (v.)

saram (사람) person

saranghada (사랑하다) love (v.)

satang (사탕) candy

seoda (서다) stop (v.), stand (v.)

seojjok (서쪽) west

seolral (설날) New Year's Day

seongham (성함) name (n.) (honorific of 이름)

seonmul (선물) present (n.), gift

seonsaengnim (선생님) teacher

seulpeuda (슬프다) sad (adj.)

seupgwan (습관) habit

seuweteo (스웨터) sweater

shigan (시간) hour

shiheom (시험) exam, test (n.)

shikkeureopda (시끄럽다) noisy (adj.)

shilta (싫다) hateful (adj.)

shinbal (신발) shoes

shinggeopda (싱겁다) bland (adj.)

shinnada (신나다) excited (adj.)

shyaweo (샤워) shower (n.)

shyupeo (슈퍼) supermarket

son (손) hand (n.)

ssada (싸다) cheap (adj.), pack (v.)

ssal (쌀) rice (uncooked)

ssauda (싸우다) fight (v.)

sseuda (쓰다) bitter (adj.)

ssitda (씻다) wash (v.)

su (수) ability

sukje (숙제) homework

sul (술) alcohol

tachida (다치다) hurt (v.)

tada (타다) ride (v.), take (v.), burn (v.)

taechung (대충) approximately

taehaksaeng (대학생) university student

taek (댁) house, home (honorific of 집)

taeryak (대략) approximately

taeshin (대신) instead

taeum (다음) next time

takda (닦다) brush (v.)

tal (달) month, moon

talda (달다) sweet (adj.), sugary (adj.), hang (v.)

talrida (달리다) run (v.)

tambae (담배) cigarette

tanggida (당기다) pull (v.)

tangshin (당신) you (used primarily by couples)

tari (다리) leg, bridge

tashi (다시) again

teiteuhada (데이트하다) date (v.)

telrebijeon (텔레비전) television

teo (더) more

teopda (덥다) hot (adj.)

teowi (더위) heat (n.)

teung (등) back (body part)

teuraibeo (드라이버) screwdriver

teureogada (들어가다) enter (v.)

teureom (드럼) drum (n.)

teurida (드리다) give (v.) (honorific of 주다)

teushida (드시다) eat (v.) (honorific of 먹다)

teutda (듣다) listen (v.)

toduk (도둑) thief

toeda (되다) become (v.)

tolda (돌다) turn (v.)

ton (돈) money

tongjjok (동쪽) east

tongmul (동물) animal

tongsaeng (동생) sibling (younger)

topda (돕다) help (v.)

toragada (돌아가다) return (v.)

ttae (때) time (n.)

ttaemun (때문) because of

ttaerida (때리다) beat (v.)

ttal (딸) daughter

ttatteutada (따뜻하다) warm (adj.)

tteok (떡) rice cake

tteonada (떠나다) leave (v.)

ttereojida (떨어지다) fail (v.)

ttoneun (또는) or

ttwida (뛰다) run (v.), jump (v.)

twi (뒤) back (n.)

uija (의자) chair

uisa (의사) doctor

ulda (울다) cry (v.)

unjeon (운전) driving (n.)

uri (우리) we (plain)

utda (웃다) laugh (v.), smile (v.)

uulhada (우울하다) gloomy (adj.), depressed (adj.)

uyu (우유) milk (n.)

wa (와) wow!

wae (왜) why

wang (왕) king

wi (위) upper

wiheom (위험) danger

yaegi (얘기) story (tale)

yaegihada (얘기하다) talk (v.)

yagu (야구) baseball

yak (약) approximately

yaksok (약속) appointment, engagement

yatda (얕다) shallow (adj.)

ye (예) yes

yeodongsaeng (여동생) sister (younger)

yeogi (여기) here

yeogweon (여권) passport

yeoja (여자) woman

yeojjuda (여쭈다) ask (v.) (honorific of 묻다)

yeol (열) fever

yeolshimhi (열심히) hard (adv.)

yeonghwa (영화) movie

yeonse (연세) age (n.) (honorific of 나이)

yeonseup (연습) practice (n.)

yeop (옆) side (n.)

yeoreobun (여러분) you all (honorific of 너희)

yeoreum (여름) summer

yeppeuda (예쁘다) beautiful (adj.), pretty (adj.), cute (adj.)

yojeum (요즘) nowadays

yuri (유리) glass

English-Korean Glossary

ability su (수)

adult eoreun (어른)

again tashi (다시)

age (n.) nai (나이), yeonse (연세) (honorific)

airplane pihaenggi (비행기)

alcohol sul (술)

all modeun (모든)

always hangsang (항상)

and keurigo (그리고)

animal tongmul (동물)

anyway eojjaetdeun (어쨌든)

apartment apateu (아파트)

appetite immat (입맛)

apple sagwa (사과)

appointment yaksok (약속)

approximately cheongdo (정도), yak (약), taeryak (대략), taechung (대충), jjeum (쯤)

area (extent) neolbi (넓이)

arm pal (팔)

ask (v.) mutda (묻다), yeojjuda (여쭈다) (honorific)

at least cheogeodo (적어도)

atmosphere (ambience) punwigi (분위기)

back (body part) teung (등)

back (n.) twi (뒤)

bad (adj.) madeopda (맛없다)

bag (n.) kabang (가방)

ball kong (공)

ballpoint pen polpen (볼펜)

baseball yagu (야구)

bean kong (콩)

beat (v.) ttaerida (때리다)

beautiful (adj.) yeppeuda (예쁘다)

because of ttaemun (때문)

become (v.) toeda (되다)

bed chimdae (침대)

believe (v.) mitda (믿다)

bicycle chajeongeo (자전거)

big (adj.) keuda (크다)

birthday saengil (생일)

bitter (adj.) sseuda (쓰다)

black (adj.) keomda (검다)

bland (adj.) shinggeopda (싱겁다)

body mom (몸)

book (n.) chaek (책)

boring (adj.) chaemieopda (재미없다)

brain meori (머리)

bread (n.) ppang (빵)

breakfast (n.) achim (아침)

bridge (n.) tari (다리)

brother (younger) namdongsaeng (남동생)

brother, sibling hyeongje (형제)

brush (v.) takda (닦다)

building keonmul (건물)

burn (v.) tada (타다)

busy (adj.) pappeuda (바쁘다)

but keureochiman (그렇지만)

buy (v.) sada (사다)

cake keikeu (케이크)

candy satang (사탕)

cat koyangi (고양이)

catch (v.) japda (잡다)

cell phone haendeupon (핸드폰)

chair uija (의자)

cheap (adj.) ssada (싸다)

cheating (n.) keonning (컨닝)

chest kaseum (가슴)

child ai (아이)

Christmas keuriseumaseu (크리스마스)

cigarette tambae (담배)

classroom kyoshil (교실)

clear (sunny) (adj.) makda (맑다)

close (nearby) (adj.) kakkapda (가깝다)

clothes ot (옷)

cloudy (adj.) heurida (흐리다)

coffee keopi (커피)

cold (adj.) chupda (춥다)

cold (illness) (n.) kamgi (감기)

cold (n.) chuwi (추위)

color (n.) saekkkal (색깔)

come (v.) oda (오다)

comfortable (adj.) pyeonhada (편하다)

company (business) hoesa (회사)

concept kaenyeom (개념)

cookie kwaja (과자)

cough (n.) kichim (기침)

country nara (나라)

cry (v.) ulda (울다)

cucumber oi (오이)

curry kare (카레)

cut (v.) kkakada (깎다)

cute (adj.) yeppeuda (예쁘다)

dad appa (아빠)

danger wiheom (위험)

date (v.) teiteuhada (데이트하다)

daughter ttal (딸)

daughter-in-law myeoneuri (며느리)

day nat (낮), nal (날)

day after tomorrow more (모레)

day before yesterday keujeokke (그저께)

deep (adj.) kipda (깊다)

delicious (adj.) mashitda (맛있다)

depressed (adj.) uulhada (우울하다)

depth kipi (깊이)

die (v.) chukda (죽다)

difficult (adj.) eoryeopda (어렵다)

dinner cheonyeok (저녁)

disappear (v.) sarajida (사라지다)

discount (v.) kkakada (깎다)

disease pyeong (병)

dislike (v.) shilta (싫다)

distance keori (거리)

distant (adj.) meolda (멀다)

distressed (adj.) koeropda (괴롭다)

do (v.) hada (하다)

do well (v.) chalhada (잘하다)

doctor uisa (의사)

draw (v.) kkeulda (끌다)

dream (n.) kkum (꿈)

dream (v.) kkuda (꾸다)

drink (v.) mashida (마시다)

driving (n.) unjeon (운전)

drum (n.) teureom (드럼)

ear kwi (귀)

east tongjjok (동쪽)

eat (v.) meokda (먹다), teushida (드시다) (honorific)

end (n.) kkeut (끝)

enter (v.) teureogada (들어가다)

evening cheonyeok (저녁)

every modeun (모든)

everybody modu (모두)

exam shiheom (시험)

excited (adj.) shinnada (신나다)

exist (v.) itda (있다), kyeshida (계시다) (honorific)

expensive (adj.) pissada (비싸다)

experience (n.) cheok (적)

eye (n.) nun (눈)

face (n.) nat (낯), eolgul (얼굴)

fail (v.) tteeojida (떨어지다)

fall (autumn) kaeul (가을)

family kajok (가족)

farewell (n.) chakbyeol (작별), ibyeol (이별)

fast (adj.) ppareuda (빠르다)

father, dad abeoji (아버지)

feelings kibun (기분)

fever yeol (열)

fight (v.) ssauda (싸우다)

first meonjeo (먼저)

fitness helseu (헬스)

flavor mat (맛)

floor (story) cheung (층)

flu kamgi (감기)

food eumshik (음식)

foot pal (발)

foreign country oeguk (외국)

forget (v.) itda (잊다)

free (available) (adj.) hangahada (한가하다)

fried rice pokkeumbap (볶음밥)

friend chingu (친구)

front (n.) ap (앞)

frozen (adj.) eolda (얼다)

fun (adj.), funny (adj.) chaemiitda (재미있다)

garden (n.) madang (마당)

get angry (v.) hwanada (화나다)

get up (v.) ireonada (일어나다)

gift seonmul (선물)

give (v.) chuda (주다), teurida (드리다) (honorific)

glad (adj.) kippeuda (기쁘다), pangapta (반갑다)

glass yuri (유리)

gloomy (emotion) (adj.) uulhada (우울하다)

go (v.) kada (가다)

good (adj.) chota (좋다)

goodbye annyeonghi kaseyo (안녕히 가세요), annyeonghi kyeseyo (안녕히 계세요)

grandfather harabeoji (할아버지)

grandmother halmeoni (할머니)

grape podo (포도)

greeting (n.) insa (인사)

habit seupgwan (습관)

hair meori (머리)

hand (n.) son (손)

handsome (adj.) meotjida (멋지다)

hang (v.) talda (달다)

happily cheulgeopge (즐겁게)

happiness haengbok (행복)

happy (adj.) kippeuda (기쁘다), cheulgeopda (즐겁다), haengbokada (행복하다)

hard (adv.) yeolshimhi (열심히)

hate (v.) shilta (싫다)

head meori (머리)

healthy (adj.) keonganghada (건강하다)

heart maeum (마음)

heat (n.) teowi (더위)

heaven haneul (하늘)

heavy (adj.) mugeopda (무겁다)

hello annyeonghaseyo (안녕하세요)

help (v.) topda (돕다)

here yeogi (여기)

high (adj.) nopda (높다)

hold (v.) chapda (잡다)

holiday hyuil (휴일)

home chip (집), taek (댁) (honorific)

homework sukje (숙제)

honey kkul (꿀)

hot (adj.) teopda (덥다)

hot pepper kochu (고추)

hour shigan (시간)

house (n.) chip (집), taek (댁) (honorific)

how eotteota (어떻다) (adj.), eotteoke (어떻게)

how much eolma (얼마)

human being ingan (인간)

hurry ppalri (빨리)

hurt (v.) tachida (다치다)

husband nampyeon (남편)

I na (나), cheo (저) (honorific)

illness pyeong (병)

inside (n.) an (안)

instant noodles ramyeon (라면)

instead taeshin (대신)

interesting (adj.) chaemiitda (재미있다)

Internet inteonet (인터넷)

irritated (adj.) jjajeungseureopda
(짜증스럽다)

jeans cheongbaji (청바지)
job chigeop (직업), il (일)
jump (v.) ttwida (뛰다)
just (adv.) keunyang (그냥)

king wang (왕)
know (v.) alda (알다)
Korea hanguk (한국)
Korean barbecue bulgogi (불고기)
Korean language hangugeo (한국
어)

ladder sadari (사다리)
land (n.) nara (나라)
language eoneo (언어)
laptop noteubuk (노트북)
large (adj.) neolda (넓다)
last (time duration) (v.) keolrida
(걸리다)
last month chinandal (지난달)
last night eojetbam (어젯밤)
late (adj.) neutda (늦다)
later ittaga (이따가)
laugh (v.) utda (웃다)
laundry ppalrae (빨래)
learn (v.) paeuda (배우다)
leave (v.) tteonada (떠나다)
left (direction) oenjjok (왼쪽)
leg tari (다리)
lend (v.) pilryeojuda (빌려주다),
pilryeodeurida (빌려드리다)
(honorific)
length kiri (길이)
license (n.) myeonheo (면허)
lie (down) (v.) nupda (눕다)
life sam (삶)
light (in weight) (adj.) kabyeopda
(가볍다)
like (v.) choahada (좋아하다)
line (n.) chul (줄)
lion saja (사자)

listen (v.) teutda (듣다)
little (a little) chom (좀), chogeum
(조금)
live (v.) salda (살다), chinaeda (지
내다)
long (adj.) kilda (길다)
look around (v.) kugyeonghada
(구경하다)
love (v.) saranghada (사랑하다)
lower arae (아래)
luggage chim (짐)
lunch cheomshim (점심)

madam ajumma (아줌마), ajumeoni
(아주머니)
man namja (남자)
marry (v.) kyeolhonhada (결혼
하다)
means (n.) chul (줄)
meanwhile hanpyeon (한편)
meet (v.) poda (보다), poepda
(뵙다) (honorific), mannada
(만나다)
middle chung (중)
milk (n.) uyu (우유)
mind (n.) maeum (마음)
miss (title) agassi (아가씨)
miss (v.) nochida (놓치다)
mom eomma (엄마)
money ton (돈)
month tal (달)
mood kibun (기분)
moon tal (달)
more teo (더)
morning achim (아침)
most (superlative) cheil (제일)
mother eomeoni (어머니)
mountain san (산)
mouth (n.) ip (입)
movie yeonghwa (영화)
much mani (많이)
music eumak (음악)
mute (n.) peongeori (벙어리)
my nae (내), che (제) (honorific)

name (n.) ireum (이름), seongham
(성함) (honorific)
narrow (adj.) chopda (좁다)
near (adj.) kakkapda (가깝다)
neck mok (목)
new sae (새)
no aniyo (아니요), anyo (아뇨)
noisy (adj.) shikkeureopda (시끄
럽다)
north pukjjok (북쪽)
nose ko (코)
not know (v.) moreuda (모르다)
notebook noteu (노트)
now chigeum (지금)
nowadays yojeum (요즘)
nurse (n.) kanhosa (간호사)

occupation chigeop (직업)
office hoesa (회사)
often chaju (자주)
oil (n.) kireum (기름)
old heon (헌)
or ttoneun (또는)
outlet (electricity) konsenteu (콘센
트)
outside (n.) pakkat (바깥)
owl olppaemi (올빼미)
oyster kul (굴)

pack (v.) ssada (싸다)
painful (adj.) apeuda (아프다)
pants paji (바지)
parents pumonim (부모님)
part (v.) heeojida (헤어지다)
party (n.) pati (파티)
passport yeogweon (여권)
pay (v.) naeda (내다)
peacefully annyeonghi (안녕히)
person saram (사람)
phlegm karae (가래)
photo sajin (사진)
pleasant (adj.) cheulgeopda
(즐겁다)
please chom (좀), chebal (제발)

plenty (adj.) manta (많다)

police kyeongchal (경찰)

practice (n.) yeonseup (연습)

present (gift) (n.) seonmul (선물)

pretty (adj.) yeppeuda (예쁘다)

price (n.) kap (값), kagyeok (가격)

prick (v.) jjireuda (찌르다)

problem munje (문제)

pull (v.) tanggida (당기다)

push (v.) milda (밀다)

quit (v.) kkeunta (끊다)

rain (n.) pi (비)

read (v.) ikda (읽다)

really cheongmalro (정말로)

rearview mirror paengmireo (백미러)

recover (v.) natda (낫다)

reduce (v.) churida (줄이다)

restaurant eumshikjeom (음식점)

restroom hwajangshil (화장실)

return (v.) toragada (돌아가다)

rice (uncooked) ssal (쌀)

rice cake tteok (떡)

ride (v.) tada (타다)

room (n.) pang (방)

run (v.) talrida (달리다), ttwida (뛰다)

sad (adj.) seulpeuda (슬프다)

salty (adj.) jjada (짜다)

school (n.) hakgyo (학교)

screwdriver teuraibeo (드라이버)

season (n.) kyejeol (계절)

see (v.) poda (보다), poepda (뵙다) (honorific)

sell (v.) palda (팔다)

shallow (adj.) yatda (얕다)

shape (n.) moyang (모양)

shoes shinbal (신발)

short (adj.) jjalda (짧다)

shower (n.) shyaweo (샤워)

sibling (younger) tongsaeng (동생)

sick (adj.) apeuda (아프다)

side (n.) yeop (옆)

side dish panchan (반찬)

singer kasu (가수)

sir ajeossi (아저씨)

sister chamae (자매)

sister (younger) yeodongsaeng (여동생)

sit (v.) anda (앉다)

size (n.) keugi (크기)

skin (n.) pibu (피부)

sky haneul (하늘)

sleep (n.) cham (잠)

sleep (v.) chada (자다), chumushida (주무시다) (honorific)

slip (v.) mikkeureojida (미끄러지다)

small (adj.) chakda (작다)

smell (n.) naemsae (냄새)

smile (v.) utda (웃다)

snow (n.) nun (눈)

so (like this/that) keureoke (그렇게)

so (therefore) keuraeseo (그래서)

so (very) aju (아주), cham (참)

social sahoejeok (사회적)

soldier kunin (군인)

someday eonjenga (언젠가)

sometimes kakkeum (가끔)

son adeul (아들)

song norae (노래)

soup kuk (국), chuk (죽)

south namjjok (남쪽)

speech mal (말), malsseum (말씀) (honorific)

spicy (adj.) maepda (맵다)

spring (the season) pom (봄)

squid ojingeo (오징어)

stand (v.) seoda (서다)

star pyeol (별)

steamed rice pap (밥)

steering wheel haendeul (핸들)

stew (n.) jjigae (찌개)

stop (v.) seoda (서다)

story (tale) yaegi (얘기)

straight (direction) chuk (죽)

study (v.) kongbuhada (공부하다)

studying (n.) kongbu (공부)

subway chihacheol (지하철)

sugary (adj.) talda (달다)

summer yeoreum (여름)

supermarket shyupeo (슈퍼)

sweater seuweteo (스웨터)

sweet (adj.) talda (달다)

tail (n.) kkori (꼬리)

take (v.) tada (타다)

talk (v.) malhada (말하다), malsseumhashida (말씀하시다) (honorific), yaegihada (얘기하다)

taste (n.) mat (맛)

tea cha (차)

teacher seonsaengnim (선생님)

telephone (n.) cheonhwagi (전화기)

television telrebijeon (텔레비전)

test (n.) shiheom (시험)

thank you kamsahamnida (감사합니다), komapseumnida (고맙습니다)

that (far away) cheo (저), cheogeot (저것)

that (nearby) keu (그), keugeot (그것)

therefore keuraeseo (그래서)

thief toduk (도둑)

think (v.) saenggakada (생각하다)

this i (이), igeot (이것)

this (time) ibeon (이번)

thought saenggak (생각)

throat mok (목)

tightly kkwak (꽉)

time (n.) ttae (때)

tired (adj.) pigonhada (피곤하다)

tiresome (adj.) kwichanta (귀찮다)

tissue (Kleenex) hwajangji (화장지)

today oneul (오늘)

together kachi (같이)

tomorrow naeil (내일)

too (much) neomu (너무)

tooth i (이)

tour (n.) kwangwang (관광)

toy (n.) changnangam (장난감)

troublesome (adj.) kwichanta (귀찮다)

trust (v.) mitda (믿다)

turn (v.) tolda (돌다)

undress (v.) peotda (벗다)

university student taehaksaeng (대학생)

upper wi (위)

USA miguk (미국)

used heon (헌)

usually potong (보통)

very aju (아주), cham (참)

waist heori (허리)

wake up (v.) ireonada (일어나다)

walk (v.) keotda (걷다)

wallet chigap (지갑)

warm (adj.) ttatteutada (따뜻하다)

wash (v.) ssitda (씻다)

wastebasket hyujitong (휴지통)

watch (v.) poda (보다)

we uri (우리), cheohui (저희) (honorific)

wear (v.) ipda (입다)

weather (n.) nalssi (날씨)

week chu (주)

weekday pyeongil (평일)

weekend chumal (주말)

weight muge (무게)

well (adv.) chal (잘)

west seojjok (서쪽)

what mueot (무엇)

when eonje (언제)

where eodi (어디)

white (adj.) hayata (하얗다)

white (the color) hayansaek (하얀색)

who nugu (누구)

why wae (왜)

wife anae (아내)

window changmun (창문)

winter kyeoul (겨울)

woman yeoja (여자)

work (n.) il (일)

wow! wa (와)

yard madang (마당)

yes ye (예), ne (네)

yesterday eoje (어제)

you (plain) neo (너)

you (used primarily by couples) tangshin (당신)

you all neohui (너희), yeoreobun (여러분) (honorific)

your (plain) ne (네)

Answer key, page 144

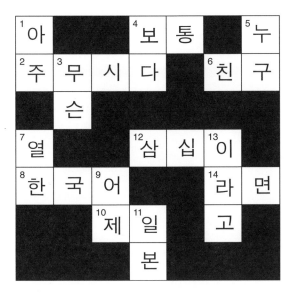

 Notes

 Notes

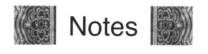

Notes

 Notes

 Notes